SAFARI PRESS

SAFARI PRESS ®

PLACE
POSTAGE
HERE

SAFARI PRESS
P.O. Box 3095
Long Beach, CA 90803-0095, USA

Ask the Grizzly/ Brown Bear Guides

Alaskan brown bears attract hunters from all over the world. Here Roderick Wurfbain from England poses with his magnificent 10½-foot brown bear. (Safari Press photo library)

Ask the Grizzly/ Brown Bear Guides

By J. Y. Jones

Safari Press Inc.

Jones, J. Y.

First edition

Safari Press

2011 Long Beach, California

ISBN 978-1-57157-346-9

Library of Congress Catalog Card Number: 2009928192

10 9 8 7 6 5 4 3 2 1

Printed in China

Dedication

It is Easter Sunday 2008 as I pen the dedication for the fifth in this series of books. I am on a plane over Thailand, on my way to try to open up Nepal to Western hunters again for the first time in years. An acquaintance was unsuccessful in his attempt to do the same last year, and spent the better part of two weeks in a Katmandu hotel waiting to go hunting. Permission was never granted, however, and I am a bit apprehensive that the same fate could befall me. I have learned to trust in the God who delivers me from all troubles, though, and I am certain that whatever the outcome, it will be best in the long run.

I always, it seems, dedicate these *Ask the Guides* books to the people who really produce them, the guides and outfitters who have participated in the interview process. I also include those worthy top-echelon guides who, for one reason or another and through no fault of their own, were not included.

Additionally, I must single out the various game departments that are doing such a grand job of managing the subject animal, in this case brown bears and grizzlies. These animals are particularly well managed in Alaska and the Yukon, and to a lesser extent in the Northwest Territories. This last province gets high marks for its barren-ground grizzly program but a zero for its lack of management of the valuable interior grizzly of its western mountains. I would single out the government of British Columbia for a low ranking in this dedication, because of its extreme susceptibility to "ballot-box biology," as one of the featured guides herein has termed it. The grizzlies there are being so lightly harvested that the population is, paradoxically, likely to suffer as bear-human conflicts increase, cub mortality skyrockets, and the population shifts toward older boar grizzlies. This situation dramatically suppresses the desired dynamic, an age-diverse population like those found in places where science-based management prevails.

Nobody knows what the future holds for hunting these great bears, but my own world view and my experience indicate that the right to hunt them will come under increasing attack. Traditional ties to the land and to stewardship of animal resources are increasingly being forgotten, and hunter recruitment is at an all-time low. I feel so greatly blessed by God to have lived at a time when the art of the outdoors could be ingrained in me as a young boy, and then be lived out to the fullest over the course of my life. I believe the push for global vegetarianism may eventually spell the end of hunting and the way of life that is so precious to all hunters. Until that happens, I plan to keep right on hunting and teaching my grandchildren to do the same. It is for them that I work to keep our right to hunt and bear arms, for I have, for the most part, already had my day.

With these thoughts in mind, I add to this dedication the National Rifle Association, Safari Club International, the North American Hunting Club, and all other organizations dedicated to fighting these disturbing trends leading away from our precious outdoor heritage.

I also dedicate this book to my family, for my wife, Linda, has given up countless hours of time with me so I could produce this work, and I have missed many grandkid events while I did interviews and typed them up. I love my two daughters, Amber and Rachael, and their husbands, Michael and Chris, more than I can say. And how could I possibly say how much I love my five grandchildren?

While the Himalayas loom ahead of me, I dedicate this book last, as always, to the triune God of the Bible, Father, Son, and Holy Spirit, who created the universe and all it contains, including this magical range of mountains that is the highest in the world. My Lord Jesus Christ also created *Ursus arctos* in all the animal's power and splendor. The bears mentioned in the Holy Bible are brown bears like those of North America, and are always symbols of power, though sometimes they are a mechanism of God's wrath against ungodly behavior. Most often they are under man's dominion in some way. If we voluntarily abrogate that God-ordained dominion, the future becomes highly uncertain for both humans and brown bears.

Table of Contents

FOREWORD

In his series of books, of which this is one, that ask the various kinds of hunting guides around the world about matters important to hunters they accompany and the secrets to success on the hunt, J. Y. Jones provides a tremendous service to the hunting fraternity in general and to individual hunters personally. Simply put: Follow the advice of the guides included in this book, and any bear hunt will go better than it would absent attention to the salient details they provide.

In reading this book, it is abundantly clear that there are things a hunter must consider and do ahead of time that are intuitive, and then there are the not-so-obvious nuances. The secret is to address all of them. If, as they say, the devil is in the details, then it stands to reason that salvation is in the overall. Although details are important to address, it is the entire hunting experience that really matters. And the guides included in this book can literally help each hunter to realize at least his or her potential, and probably even more than that if the sportsman is willing to team-up and do it right.

J. Y. has included herein an all-star list of bear hunting guides, and that matters. It matters because these folks are the true experts. They have been there. They have done it. But more than that, they possess that rare ability to relay in meaningful and real terms what they have learned in a way that improves the experience for others.

Bears are incredible beasts. In North America I have hunted them from Alaska through Canada and all the way to where the southern end of the Rocky Mountains tails off into Mexico. I have hunted bears literally where Ben Lilly traipsed decades before, and have pursued the bruin in the exact area where the last of the California browns was taken earlier in the twentieth century.

There exists a culture of the bear hunt. To be able to appreciate this elevated state, it is crucial that the hunt itself be correct. Advice in this book can help any hunter, new or veteran, to have a better and more fulfilling experience. That in turn opens the door to a higher and more complete appreciation and understanding of the bear itself.

In all of nature there is no animal quite like the bear. In some ways bears are much like we humans are. In other ways they represent some things that we wish we were. In all things, they are wonderment.

It is said among soldiers that there are no atheists in the foxhole. A similar thought might be applied to bears and those who truly hunt them properly. There simply is no way that a person can be in the presence of these magnificent beasts and not recognize, indeed celebrate, both the existence and the presence of the Creator.

For that, I join all of those who hunt the bear and give thanks. And thanks to J. Y. for his effort in this book, which provides the key to open this fascinating aspect of the natural world to those who wish to realize the epitome of pursuing one of nature's most perfect animals.

Steve Comus
Director of Publications
Safari Club International

Introduction and Acknowledgments

It has indeed been a pleasure finding the right brown bear and grizzly guides, accumulating the needed interviews, putting together an astounding layout of photos, and then doing the hard, unseen work required thereafter. First, after each interview I typed up all the information myself, as I have with every one of my books. I never use a secretary and never press my business employees or my wife (who types rather well) into doing a single keystroke for me. As with my nine books that preceded this one, I have been the first and only typist. I also approach every interviewee in the *Ask the Guides* series myself, never depending on go-betweens or mutual friends.

However, there is one requirement that I have tried not to breach in any way: Either I must know the guide or outfitter I'm to interview on a personal basis and have been on a hunt with him, or else the outfitter must be strongly recommended by one of many hundreds of hunter-friends logged in my e-mail address book. Most, of course, fall into this latter category, because one can have personally hunted with only a limited number of guides. I believe I have recognized in this section every single person who has submitted a name, whether I was able to utilize the individual or not, and all of them are listed at the end of this section.

It has indeed been rare for an invited guide or outfitter to decline to participate in one of these books. In fact, only two guide/outfitters so far, out of queries to seventy-six, have declined to participate. One guide submitted to the interview (painstakingly typed up and edited by me) but had to be cut from the book because he either couldn't or wouldn't send me the required pictures.

How problematic the task of getting the featured guides and outfitters to send pictures has varied vastly. The extreme case was the individual above, who was cut out entirely from an early book in the series. Most have sent tons of pictures—from which I could choose only the best, a real pleasure for me. About a fourth of the interviewees required some degree of arm-twisting, particularly on the photo for their biographical page. Eventually all featured guides have sent in at least the minimum of a good head-and-shoulders photo of themselves, plus a kill photo. I make it clear up front, and have them commit to it on tape, that I have permission to use their photos and interview in the book, and that they will send the photos. This has, by and large, worked out quite well.

There seems to be more interest in the big bears—or at least the guides are more verbose—than for the other animals featured in this series. This book has 25 percent more words than any of the others, in part because of the enthusiasm of the guides for the unique hunts they conduct for perhaps the grandest game animal in North America or the world. As well, many have harrowing tales of narrow escapes that take time to tell and dangerous situations that are painful to relate, and three featured guides have been mauled by either a grizzly (two) or a brown bear (one). Such incidents tend to be explained in greater depth, and I've let them tell their tales as they please with minimal attempts to limit their length. I believe the reader will find these many anecdotes riveting, entertaining, and thought-provoking.

A word on the book's layout is necessary. This is the most asymmetrical book in the series in terms of numbers of guides used for each section. By far the majority of hunts for *Ursus arctos* in North America are for the Alaskan brown bear, and more of these animals are harvested than any of the other categories. This is because these hunts generally offer a higher success rate and potential for a bigger bear.

Moreover, there are three distinct types of hunts for this bear, so I have included two experienced guides for each kind of hunt: two from the Alaska Peninsula, two from Kodiak Island, and two from southeastern Alaska. Each of these three hunts is distinctive, and the differences are brought out in the text. For two reasons, I interviewed only two guides for the coastal British Columbia grizzly bear: First, there aren't many outfitters for coastal grizzlies anymore because the province has ratcheted back its grizzly hunting, which is a result of pressure from an uninformed public willing to disregard scientific facts. This has driven at least one major outfitter to sell his area to an antihunting group, closing forever a superb, pristine area that will soon have few females with cubs but a preponderance of large, cannibalistic adult males. The remaining British Columbia guides are severely restricted in the number of hunting permits they are issued annually.

Because of the diversity of terrain and the vast differences in hunting situations, I included three each for interior Alaska grizzlies and interior Canadian grizzlies (British Columbia and the Yukon). For the barren-ground grizzly, only a handful of which are taken by sport hunters annually and for which there is a lower level of diversity in hunting techniques and methods, I interviewed only one, Inuvialuit guide James Pokiak, who guided me to my own barren-ground grizzly in 1996.

In some instances there seems to be a great conflict in the answers given by the guides, even within the same section, especially regarding calibers, bullet construction, and recommendations. These differences are usually related to the terrain in which the guide operates, either wide open or close-quarters, so as you assess the usefulness of answers that appear to be at odds, please be cognizant of the different hunting situations represented in this book.

I acknowledge the following individuals for suggesting guides and outfitters for this book: Craig Boddington, Jimmy Rosenbruch, Ludo Wurfbain, Jerome Knap, Keith Atcheson, Darren DeLuca, Dave Fyfe, Jeff Neal, Eric Mikkelson, Brent Sinclair, and Terry and Ruth Wilkinson. If I missed anyone, please let me know and we'll make a correction in the second printing of the book.

Thank you for your interest in this book and the others in this series. The featured guides have over three hundred years of accumulated guiding experience, so the amount of studied observation is vast. I hope you enjoy reading it as much as I have enjoyed putting it together. May God bless you in your own hunting and watch over you in this sometimes dangerous passion we all hold so dear.

You will spend a lot more time glassing than walking, so you cannot afford to buy anything but the best binoculars and boots. (Safari Press photo library)

Chapter 1

MEET THE GRIZZLY/BROWN BEAR GUIDES

It is with great pleasure that I introduce dedicated hunters everywhere to perhaps the best assemblage of grizzly/brown bear guides ever featured in one piece of literature.* These guides are the most experienced group I could find, and each has guided for an average of more than twenty-five years. Most are still actively outfitting and guiding, though a couple of them are now retired. All possess a wealth of information to share, and what they have to say may open your eyes to a whole new world with respect to guide-client relations. I believe that anyone who has ever been on a guided hunt will find helpful information somewhere in the pages of this book.

These guides share a large number of characteristics in common with each other and with guides featured in other books in this series. They universally place a high premium on hunter ethics, honesty, integrity, hard work, patience, dependability, and persistence. They all desire their hunters to come well prepared in every possible way, and they go into great detail delineating how one goes about doing this. They have unique information to share, so the reader should never get bored.

These guides are truly excellent representatives of the outdoor fraternity, and I think you'll agree they all offer invaluable insights into the world of grizzly/brown bear hunting. I can't think of a sufficient way to repay them for imparting their wealth of experience to us, so thank them yourself when you see them . . . and enjoy the information here to the utmost!

*Each guide can be found here in the sequence they appear in the book, with a brief summary of their backgrounds and experience, contact information, and a recent photograph. The material included here is taken directly from interviews with the guides and some cases from printed material they supplied. Most information in this book has been obtained by means of telephone interviews with each guide, and is essentially as they said it.

Dennis Harms
Alaska Trophy Safaris
P.O. Box 670071
Chugiak, AK 99567
907-696-2484
www.alaskakodiakbear
huntingsafaris.com
alaskatrophy@yahoo.com

Dennis Harms grew up in Wisconsin with a dream to hunt moose, bears, and other big game. He finished high school there, and in 1965 graduated from Wisconsin's South State University. He went to Alaska afterward and became a registered guide in 1968, guiding for virtually all available big-game species including walrus and polar bear. Besides running a few fishing camps, he has done no work other than guiding hunters.

He began guiding on Kodiak Island for brown bears in 1970 and continues to do so today. He also has vast experience in southeastern Alaska guiding for brown bears, starting in 1974 and finishing his operation there in 1991. The season dates were different enough that he was able to guide in both places each season. In southeastern Alaska he used boats—something of a tradition there.

From 1972 to 1988 he also operated a camp on the Alaska Peninsula, where he hunted primarily for moose and caribou, but he also guided and outfitted for Alaska Peninsula brown bears as well. He even has interior grizzly experience, spanning the years 1968–2000. Most of his interior grizzly experience came on mixed-bag hunts where the bears were taken incidentally, though he did take some hunters specifically for grizzly. He had one of the few Alaska Range horseback hunts, and took quite a few grizzly bears from that operation, which was directed at sheep, moose, and caribou in addition to bears.

Dennis currently outfits on the Alitak Peninsula, the farthest southwest corner of Kodiak, a unique area in that it was the only part of the island not covered by glaciers during the Ice Age. Bears there have larger heads and slightly smaller bodies, as a rule, as compared to other Kodiak bears. His second area is also on the southwest part of Kodiak in the Frazier Lake area, where the bears have truly large bodies. His third area, the brushy country around Uganik Bay, is more difficult to hunt but produces some real monster brown bears.

Dennis has limited his operations in recent years to Kodiak brown bears, making him one of the few outfitters to do this. He has taken over three hundred brown bears for his clients and has personally been in on about seventy-five of those kills. He has nine brown bear permits for the spring hunt and two permits in the fall.

Dennis has been married to his wife, Cheryl, since 1962, and they have two daughters who are both physicians. His girls are married and have presented the Harms seniors with three grandchildren.

Dennis maintains an extensive hunting library and subscribes to virtually all the hunting magazines. He highly recommends two books by Marvin H. Clark Jr., *Last of the Great Brown Bear Men* and *Track of the Kodiak*. Another book he recommends is Harry Dodd's 2007 title, *Kodiak Island and Its Bears,* a volume filled with years of in-depth research.

Gary "Butch" King
Wildman Lake Lodge/Cinder River Lodge
2024 Stonegate Circle
Anchorage, AK 99515
907-522-1164
www.wildmanlodge.com
hunt@wildmanlodge.com

Butch King was born and raised in Anchorage, where his father owned a sporting-goods store and flew as a bush pilot. Butch started young in the guiding and outfitting business. In 1966 at age twelve he shot his first grizzly. That same year he began working as a camp boy for legendary brown bear and polar bear guide Lee Holen. Holen owned the Wrangell Mountain Lodge and hunted polar bears out of Point Hope, Alaska, and he also owned Cinder River Lodge on the Alaska Peninsula.

Butch became a pilot in 1968 and finished high school in 1971. He then became a pilot-guide for Holen, working out of Cinder River Lodge. Holen retired in 1983, and Butch immediately bought his area and has owned it ever since. That area has expanded significantly since Butch bought out his neighbor, Keith Johnson, and added Wildman Lake Lodge to his guiding operation. Today Butch's hunts for brown bear are conducted out of both these lodges, and he personally runs Wildman Lake Lodge. He has another highly experienced brown bear master guide running Cinder River Lodge, that being Brad Adams, who himself has almost twenty years in the business. His area starts at the north end of Amber Bay on the Pacific side of the Alaska Peninsula and includes Mount Aniakchak, the highest volcano in this region, in the heart of the Aniakchak National Preserve. The area continues southward on the Pacific side to near the village of Perryville, excluding native lands. The line then crosses the peninsula to a place called Cape Cinnamon, where the walrus haul out frequently, on the Bristol Bay side, and then goes north to the mouth of the Cinder River. The area encompasses about two and a half million acres in total, as large as all of Kodiak Island.

Butch has outfitted hundreds of hunts for brown bear over the years, and additionally has guided some hunts for grizzly in the western Arctic and in the Wrangell Mountains. His hunters have taken more than three hundred fifty brown bears over the years "since we got computers," and he carefully keeps records on each bear taken. He estimates that before computers and his current record-keeping system, he took perhaps an additional hundred brown bears, for a total of close to four hundred fifty kills. In addition to his brown bear operation, he runs an extensive sport-fishing business.

Butch isn't a big reader of the hunting literature, having experienced so many hunting adventures of his own. He does enjoy the renovated *Sports Afield* magazine, some of the magazines from Petersen's Publishing, and the Safari Club International magazine *Safari*.

He has been married to his wife, Kathy, for some sixteen years, and she helps with the daily operation of their guiding business. Butch has two daughters. He is one of the very few outfitters who actually lives in his guiding area during the spring, summer, and fall. After living through fifty Alaska winters, he now heads for the Lower Forty-Eight to live in more hospitable weather during the harshest time of the year in Alaska.

Mike Munsey
Munsey's Bear Camp
Amook Pass
Kodiak, AK 99615
907-847-2203
www.munseysbearcamp.com
mmunsey@starband.net

Mike's parents started Munsey's Bear Camp back in 1956, the year he was born, and except for a stint in college Mike has lived in the camp his entire life. He started helping his father, master guide Park Munsey, in guiding hunters as soon as he was old enough. He got his own guiding license when he was only nineteen, bought the camp from his parents in 1980, and has been running it since that time. In 1996 Mike received his master guide license.

Mike and his wife, Robin, operate in Uyak Bay and Spiridon Bay on Kodiak Island. This is the same area in which Mike's father guided, and in 2006 the Munsey family celebrated fifty years of guiding, all in this same area.

Having been raised in the business, Mike was taught all facets of bear guiding by his father. His mother home-schooled Mike as well as his brother and sisters. During those years Mike would spend a half-day in class and the other half-day helping his father run his bear hunts. Mike went off to college at the University of Alaska in Fairbanks and at the University of Hawaii, and then returned and bought the camp. He married Robin in 1984, and they have since been running Munsey's Bear Camp together.

Mike admits he doesn't keep an exact count but estimates he has personally guided hunters to well over a hundred brown bears through the years. He further estimates that over the fifty years Munsey's Bear Camp has been in business, almost one thousand bear hunters have taken about eight hundred Kodiak bears. Mike's operation takes twelve bear hunters per year, distributed in three areas: North Uyak, South Uyak, and Spiridon Bay.

Mike enjoys reading *Outdoor Life*, *Sports Afield*, and the magazine of the Alaska Professional Hunters Association.

It is big country and it takes patience to find bears. (Safari Press photo library)

Scott Newman
Alaska Bear Guides LLC
P.O. Box 1348
Petersburg, AK 99833
907-723-1053
www.alaskabearguide.com
info@alaskabearguide.com

Scott Newman began guiding for brown bears in 1988, initially working for several other outfitters before starting his own business in 1992. He lives in Petersburg and guides primarily in the Admiralty Island area in southeastern Alaska. He has had a passion for bears since he was only six years old. He used to go to the town dump and watch the hulking animals, and he states that at this tender age he had already decided he wanted to be a bear guide.

When Scott was younger, he fished quite a bit commercially for halibut, salmon, and crab, and states matter-of-factly that after watching some forty-year-old fishermen, he decided he didn't want to be in their kind of shape when he reached their age! He is an instrument-rated commercial pilot and flew for several years before settling on the guiding business.

He grew up hunting brown bears and has taken about two hundred of the animals since starting his guiding operation. He has an allocation of ten brown bear hunters per year, but he also takes an occasional black bear.

Scott has three daughters ages four to fourteen, and his oldest girl has been developing into quite a hunter herself.

Scott isn't a big reader and feels that he knows more about bears than most people who write stories in the average magazine.

Peter Klaui
North Coast Adventures
Box 13 RR#2
Galiano, BC, Canada V0N 1P0
250-539-5751/250-830-7434
www.ncasafaris.com
info@ncasafaris.com

Peter no longer actively guides for coastal grizzlies, but he did so for many years and still outfits hunts for the big bears. In addition, he has twenty-five years of experience as a commercial fisherman. Peter was born and raised in Calgary, Alberta, and went to the University of British Columbia in Vancouver. He is married and has a daughter and a son; his son is an active guide who, Peter hopes, will someday take over the family business.

After guiding and fishing for most of his life, Peter purchased an extensive guiding area on the British Columbia coast north of Vancouver. His area parallels the center of Vancouver Island and runs northward to the same latitude as the northern tip of that island. Extending inland a long way, it encompasses seven to eight thousand square miles.

Peter has personally guided clients to more than twenty coastal grizzlies since purchasing the area in 1995, but several guides who work for him have taken many more. Over the years before he obtained the area, it produced perhaps hundreds of bears for hunters. His operation is now on a very conservative quota system, and he takes a maximum of five grizzly hunters per year.

Alisha "Mutts" Rosenbruch-Decker
Glacier Guides, Inc.
P.O. Box 219
Gustavus, AK 99826
907-697-2252
www.glacierguidesinc.com
wildlifeheritage@yahoo.com

Guiding for Alaska brown bears has been a way of life for Alisha "Mutts" Rosenbruch-Decker since she was a small child. She readily states that she has never known, or wanted to know, any other way of life.

Mutts was raised in a hunting camp, so her initiation into brown bear hunting was all-encompassing and complete. Her family operation, Glacier Guides, Inc., operates in Southeast Alaska on the famous "ABC" islands of Admiralty, Baranof, and Chichagof. These islands boast phenomenal concentrations of brown bears. Admiralty Island, in fact, has the highest density of brown bears in the world, nearly 2.5 per square mile.

Mutts was home-schooled aboard the family vessel at sea, with schedule adjustments so she could be involved in the field. She began classes in early July and was finished in time to be off during the spring bear season. From the time she was eight, Mutts was in the field every day of bear season. For the next ten years she was involved in every aspect of the hunt—skiff tending, trophy judging, stalking techniques, area familiarity, skinning, and learning to adjust to individual client needs and abilities.

At age eighteen, the earliest she could apply, the state of Alaska issued her an assistant guide license, and again at the earliest possible age (twenty-one) she received her registered guide license. In truth, by that time Mutts had over thirteen years of brown bear hunting-guiding experience. Despite her vast experience, she cannot receive a master guide license until she has twelve years of experience as a registered guide, and that is still a few years away at her young age.

She is following in the footsteps of her parents, Jimmie C. and MaryAnn Rosenbruch, who both hold Alaska master guide licenses, as does her brother, Jimmie "Bud" Rosenbruch. At age sixteen she received the Safari Club International's Young Hunter of the Year award. In 2008 Mutts was the recipient of SCI's North American Professional Hunter of the Year award, which her father, Jimmie, had received back in 2001, making them the first-ever father-daughter team to achieve this honor. In March of 2005 Mutts was the first woman ever to appear on the cover of *Outdoor Life,* where she was named as one of North America's top female guides.

In the offseason Mutts and her husband of eight years, Zach Decker, operate their Wildlife Heritage Taxidermy business. Mutts went to taxidermy school to improve the quality of her personal mounts, and this led to their business. They specialize in life-size dioramas of Alaskan trophies, and they also do dioramas and habitat displays for the Rosenbruch World Wildlife Museum in St. George, Utah (www.rosenbruch.org). Hunting is clearly her passion, and she and Zach are dedicated to continuing the family legacy.

Mutts is a life member of the NRA and SCI, and she regularly reads *American Hunter, Safari,* and *Safari Times.* She also reads the *Alaska Professional Hunter* magazine. She recommends Craig Boddington's book *The Perfect Shot—North America* for information on correct shot placement and animal anatomy.

Tracy Vrem
Blue Mountain Lodge
P.O. Box 670130
Chugiak, AK 99567
907-688-2419
www.bluemountainlodge.com
tracy@bluemountainlodge.com

Tracy Vrem is a native Alaskan whose father came there in 1948 from North Dakota looking for a higher-paying job. He and Tracy's mother drove up the Alcan Highway to start a new life. Tracy has three siblings, and his oldest brother, Kelly, is also a master guide. His father is now retired, but his mother has been the cook for his operation since he purchased it. Tracy married his wife, Linda, also a native Alaskan, in 1995, and they have three children.

Tracy had a best friend whose father, George Needels Sr., had a hunting operation on the Alaska Peninsula. Tracy was able to spend two weeks there in October every year during high school in the 1970s, doing odd jobs such as washing dishes, working on skins and capes taken by clients, and cleaning ptarmigan. Tragically, his good friend George Needels Jr. and George's sister Terri died in a Super Cub crash in 1978, devastating their parents and all who knew them.

Tracy guided his first brown bear hunt for George Sr. in 1979, when he was only nineteen years old, taking a client from Germany. He readily admits that he had an awful lot to learn back then. However, he enjoyed such experiences so much that he decided to make guiding his life's work. He bought the entire operation from Needels just four years later, in 1983. His guiding area is in Unit 9E and extends from the Pacific Ocean to Bristol Bay, taking in the drainages of Becharof and Upper Ugashik Lakes.

Tracy has vast hunting experience for all species in Alaska, but most of his time has been spent on the Alaska Peninsula. He has personally guided almost fifty hunters to brown bears, and his operation has produced more than two hundred fifty of these trophy animals. He is permitted to take thirteen bears on the Alaska Peninsula and Becharof Refuge, and to take from one to three bears from state land every bear season.

As for his literary preferences, he reads all the documents produced by the Alaska Department of Fish and Game. Tracy also reads several hunting magazines for entertainment, though he states he seldom gets any new knowledge of brown bears from such articles.

Guy Anttila
P.O. Box 319
Atlin, BC, Canada V0W A1O
250-651-7784
www.guyanttilas
biggamehunts.com
info@guyanttila-hunts.com

Guy Anttila began guiding for coastal grizzly bears in 1978, when he purchased a guiding area in the Coast Range of northwestern British Columbia. Guy lives in the town of Atlin with his wife, Elsie, who has been with him since the start of his hunting operation. They were married in 1966 but have no children. He recently opted for retirement after thirty years in the business.

Even as a young boy Guy was attracted to wilderness and wild things. He enjoyed trapping muskrats, often skipping school to check his traps. Back in those days, hunting always seemed to be an overriding priority and he learned well the necessary techniques. Guy's education on grizzlies has come from living with and hunting the bears, and he states that this in itself gave him the most interesting and educational classroom possible.

He has never kept a log of the numbers of grizzlies his hunters have taken over the years, but he admits that in the early days prior to quotas, his clients did occasionally number in the low teens in a single year, so his take of grizzlies likely is in the range of at least a couple of hundred. In recent years the number of hunters passing through his camps has unfortunately been dropping gradually as politics has taken hold; as one example, British Columbia biologists actually try to convince interested parties how few bears there are in the forest. Guy states flatly that the population of grizzlies in British Columbia has never been better, and the new political climate is actually a threat to grizzlies rather than a protection.

He admits that he cannot honestly recommend to hunters which books to read in preparation for a grizzly hunt, because he hasn't had time to keep up with the available literature.

Because bears love to come to the beach and rummage around for something to eat in the spring, keep an eye on the water's edge. (Safari Press photo library)

Dave Leonard
Mountain Monarchs
of Alaska LLC
35555 Spur Highway PMB 300
Soldotna, AK 99669
907-283-4010
907-252-4952 (cell)
www.mountainmonarchs.com
mountainmonarchs@alaska.com

Dave Leonard grew up in a hunting family in Louisiana, where he was well schooled in the outdoors. He moved to Georgia while quite young and there extended his hunting education. As a young man Dave wanted to go to Alaska to work in the summer, so he wrote to many well-known outfitters and eventually, between his junior and senior years in high school, went to work in the Wrangell Mountains for Buck Conkle, one of the old-time Alaska outfitters. He primarily pursued Dall sheep, but many grizzlies roam the Wrangells as well, and his hunters took quite a few.

He states that from childhood he always wanted to be a big-game guide, so with his Alaska forays he was simply following his dream. He did return to Georgia and finish up his high-school education, but then his hunting, guiding, and commercial fishing careers took off and he stayed close to the land and never pursued higher formal education. He claims to have a master's degree in the school of hard knocks.

Today Dave guides in the Noatak River country north of Kotzebue in the western Arctic, in the western end of the Brooks Range. He has taken about two hundred interior grizzlies with clients over the years, counting his years of guiding and those taken by other guides within his current operation. For grizzlies, he takes an average of six to eight hunters per year, and many more for other species, including brown bears on the Alaska Peninsula.

Dave's wife is from Australia, and he met her in a furrier shop in Alaska. They have been married for many years but have no children.

Dave reads all the publications of the clubs to which he belongs, such as the SCI publications, and he also reads *Petersen's Hunting.* He likes almost anything written by Craig Boddington, calling Craig a hunter's hunter with much valuable insight.

Many hunters lack the patience and stamina to glass for bears day after day—but the payoff can be huge! (Photo courtesy of Tracy Vrem)

Joe Mott
Stoney River Lodge
(Outfitter Curly Warren)
P.O. Box 62
Sleetmute, AK 99668
907-526-5211/307-856-5258
www.stoneyriverlodge.com
srl1@starband.net
rangepainter@bresnan.net

Joe Mott, who lives in Riverton, Wyoming, readily admits he took up hunting only after he was an adult. In 1985 he had a friend who had begun doing some work for outfitter Curly Warren of Stoney River Lodge. Joe had already begun guiding for elk in Wyoming when, after elk season, he got a call asking if he could oversee Warren's lodge for a winter. He drove up the Alcan Highway, spent the winter at Stoney River Lodge, and then stayed on to guide for bear when springtime came in 1986. He has guided for interior grizzlies and coastal brown bears every year since.

Joe has been married "a long time" and has a daughter and two granddaughters.

Stoney River Lodge is in Alaska's Game Unit 19, but its area also laps into part of Unit 17, a brown bear area. Over the years, Joe has guided clients to over a hundred bears, about 75 percent of them in the interior grizzly area. The grizzly season has changed over time, and for many years the lodge hosted four groups of three hunters, each group for a ten-day hunt. Joe often would guide nine out of the twelve hunters, because he was the main guide most of those years. In recent years Stoney River Lodge has established more camps in the outlying areas to spread out the hunting. Joe guides in both the spring and fall for grizzlies, but due to changes in hunting seasons and the way the lodge operates, he now usually guides only five hunters per year.

He is a member of several hunting and shooting organizations, including the National Rifle Association, and he reads their literature. Like many guides, he gets enough hunting without having to do a lot of reading about it.

A genuine 10½-foot bear is rare, but every year a few dozen of them get shot in Alaska because of the excellent management of the bear population. (Safari Press photo library)

Ask the Grizzly/Brown Bear Guides

Larry Rivers
(Master Guide, Retired)
Box 107-I
Talkeetna, AK 99676
907-733-2473
www.larryrivers.com
larry@larryrivers.com

Larry, the product of a Kansas farm, says he grew bigger as a teenager in Colorado, though he is small in stature and says he never did really grow up. He moved to Alaska in 1962, at first living there only during summer and attending college in Colorado the rest of the year. He spent some time in Hawaii as well. Larry has two college degrees, one in marketing and one in management.

One summer he met a young nursing student on a blind date in Colorado, and ultimately married Naomi in 1969. Naomi and Larry have three offspring, a son and two daughters. Tragically, Naomi was killed in a motorcycle accident in 2000. Some months later one of Larry's friends was killed in an automobile accident, and after another year Larry married his friend's widow, whose name is Robin.

Larry Rivers started both guiding and flying as a bush pilot in 1972, working for Clark Engle. His first quarry was the grizzly, but later he expanded to brown bears. What got him interested in guiding? Well, mainly he needed a job! Back in the early 1970s, before the Alaska Pipeline project began, very few jobs were available in Alaska. He was living in a remote cabin eight or nine miles from the nearest road. One day as he walked through the village of Talkeetna, a friend leaned out a door and yelled, "Hey, Larry, do you want to guide?" The friend had Clark Engle on the radio, and he put Larry on with him and that's how it all got started. On Monday he didn't even have a guiding license, and on Friday he was a guide!

Larry has guided for grizzlies and brown bears all over Alaska, including the Wrangells, the Brooks Range, the Talkeetna Mountains, and the Alaska Peninsula. He has owned lodges in the Talkeetna and Brooks Ranges. Everywhere he's guided there have been grizzly bears, except for Unit 9, which is purely brown bear. He has also guided in Russia for the Siberian brown bear, very similar to the North American grizzly. Larry's operations took about one hundred forty interior grizzlies over the years, in addition to a substantial quantity of bears classified as browns.

Though retired now from active guiding and outfitting, Larry is well-respected in Alaska and has been president of the Alaska Professional Hunters Association.

He enjoys reading quality hunting books, especially the classics, but is rather turned off by many of the current hunting magazines because they are repetitive and often not truthful, in his opinion. When he does read a magazine, he gravitates toward *Sporting Classics* and a new one called *Under Wild Skies*. He receives and selectively reads *Safari* and *Wild Sheep*.

Larry is one of only two retired guides featured in this book, and much of his interview comes across in the past tense, so the reader should be aware why this is the case.

Darwin & Wendy Cary
Scoop Lake Outfitters
5615 Deadpine Drive
Kelowna, BC, Canada V1P 1A3
250-491-1885
www.scooplake.com
info@scooplake.com

Darwin has been outfitting for Canadian interior grizzly bears for many years, though in recent years he has ceased to be an active field guide. He grew up in an outfitting family, his parents owning a guiding area in northern British Columbia from 1960 through 1982. He was born in 1959, so he truly grew up in the business. He guided his first grizzly hunt at age seventeen, even before he could obtain a guiding license, at a time when his father was short of guides. Today he and his wife, Wendy, to whom he has been married for "twenty-something years," have two daughters.

His outfitting area is in northeast British Columbia, a hundred air miles from the nearest road and about a hundred miles southeast of Watson Lake, Yukon. His area actually corners into a guiding area in the Cassiar Mountains where this author took his first wild sheep in Canada in 1986. In 1992 Darwin bought his current area, which is adjacent to the one his parents owned all those years. He's been in that sector of British Columbia pretty much all his life. He started flying as a pilot when he was only sixteen and has been at it for some thirty-two years.

If you count his own operation and that of his parents, he's been involved in taking over one hundred grizzly bears. He readily points out that in the "good old days" his operation took four to five grizzlies per year, but since the infamous political closure of British Columbia grizzly hunting in 1996–1997, they are limited to only three a year. Today they shoot more nuisance grizzlies than those taken by legally licensed hunters, something he says is a direct result of the overly conservative quotas assigned by the British Columbia government.

Darwin accepts three hunters per year for grizzly, but takes them on a trophy-fee basis only. Most hunters seek either mountain goat or moose, or a combination, and the grizzly, if it comes, is a bonus animal. Typically, all his hunters see grizzlies, but less than half kill a bear. The tag for a grizzly in British Columbia costs $1,000, and if a bear is taken the government garnishes another $1,000 of the trophy fee. He points out that few of his hunters are interested in bears at these prices and these odds, but he does usually take his three bears during the season.

Thanks to his position as an outfitter, Darwin gets all kinds of hunting magazines, even though he doesn't actually subscribe to them. He likes *Wild Sheep, Safari, B. C. Hunter,* and a number of others. He also likes the old hunting biographies in book form by earlier writers so he can see what hunting was like in the past and compare it to the present.

Ron Fleming
Love Brothers and Lee, Ltd.
RR#1-L-42
Kispiox Valley Road
Hazelton, BC, Canada V0J 1Y0
250-842-6350
www.lovebroslee.com
lovebroslee@bulkley.net

Ron Fleming says that from an early age of perhaps eight, all he could think about was trapping. He caught lots of muskrats and even admits to taking a few of the neighborhood cats! It quickly became a way of life for him. His family lived in Prince George, British Columbia, and his father worked in the logging industry. He says he was never interested in following in his father's footsteps, being drawn to more appealing outdoor pursuits, especially hunting.

An older friend went north one summer and guided for outfitter Tommy Walker, and the photos he brought back ignited a strong desire in Ron to do the same thing. The pictures showed hunting camps, packtrains with caribou antlers tied on, bear hides tacked on the side of a cabin, sheep horns, clients with trophies, and the like. He decided—on the basis of those pictures, his friend's experiences, plus his natural inclination—that he had to go there.

At first Ron wanted only a summer job in the north, so he tracked down the outfitter to see if he could work. Unfortunately, Walker wasn't interested in hiring a fresh-out-of-high-school kid. However, he changed his mind when Ron volunteered to work for free. That experience started Ron's guiding career in 1967. He worked mostly as a wrangler for two years, but in the process he learned the habits of the grizzly, how to skin one, and how to hunt them.

A huge opportunity opened for him just two years later, in 1969, when he joined the outfit of Love Brothers & Lee and began guiding for grizzlies right away. He has since purchased all interest in that same outfit. His guiding area is in extreme northwestern British Columbia, centered on the headwaters of the Skeena River and the Finlay River. He and his first wife had one son before she died of cancer almost at the time of the birth. Ron took the new baby, only two months old, into the bush on a spring grizzly hunt, doing double duty as a single parent and a grizzly guide. On that hunt he took out a client from Ontario who killed a big grizzly. That baby is now grown and has presented Ron with two granddaughters. Ron married his present wife, Brenda, twenty-six years ago, and they now have a daughter as well.

Ron has a quota of three grizzlies a year in his hunting area, and usually takes two hunters in the spring and one in the fall. Ron's hunters have taken some sixty interior grizzlies over the years.

Ron recommends that hunters read and learn about the animal itself rather than concentrating on hunting magazine stories, which he believes are often sensationalized to the point of making a hunter spooky.

James Pokiak
Pokiak Guiding and Outfitting
P.O. Box 131
Tuktoyaktuk, NT, Canada X0E 1C0
867-977-2170
ookpiktours@yahoo.ca

James was born and raised in Canada's Arctic in the village of Tuktoyaktuk, near where the Mackenzie River empties into the Beaufort Sea. He began his guiding career in the 1980s when his local Hunter-Trapper Association set aside some big-game tags for visiting sportsmen. He guides for muskoxen, polar bears, caribou, and, of course, barren-ground grizzlies. A number of criteria were set by his peers when Tuktoyaktuk's hunting program was instituted, and he states that he was one of the lucky ones able to meet those criteria and begin guiding hunters. His guiding area is a vast area of Arctic tundra stretching from the Yukon border on the west side to the Horton River on the east.

James is unique in this entire *Ask the Guides* book series in that so far he is the only featured genuine Native American, a member of the Inuvialuit people. His native language is somewhat akin to the Inuit tongue spoken farther east, but it is also distinct. He speaks English perfectly, however. James has been married for many years to Maureen, who is from Saskatchewan, and they have a son and two daughters. He met Maureen when she came to Tuktoyaktuk as a young teacher.

James learned to hunt and guide by observing and participating with others, including community elders and an uncle who is a hunter and guide. He emphasizes that his education in hunting came because others taught him, and he counts himself fortunate to have been in a position to take advantage of that time of learning.

His quota of grizzly bears is small, never more than two per year, and some years he doesn't get a tag at all. Tuktoyaktuk has eight outfitters and all are vying for the sportsmen tags allocated by the Hunter-Trapper Association.

He likes to read any big-game magazine but especially enjoys Safari Club International's publication *Safari.*

Now back in camp, it is all smiles. The trophy's won, and the hard physical effort is forgotten. (Safari Press photo library)

Chris Widrig
Widrig Outfitters Ltd.
139 Falaise Road
Whitehorse, YT, Canada Y1A 3C8
867-393-3802
www.widrig.yk.ca
chris@widrigoutfitters.com

Chris Widrig began guiding in 1973 for his grandfather, George Dalziel, who was one of the original British Columbia outfitters. Chris admits he was just a kid at the time, but the experience inspired him to later purchase his own outfitting area in the Yukon. His guiding area, 275 miles northeast of Whitehorse in the Mackenzie Mountains, is roadless and extremely remote—the whole region is untouched wilderness. All of his hunters are flown into the hunting area from Whitehorse.

Chris not only is the outfitter but he actively guides as well. He takes some twenty-eight hunters per year, and his primary species are interior grizzly, Dall sheep, mountain caribou, and Alaska-Yukon moose. His hunters have taken dozens of grizzly bears over the years, including several every hunting season, but he isn't sure exactly how many.

He has a boy, Ryan, who is fifteen years old, and a daughter, Deban, who is ten.

Chris regularly reads all the usual hunting magazines but is reluctant to recommend any one as his favorite.

Section I

HUNTING BROWN BEARS IN ALASKA

Chapter 2

SELECTING AN OUTFITTER

What should a hunter look for in an Alaskan brown bear outfitter/guide?

Dennis Harms: Regardless of the species hunted, and even for a fishing guide, I recommend that you find someone with honesty and integrity. There are so many variables all the time that using such a guide is important. For example, if an outfitter encounters a guy who's badly out of shape but wants to hunt brown bears, the outfitter should be honest enough to tell the prospective hunter whether he can offer the kind of hunt the client is able to do.

Beyond honesty, ambition is pretty high on the quality list of the outfitter because this business is very hard work and you've got to want to do it badly enough to do it well. Experience is definitely important, and so is the desire to hunt hard for a good trophy animal. The ability to judge bears is also essential because in Alaska it's relatively easy to go out and find just any bear, while it's relatively tough to get your client a really big one. The difference is ambition, experience, and the ability to judge the animals. Lots of guides can take you out and get you a bear, but it's a challenge to take a hunter out and get him a ten-foot boar.

Gary "Butch" King: The potential hunter should look for more than experience in hunting brown bears. He needs an outfitter who has conquered the logistics of putting on the hunt, which leans more heavily on the outfitter aspect than on the guiding aspect. Getting the hunter in front of a bear isn't actually the most difficult part of the job. The hardest chore is to get the hunter properly outfitted and prepared, which means having the hunt supported by good equipment and permanent buildings and structures within the guiding area. This is in contrast to what I refer to as a

A good outfitter on Kodiak should have reliable and safe access to his guiding area. (Photo courtesy of Dennis Harms)

"pup-tent gypsy," who may or may not own an airplane and who has a backpack tent and a Coleman stove. That type of outfitter cannot support your hunt in a manner that is proper and safe. The guide on the ground with the hunter is about 10 percent of what it takes to conduct a hunt. The rest of it is equipment, logistics, and getting proper food into the camp. You've got to be able to access that camp as necessary, and that requires an airplane most of the time.

Mike Munsey: I would say longevity is the number one priority. Make sure your outfitter has been in the business long enough to know what he is doing. Also, check references, especially those of unsuccessful hunters. An unsuccessful hunter will sometimes give you a more honest assessment of a hunt because he is not biased by the fact he got a bear. But watch out for someone who's just upset that he didn't get a bear and doesn't really have anything to complain about. On the other hand, a successful hunter might be so excited about scoring

Good equipment is the mark of a good outfitter; the Kodiak scenery is free! (Photo courtesy of Dennis Harms)

that he will ignore some major problems with the hunt, such as quality of equipment, availability of game, etc. So you need to check all references to get a feel for the operation. Ask the guide for names and addresses of all that outfitter's hunters from the past year.

Scott Newman: To a great extent it depends on the hunter's priorities. There are primarily three areas of Alaska that offer the hunter an opportunity to take a coastal brown bear: the Alaska Peninsula, Kodiak Island, and Southeast Alaska. Hunting style in the three areas varies a lot in many aspects. Here in Southeast, it's primarily a boat-hunting operation. We do have a lot of bears, too. We hunt from the boat, glassing beaches and estuaries. This kind of hunting is for people who want accommodations that are a little more secure and comfortable than a tent. Too, I think our area is one of the most beautiful places in the world to hunt, even though we don't get quite the size of brown bear as the average on Kodiak or the Peninsula. Our skulls seldom reach 27 inches, and our average in fact is 24½. That's still a very nice bear, and we've got a high-density population.

Alisha "Mutts" Rosenbruch-Decker: There are a number of factors involved in selecting a reliable outfitter/guide. Experience is clearly a major factor in a hunter's chance of success. When looking at a prospective outfitter, consider the area and how well that outfitter knows that area. Also find out how far in advance the outfitter is booked. It should raise a red flag when an outfitter has several same-year openings. Certainly a cancellation or similar circumstance may yield an opening or two at times in any operation, but an outfitter with numerous openings could indicate a struggling success rate. Hunters should carefully examine an outfitter's authorization for hunting the area advertised. For example, make sure that if an outfitter hunts National Forest lands, his Forest Service permit is current and valid.

Tracy Vrem: A person should look for experience, a good reputation, and how the prospective area is accessed. A good guide or outfitter should be able to provide plenty of positive references as well.

What are (a) the most important single characteristic and (b) the worst possible deficiency in an Alaskan brown bear guide?

Dennis Harms: The most important characteristic is a strong desire to take a trophy male bear, combined with the ability to identify such a bear. The worst thing would be the opposite, the guide who's both lazy and unable to judge bears.

Gary "Butch" King: The most important characteristic is that the outfitter is well-established with permanent physical assets in the guide area, meaning a base camp that is strong and substantial enough to withstand anything the weather can throw at it. Weather is surely going to trash a few spike camps from time to time, and when that happens, you've got to be able to fall back to a good facility, reorganize, and redeploy. If you don't have that permanent facility within the area, you can't do that. Also make sure your outfitter has the transportation logistics conquered, and that doesn't mean one airplane. It means several planes and several pilots so there are options

A comfortable base lodge is a fine asset before and after the hunt, and is essential if one needs to leave the field and regroup. (Photo courtesy of Gary "Butch" King)

if one is disabled for some reason. That allows the outfitter to handle almost any situation without having to call on the Coast Guard or his neighbor. The worst deficiency is the opposite of the guy described above—the "pup-tent gypsy" who has no capability to back up his operation with multiple assets.

Mike Munsey: It depends on whether you are talking about the guide who accompanies a hunter in the field or the guide/ outfitter who books the hunt. I'll discuss both, and will refer to the personal guide as "guide" and to the guide who books the hunt as "outfitter."

It takes many important characteristics to make a good guide, and it's hard to single out one. Some are obvious, like safety and courtesy. If I had to choose one single characteristic of a guide, I would probably say experience, because it's the hardest one to fake. Either you have it or you don't. It's important for spotting game, for making a stalk, for judging animal size—pretty much all facets of what a guide does. All of these improve with experience. The worst deficiency is the guide who has his own agenda and pushes a hunter to shoot a substandard bear to get the hunt over and done. When this happens, the hunter isn't going to be happy with the bear. The guide could just be in a rush to finish the hunt—for many different reasons—but he needs to realize he's being paid to make sure the hunter has a good, safe hunt, not just to produce a bear.

Regarding outfitters, the single most important characteristic would be honesty, and not having it is the worst deficiency. If a hunter knows ahead of time what kind of camp he's coming to and what kind of hunting he'll be doing, it just makes for a better hunt and eliminates any unpleasant surprises when a hunter arrives.

Scott Newman: That's a tough question, but I'd say the most important characteristic is the ability to handle tough situations, like a bear charge. I've been charged several times, one or two of which were serious and most of which were false charges. The worst possible deficiency would be a guide who fails to rank safety first and thereby puts his client at risk.

Alisha "Mutts" Rosenbruch-Decker: I believe the single most important characteristic is a true passion for hunting the animal, which ensures a focused brown bear guide. This passion also generates energy, motivation, and the effort that will often produce an excellent trophy.

Energy, passion, and effort may not be enough, though. A true connection to these magnificent animals—almost a spiritual connection—is a rare and yet very important factor that makes for a superior brown bear guide. The worst possible guide deficiency is a lack of respect for these animals. This attitude breeds a profound lack of drive to truly know these great bears. If a guide does not know the quarry, consistent positive results and a high-quality trophy harvest are not possible.

Tracy Vrem: I'd rank honesty, experience, and organization as pretty much equally important characteristics. The worst deficiencies are dishonesty and laziness.

Is there any exceptional qualification for being an Alaskan brown bear guide that may not apply to other types of guiding?

Dennis Harms: I've guided for everything in Alaska over the years, and the thing that stands out most of all in brown bear hunting is the tremendous amount of patience required. You go to a hill or knob and glass for days, and if the guide doesn't have the patience to stick with the optics, he'll be terrible at hunting brown bears. You can sit on that hill for three days and see absolutely nothing, and at dark on the third day a ten-foot bear can come moving through the brush.

Gary "Butch" King: These are big, dangerous animals, and experience being around brown bears is extremely important. I wouldn't take a Montana elk guide, even if he has guided hundreds of elk hunters, and put him out there as a brown bear guide if he's never even seen one. I keep going back to logistics being 90 percent of the hunt, and I know it isn't very exciting gathering supplies and the like, but if it's not done thoroughly and well, then you're

Good equipment and good organization lead to better chances of a successful hunt. (Photo courtesy of Gary "Butch" King)

Scott Newman's base camp and skiff for hunting brown bears. (Photo courtesy of Scott Newman)

being shortchanged. In Montana, all a guide needs is a rifle and a pickup truck. That's far from the case in outfitting for brown bears in Alaska. My business has been successful because I've had the ability to keep an overview of everything that's going on with my operation, mainly because I'm a pilot with several airplanes. I can check on camps, I can get supplies there when they're needed, and I can pull the camp quickly when the hunt's over. In our country, if an outfitter isn't a pilot, he's at a great disadvantage.

Mike Munsey: The ability to spot game is universally important among guides, but it's probably even more so for bear guiding on Kodiak because so much of the day is spent glassing. Also, being a good seaman is important in those areas where a boat is used. We do not hunt out of boats, but we use boats to get around the hunting area and to get to and from camp. A good understanding of weather patterns, wind, and waves is crucial to a safe and successful trip.

Scott Newman: You can easily get yourself into a dangerous situation when guiding for brown bears, so you've got to know how to get yourself out.

A Bob Delaney photo taken in Scott Newman's area—a good area should have salmon streams and plenty of bears. (Photo courtesy of Scott Newman)

Alisha "Mutts" Rosenbruch-Decker: The Alaskan brown bear is truly a special animal. This large predator clearly has different qualities and personality traits from most other game species. Most certainly, different elements are required to be a regular winner when guiding for and hunting these creatures. Brown bears are highly intelligent and have an uncanny capacity to avoid human contact. To become truly successful at hunting them, a guide must learn to think like a bear. Becoming totally immersed in a brown bear's way of life is a very important element to consistent success.

Tracy Vrem: Patience and knowing every square mile of your guide area are absolute essentials in this business.

Does your area boast a really good source of protein to help bears grow big (salmon streams, plentiful ungulates, large ground-squirrel population, etc.)?

Dennis Harms: I've probably got a little different take on that question than most people. I believe the size of bears in a given area is determined by heredity, but this potential has been influenced heavily by available food over the past several hundred years. If an area has a huge supply of salmon year in and year out, along with good vegetation, you're not going to have a great big bear starve to death. In the eastern Wrangell Mountains, which is now a park where we used to hunt sheep, we saw lots of grizzlies. However, they were the smallest grizzlies I've ever seen in my life. I think the reason they were small was that very little quality food existed there, just the occasional ground squirrel and whatever else the bears could pick up. If a ten-foot Kodiak bear were suddenly plopped down there, he'd starve to death. But those scrappy little grizzlies living there didn't need a huge diet to keep alive, so they did fine. I don't think such a change happens just during the lifetime of a single bear; it happens over dozens of generations. Where there's a big food supply, you certainly have bigger bears, but I think the relationship of big bears to a good food supply is more complicated than meets the eye.

Luxury aboard Mutts' family boat, Alaska Grandeur. (Photo courtesy of Alisha "Mutts" Rosenbruch-Decker)

Scenic grandeur with the Rosenbruch's boat in the background. (Photo courtesy of Alisha "Mutts" Rosenbruch-Decker)

Good salmon streams in Southeast Alaska mean plenty of bears! (Photo courtesy of Alisha "Mutts" Rosenbruch-Decker)

Gary "Butch" King: In our area we have over a hundred salmon streams. The reason the largest bears in the world come from the Alaska Peninsula and Kodiak Island is that they have fish every month they're out of hibernation, except for May. In May here on the Peninsula, moose calves are the bears' primary source of protein. Both the Alaska Peninsula and Kodiak Island have salmon streams coming from both the north and the south sides. When things are slow on one side, the bears cross the mountains and feed on the other side. There's just no given week that a brown bear has to go around with an empty belly—there is always an abundance of fish. The more food they have, the bigger they grow.

Mike Munsey: Uyak and Spiridon Bays have two of the most important salmon spawning streams on the west side of Kodiak Island. That, plus an abundant supply of berries, provides ample protein for large bears. Bears on Kodiak don't prey much on ungulates or ground squirrels, mainly because of the dependable source of fish protein.

Make certain your outfitter has the skills and the salt to prepare your trophy. (Photo courtesy of Tracy Vrem)

Scott Newman: We've got plenty of salmon streams, the primary source of protein for our bears. We hit those streams pretty hard in the fall.

Alisha "Mutts" Rosenbruch-Decker: Southeast Alaska hosts an incredible number of wild salmon streams. The portions of unspoiled temperate rainforest in the Tongass National Forest support an immense biomass of salmon. This is a huge source of protein because these salmon spawn in small, easily accessible streams. Combine this with a moderate climate and a short hibernating season and you get really big boars and a prolific, dynamic population.

Tracy Vrem: Becharof Lake and Ugashik Lake have escapement of one million and six hundred thousand red salmon, respectively. The Pacific side has tremendous runs of pink, chum, and silver salmon. The state of Alaska has done a tremendous job of maintaining large, healthy salmon stocks since statehood.

These large, consistent stocks of salmon year after year provide the bears with plenty of food.

What does a good Alaskan brown bear guide do to ensure safety while hunting North America's most dangerous game?

Dennis Harms: The most important safety factor is to make sure the hunter isn't walking around with a shell in the chamber of his rifle. A lot of hunters are a little bit jumpy about hunting these bears, and if you don't watch them, they'll be locked and loaded. I had one guide who went so far as to take all the cartridges away from his hunter, and he gave them back only when they were ready to shoot.

The hunter is usually walking along behind the guide, of course, and most often the hunter's rifle barrel is pointed right at him.

Beyond that, the real danger in bear hunting is dangerous water. If it looks like it's going to blow, you're wise to stay off the water and just walk around the bay that day. Along with that, outfitters should not allow air taxis to bring hunters in during marginal weather. Some of these air taxis will fly in really crappy weather, but they have strict instructions from me that if conditions are marginal, they don't fly my hunters. Your statistical chances of getting killed by a bear are extremely small when compared to the chance of getting killed flying to camp by air taxi in poor weather.

Last but not least, you need to exert a prudent amount of care when you're around the bear, particularly in following up on a wounded one. I've been charged and my crew has been charged, and almost always it's been by a wounded bear. Still, we're always ready and we've had very few close calls over the years. In minimizing conflict with bears, it helps to keep a clean camp, hang food up in the trees, and so on.

Gary "Butch" King: One important thing is keeping a clean camp; if it's dirty it will attract bears. This is especially important in the fall, when there are sixteen hours of darkness and a lot of things can go "bump" in the night. Keeping a clean camp

The venerable Super Cub with tundra tires, the workhorse of many brown-bear operations. (Photo courtesy of Tracy Vrem)

minimizes the possibility of a bear intrusion. Also, we don't set up in the same spot year after year. We move the spike camps around so the bears don't get used to coming there to check out where we've been. We do that even though we fly out every scrap of garbage when we pull a camp. I keep two pigs back at the main camp inside an electric fence, and I feed them all the garbage from our entire operation.

Mike Munsey: A good backup weapon is essential for bear hunting. Most guides carry at least a .338 or a .375 H&H. Knowing when to fire a backup shot is crucial and comes with experience. With a wounded bear, time is also critical. You want to go after him as quickly as possible, whether that means following a blood trail or searching in the alders. I'll go more into our backup policy later.

Scott Newman: I think communication is the key. I encourage hunters to call me as often as they want before the hunt so we can talk through various aspects. By the time they actually get here, we have a limited amount of time to talk. We do try to cover well what to do and what not to do in various situations. However, I've learned that when things go wrong, the client is going to do what he's going to do, regardless!

Alisha "Mutts" Rosenbruch-Decker: Alaskan brown bears are the largest land carnivore in the world, and that's an intimidating fact. However, their reputation for being dangerous is often exaggerated. Clearly a brown bear (or even a black bear, for that matter) can kill or maim a human with ease. What is not widely known is that brown bears actually are rather gentle giants. Different bears have different space tolerances when it comes to associating with humans. A safe rule of thumb when hunting and guiding for brown bears is to hold a healthy respect so you avoid a dangerous situation.

Tracy Vrem: Firearms safety should be high on the list. Also, clear communication with the hunter about all aspects of the hunt is essential. This would include the stalk, shot placement, and any necessary steps to be taken after a bear has been shot.

Chapter 3

ALASKAN BROWN BEAR GUIDES EVALUATE THE HUNTER

What is your favorite type of hunter [personality, physical abilities, experience level, socioeconomic status, etc.]?

Dennis Harms: The element I prefer by far in a hunter is a good attitude. That's more important to me than any of the other things you list. I want the hunter to be square with me about what kind of physical shape he or she is in so I can design a hunt specifically for that person. I love a hunter with a great attitude who just loves being out there and who understands—if he isn't too physically able—that his expectations have to be lower than those of a hunter who is in great shape.

Gary "Butch" King: Physical ability is certainly a plus. Another big thing is personality. I like to say that expectation leads to disappointment. If a hunter's expectations are unreasonable, no amount of organization or quality of area or anything else can come up to those expectations. When I go on a fishing or hunting trip, I go just for the enjoyment of the experience. If a hunter comes just to kill a bear, he is here for the wrong reasons. It does help if a hunter is experienced in the woods and with firearms—these factors are more important than being an experienced bear hunter. I've had hunters who were billionaires and hunters who were factory workers, and I don't think status has any bearing on their hunting abilities.

Mike Munsey: My favorite kind of hunter is one in good physical condition who can climb and is friendly and easygoing. That is important when you are spending up to twelve days in the field and possibly sleeping in the same tent with him. Experience level is not as important. In fact, I sometimes prefer a novice hunter who will listen. Sometimes an experienced hunter thinks he knows everything there is to know. In all likelihood, regardless of how much experience a hunter has, his guide knows more about hunting these particular bears in this particular area than he does.

Scott Newman: None of the things you list are really important to me. The hunter I want to show up is the one who refuses to put pressure on the guide by repeatedly saying things like, "I want nothing but a ten-footer." That's probably the biggest mistake a hunter can make, and it can force the guide to make the wrong decision sometimes. If the hunter is more relaxed and just enjoying the hunt, the guide doesn't feel that pressure and he's a better decision-maker. If a guy has reasonable physical ability, that certainly helps.

Any hunter also ought to be able to handle his rifle in a safe and effective manner. Hunters too often handle guns carelessly, and I don't hesitate to let them know about it if I see it. You just can't afford to forget that a gun can kill somebody, and some hunters seem not to be aware of that.

I really like it when a guy is relaxed about his hunt and can afford to come back if necessary. If it's going to be a hunter's only chance ever to hunt brown bear, that's a tough situation. There's pressure you can't believe, because so many elements, such as weather, are completely out of our control. It sure removes a lot of pressure when the hunter's attitude is that it's fine whether he gets a bear or not. We try just as hard for either hunter, of course. Hunters of all socioeconomic levels have got to realize that it's a hunting trip and not a shopping trip, and hunts don't always conclude with a trophy.

Alisha "Mutts" Rosenbruch-Decker: The perfect type is the hunter who comes on a trip to actually hunt. He or she comes with the idea of having a good time, enjoying the opportunity to experience some of the most magical country on earth, and savoring the chance to pursue a magnificent creature. This kind of hunter has a personal goal in mind about what he would like to harvest as a trophy, and that's different for each hunter. When this quality hunter shows up in camp, physical shortcomings can be worked around and overcome. Guides can adjust to different personalities and generally help the hunter develop the attitude of relaxing and enjoying the adventure and the experience.

Every hunter dreams of being in a scene like this, but first comes the hard work, patience,

Experience level is an interesting element. Very often, a person who recognizes his inexperience can be the best type of client, assuming he allows himself to be taught. An experienced hunter is really hurting himself if he refuses to listen to instructions.

Social and economic status really has nothing to do with being a good or bad hunter unless wealth is used inappropriately to try to persuade a guide to do more. My favorite hunter comes to hunt brown bears—not to simply collect one. Taking a trophy brown bear is a huge element of the hunt, but it certainly is not the only element, and it may not even be the most important. There are facets of a brown bear hunt that give hunters the chance to experience something far beyond the ordinary.

Tracy Vrem: My favorite hunter has a cooperative personality. I also like for him to be physically fit enough to walk thirty minutes

and diligence. (Photo courtesy of Tracy Vrem)

at a time without a break. Ideally he'll have quite a bit of experience and have taken fifty or more big-game animals. I don't really care about a person's background or income; people are people, and socioeconomic status doesn't really matter to me.

How important is it for the hunter to be in top physical shape?

Dennis Harms: That varies greatly from one hunt area to another. In some areas the hunter has to be in great shape because there simply isn't any other way to do it, and those in poor physical condition shouldn't even consider going. That's where integrity comes in, because you've got to be willing to tell a person whether you've got a place to hunt that will match that hunter's physical ability.

Large bears have large feet. (Safari Press photo library)

Gary "Butch" King: Our hunters need to be in the best physical condition they personally can achieve. Spring hunts are usually more physically demanding than fall hunts. On a fall hunt, bears are predictable in where they're going to be. They'll either be on the river fishing or on the hill above the river sleeping it off. Once you figure out where the bear eats and sleeps, it's just a matter of hanging out in the middle until you get your chance. On spring hunts, the bear can be on the top of the mountain or on the beach or anywhere in between, because the rut is on and he's chasing the girls. The good thing is that you've got twenty hours of daylight to get to him, even if you see him a long way off, but that situation can be demanding as heck sometimes.

Mike Munsey: Physical conditioning is extremely important. Kodiak Island is very mountainous, and the larger boars are usually up on the mountain or back deep in the valleys. If a hunter can get to these areas, his chances of getting a large bear greatly increase.

Scott Newman: It's not very important in my area. Sometimes there's a significant walk to be made, and sometimes you've got to hurry to get in position for a shot. Being in good shape is helpful at those times. Most of the time, though, it's not a hurry-up situation; it's pretty relaxed, and any hunter who can walk at all can do it.

Alisha "Mutts" Rosenbruch-Decker: A hunter's physical abilities can generally be accommodated if the person has a willing personality. To ensure a truly fair chance at harvesting a trophy brown bear, any hunter should realistically be willing and able to walk roughly two miles a day on wet, slick, uneven ground in hip-length waders. Of course, any ability beyond this greatly expands the possibilities and options.

Tracy Vrem: I tell my hunters that most of the time a person gets out of a hunt what he or she puts into it. In other words,

Gun safety is a big issue in this remote country, and its practice is a major positive factor in a hunter. (Photo courtesy of Scott Newman)

Some hunters come mainly to eat, I guess—but that's OK with the Rosenbruches! (Photo courtesy of Alisha "Mutts" Rosenbruch-Decker)

the better shape you are in, the better your odds of killing a really big bear.

Should inexperienced and physically challenged hunters go after Alaskan brown bears? Why or why not?

Dennis Harms: Inexperienced hunters are no trouble as long as they can safely handle a gun. Evaluating and accommodating the experience level is the job of the guide. We can easily handle inexperience so long as the hunter is mentally prepared to deal with wind and cold and rain and all the other natural elements, and if he has a good attitude and motivation. We've had some physically challenged hunters over the years, too, and in many instances we were able to get them a bear.

I remember one guy who had a friend who was dying of cancer. The fellow also had emphysema and was just in terrible shape. His friend had to somewhat beg me to take him because I was highly skeptical about his chances. It was a fall hunt, too,

Hunter and guide heading out for a day seeking brown bears. (Photo courtesy of Alisha "Mutts" Rosenbruch-Decker)

so I scratched my head a lot and decided to put him in a camp up on a prominent knob along a river so he and his guide could see well but wouldn't have to move much. They basically traveled only from the tent to their nearby glassing place, and I figured they'd have to sit there the whole fifteen days to have a decent chance. However, on about the fourth or fifth day an exceedingly nice, big Kodiak boar came by, and the fellow made a really good shot and that was it! That man was in such bad shape he should have been in a hospital, not in the Kodiak back country, so it boiled down to designing a hunt to fit the hunter.

Gary "Butch" King: We've hosted hunters with all levels of experience. A lot of times an inexperienced hunter has no preconceived notions of how we should be doing this, so he does what he's told and is easier to guide. Physically challenged people can be accommodated up to a point. I instruct all my guides not to go too fast for such a client, and to avoid getting separated from the person. Separated simply means that

Getting up where you can see well can require some physical stamina. (Photo courtesy of Alisha "Mutts" Rosenbruch-Decker)

the guide can't reach out and touch his hunter, which he should be able to do the majority of the time.

If a guy can't get around at all, it's tough to give him a brown bear hunting experience because you have no vehicle or level ground or anything else that can help accommodate the person. Brown bear hunting is the real deal, and it's the last great hunt in North America. Unfortunately, it doesn't allow much room for hunters who aren't at least a little bit mobile. The degree of disability is directly proportional to a hunter's chances of taking a bear.

Steak night at Wildman Lake Lodge. (Photo courtesy of Gary "Butch" King)

Mike Munsey: I don't have a problem with an inexperienced hunter, assuming he is proficient with his rifle. As for physically challenged hunters, Kodiak can be a physically demanding hunt, as I mentioned previously, so I would probably recommend a fall Alaska Peninsula hunt for such potential clients. The fall Peninsula bear season is earlier than on Kodiak and the bears are still feeding on salmon more so than on Kodiak, so chances of walking a salmon stream and taking a nice bear are probably better over there.

Scott Newman: It's possible for a physically challenged hunter to score if the person has a reasonable level of proficiency with a rifle. We can get special permission to shoot from the skiff if a hunter is truly handicapped. However, it's not very easy to get within range of a brown bear that way, though we do it from time to time. If a guy can even hobble down the beach, we can probably get him a chance at a bear. It really depends on the amount of physical challenge a person is dealing with. I've had people take bears who could hardly hold a gun.

The inexperienced hunter can be a problem—I have enough problems with experienced hunters! Hunting dangerous game

Patience is a virtue when glassing for brown bears. (Photo courtesy of Dennis Harms)

is a different experience from hunting deer or elk. Still, as long as the inexperienced hunter believes in and listens to the guide, he should have a decent chance.

Alisha "Mutts" Rosenbruch-Decker: With the right attitude and a dedicated determination to have a good experience, anyone can successfully hunt brown bears. Inexperienced clients should be willing to listen to the guide and follow instructions. Physically challenged hunters need to be forthcoming from the beginning with both the outfitter and the guide. Few guides can diagnose medical conditions, and no guide can read minds. Hunters need to disclose whatever limitations they have that could affect their performance. Hunters and guides should both remember that they need to operate as a team if they are to be successful. It is not a competition to see who is in the best shape, or who can get there first, or who knows the most about the situation at hand.

Tracy Vrem: Yes, we can accommodate either category. Inexperience we handle by educating the person as we go along. For the truly physically challenged, you have to honestly discuss with them the realistic odds of success on their hunt, and make it clear their chances are reduced by their handicap, whatever it might be.

Is there any particular characteristic that would make you refuse to guide a hunter for Alaskan brown bears?

Dennis Harms: Once in a while a guy will call you and hint he'd as soon take a bear illegally if that's what it takes. When that happens, I back away immediately. I won't have anything to do with a person who's even remotely thinking like that. I also wouldn't take a person with a poor attitude, typified by a comment like, "I just want to get my bear and get the heck out of there." If you're not coming to enjoy and appreciate the privilege of seeking a truly magnificent animal, I won't take you.

Gary "Butch" King: I've been in this business a long time and can count the bad eggs I've encountered on one hand. Most of those who fall into that category simply can't understand or appreciate the degree of effort required to put on the hunt. For example, we had one guy who seemed to judge the quality of the hunt on whether the coffee creamer was in a package or in a can! I'll leave it at that.

Mike Munsey: I would not take a hunter who insisted on being able to shoot a small bear early in the hunt. I would also be hesitant to take a hunter who could devote only a few days to the hunt. I'd also refuse a hunter who insisted a guide not back him up on a wounded bear. Our policy is that if a bear is obviously wounded and is on his feet and running away, the guide shoots—and this policy is nonnegotiable.

Scott Newman: Two or three times I've turned guys down because I already knew about their questionable reputation, or they came across on the phone as too demanding. Again, it comes down to whether a hunter is willing to listen to the guide. If he demonstrates he is incapable of doing so, I wouldn't have him back in my camp under any circumstances.

Alisha "Mutts" Rosenbruch-Decker: A hunter who comes to simply collect a bear creates a difficult situation from the beginning. As a guide–outfitter, I am seeing more and more hunters who have the wrong attitude. They seem to believe that because they bought the hunt, they purchased a trophy bear. They seem to think it's within the guide's control when and where a bear will show up as well as what size it will be. Hunting in Southeast Alaska is a pure fair-chase experience. A hunter unwilling to have an open mind and enjoy this absolutely pure form of hunting has set himself up to be a failure, regardless of any bear taken.

Tracy Vrem: That would be when their check bounces! I used to constantly worry about my success rate and good references, which is not to say that I'm not concerned about such things today. However, much of the time we are only as good as the hunters we host. We simply cannot control certain elements—what shape the hunter is in, how cooperative he is, how cooperative the bears are, the hunter's marksmanship, etc. We take every legitimate step to try to ensure a successful hunt, but certain aspects are out of our hands.

What is the most dangerous thing a brown bear client can do? Can you share an instance where a client placed himself or the guide in danger?

Dennis Harms: That would be keeping a shell in the chamber. In forty years of guiding, neither I nor my crew has had an accident involving firearms, but I've had about four incidents when a supposedly unloaded rifle discharged accidentally. A low regard for firearm safety is the most dangerous thing we face. I'm far more afraid of getting shot by a hunter than I am of a charging bear. If a bear charges, you throw up your rifle and that ends that. If you get shot by a hunter, you have no control over the situation.

It's also really dangerous to go in after a wounded bear, but it's much worse if too many people are involved. You're all wearing camouflage and often the light is failing, so it's just too easy to shoot one another. I usually go in with the assistant guide and leave the hunter waiting on the edge of the alders.

A venerable old outfitter like Dennis Harms looks forward to his new crop of hunters every season. (Photo courtesy of Dennis Harms)

Gary "Butch" King: The most dangerous thing a client can do is exercise bad firearms safety. That's the guide's worst nightmare. The second most dangerous hunter mistake is failing to listen to the guide and draw on his experience. For example, we don't shoot bears that are more than two hundred yards away. We want a lung shot. If the guy lobs a long shot at a bear and makes a lousy hit, the bear is going into thick brush and someone is going to have to go in and smoke him out. That's another huge nightmare. Firepower is the only solution to this situation. It is our standard policy that if the guide thinks the bear is getting away, he shoots.

Mike Munsey: It's a huge mistake for a hunter to insist that a bear stalk be made against a guide's better judgment. Maybe the bear is in a dangerous spot or it's too late in the day for a stalk. The nights are very cold on Kodiak, especially in the fall, and nothing is more hazardous than walking through the brush and down the mountain in the dark. It's easy to break a leg or poke out an eye. I've had several instances where a hunter has insisted on climbing after a bear too late in the day, and while it turned out OK and nobody was injured, it was still an unsafe situation.

This terrific brown bear was taken in the thick alders on Kodiak Island. (Photo courtesy of Mike Munsey)

Scott Newman: There again, especially in a marine environment like where we hunt, it's not as if you're just walking along in a park. If your client is doing things you don't want him to do, a whole host of unpleasant things can go wrong. I'd say that a client who listens to the guide is a safe client.

Once I was walking up a salmon stream with a client. It was really slippery, with moss all over the logs, and I told him not to put a shell in the chamber until I said so. He did exactly the opposite and loaded the gun anyway. Then he slipped on a rock, and when I turned around to help him, the barrel of the gun was right in my face. I asked him if the rifle was loaded, and he said, "Oh, yeah, it is." I reminded him I had told him not to load it. He said, "No problem—I'll unload it." But he could have killed me right there by ignoring what I'd told him to do. He did end up shooting a bear, but things really went downhill from there. He wouldn't shoot a decent boar we got up on because I wouldn't guarantee him it was a certain size. He wound up killing a little dry sow on the last day. I put him with another guide because I just didn't want to go out with him anymore.

Alisha "Mutts" Rosenbruch-Decker: The single most dangerous thing a hunter can do is drink liquor prior to the hunt. This element reduces a hunter's ability to think and act rationally. For example, I rarely allow a hunter walking behind me to carry a bullet in the chamber. A client who insists on drinking prior to the hunt or during it without notifying the guide is often a client who disregards instructions—including our no-bullet-in-the-chamber policy. There have been uncounted times over the years when a client traversing a log has pointed a large-bore rifle directly at me. The most unnerving part of that issue is that, more times than I care to count, that rifle has been loaded and even off safety! This is a huge safety risk that can get you killed. Such a situation places all parties in much greater danger than any bear poses.

Tracy Vrem: That would be not listening to the guide, or chasing after a wounded bear without discussing it with the guide. Later we'll talk about Billy's bear, a case in point.

Chapter 4

ALASKAN BROWN BEAR GUIDES EVALUATE HUNTING ARMS

What is your favorite rifle caliber for Alaskan brown bears, and do you recommend this caliber to clients?

Dennis Harms: Well, the best caliber is the one the hunter can shoot most accurately. You've got to be able to hit the bear first. The next most important thing is bullet construction—I'll address this topic later.

In my mind the .375 H&H Magnum was made for hunting Kodiak bears. It has all the perfect characteristics: good range and fair accuracy, good brush-penetrating ability with its big bullet, and so on. Other, similar calibers are good also. I like the .375 better than I like the .378 Weatherby because the .378 kicks so badly that not many people can shoot it well. My second choice is the .338 Winchester, especially if the hunter uses a fairly heavy bullet. I'd rather the hunter carry any of these calibers than a .416 or a .458, because a bullet from these latter guns drops so fast that you may well have trajectory problems. We always try to get in close, of course, but if you have a long follow-up shot, you're at a huge disadvantage. Someone did a survey here on Kodiak a few years ago and found that about 85 percent of brown bear guides here use the .375 as their primary weapon.

Gary "Butch" King: The .375 H&H with a Swift A-Frame bullet is my favorite. It's got great stopping power, plus it can reach out if you've got a bear escaping. I do recommend this caliber for clients if they can shoot it well. We will allow clients to bring any rifle of .30-caliber magnum or larger with a minimum bullet weight of 180 grains, and we recommend the Swift A-Frame. We don't normally recommend the hunter get up into the .400+ calibers unless they're very, very familiar with the gun. You can kill a bear by putting a shot through both lungs with a

A good rest is highly useful, no matter what caliber the hunter chooses. (Photo courtesy of Scott Newman)

.243, but it will take three to five minutes for him to expire and a lot of things can happen in that amount of time, most of them not good. Too often the bear is out of control, either leaving or charging, despite a good shot, and our guide then is forced to use his backup weapon.

Mike Munsey: My favorite is the .375 H&H, and yes, I do recommend it for clients. But as I have said many times, I would rather a hunter bring a rifle he is comfortable with than go out and buy a new, larger-caliber rifle with which he is unfamiliar. As my father used to say, a good hit with a .30-06 is infinitely more effective than a miss with a .458.

Scott Newman: If I had to pick one caliber for a client, I'd take the .300 Winchester Magnum. It's got all the right combinations of speed and power. I've seen more one-shot kills with this rifle than with any other.

Alisha "Mutts" Rosenbruch-Decker: My favorite caliber for brown bears is clearly the .416. We recommend a minimum caliber of .375, with the .416 highly recommended because of superior knockdown and ballistics qualities. A .458 is also a good caliber for both brown and black bears.

Tracy Vrem: I love a .375 H&H. The ammunition is readily available, and almost every one of my guides uses this caliber as his weapon of choice. If the client has a problem and comes up short of ammo, almost any bear camp in Alaska will have extra .375 bullets.

What is your choice as a backup weapon for brown bears?

Dennis Harms: I and most of my guides use the .375. A couple of guys use a .338, but these are the only two calibers in use for backup in my organization. We had a few guides using the bigger calibers, like the .416, but a backup situation in our open country is much more likely to involve a wounded bear going away, and you can mess up a long shot with a bullet that drops sharply. Long shots are far more common than having a bear charge you at close range. If that bear is going away at 175 yards, you can reach out and get him with a .375 or a .338, but with a .458 you don't have

Only the best bow hunters are allowed on most brown bear hunts, and a heavy backup weapon is standard. (Photo courtesy of Scott Newman)

much of a chance at all. The .375 is such a good weapon because it is excellent from point-blank range out to 250 yards.

Gary "Butch" King: We use mainly the .375 and the .416. Our policy is very simple. I explain it to every hunter and to every one of my guides. During those explanations, I always use two terms: One is "under control" and the other is "in the arena." The arena is the place where you take your first shot. It might be vast or it might be tight—it just depends on what opportunity presents itself. This term refers to your clear, comfortable range of vision at the target. If the bear gets outside the arena, that means he is out of control. Under control means the bear isn't either coming or going, but rather staying put in the arena. What we want is both lungs with one shot. As long as the shot is good and the hunter has the bear under control, there's no reason for the guide to do anything except watch the game play out. If the bear decides he's going to leave the arena, it's the guide's job to stop the animal with his own weapon. As the bear is leaving the arena, you've got to hit him so hard you change his mind. A smaller caliber, like a .270 or a .30-06, just can't put enough energy into the bear to do that.

Mike Munsey: I use a .375 H&H.

Scott Newman: I've probably spent $15,000 on guns, but I only use a couple of different ones. In springtime when bears are walking on the beaches, I like to use a .338 with 225-grain Swift A-Frame bullets. It does the job. In the fall, though, I switch to the .458 because in the fall we generally walk up salmon streams and the bears are closer. You're bumping into them all the time. A gun like the .458 gives you the confidence you need if problems come up.

Alisha "Mutts" Rosenbruch-Decker: I use a .416 Remington as a backup weapon when guiding.

Tracy Vrem: Like I said in the previous question, I prefer the .375 H&H over all the others.

What is your advice on bullet weight? Bullet construction?

Dennis Harms: There is a huge selection of whiz-bang bullets out there; in fact, there's so much available that it's almost

A .308 can kill a ten-foot brown bear if the bullet is well placed—even by a ten-year-old young lady! (Photo courtesy of Dennis Harms)

a laugh from a professional standpoint. Some manufacturers put a nickel into their bullet and forty-five cents into advertising, while some others do just the opposite. It's pretty tough to make the right decision. I've had hunters show up with some oddball trash bullet recommended by their gunsmith, who's never been within five thousand miles of Alaska. I've reached the point where I won't take a hunter unless he's got a good bullet.

Adequate bullets are like the old Nosler Partition, which expands well and retains weight well. I've had hunters tell me those bullets don't mushroom well, and I ask how they know this. They tell me, well, I killed a such-and-such and dug out the bullet and looked at it. My reply is, well, you took it out of a dead animal, didn't you? It must have done all right. The Swift A-Frame, which is a Nosler knock-off, is darned good, too. Which one to use depends on which one shoots best in your particular rifle, and it's very important to test and see for yourself. I think these two bullets are the only ones I'd personally recommend without reservation, though some others out there are probably just as good.

You've also got to experiment with different powder and primer combinations to get the best accuracy. But you just can't experiment while you're hunting—it's a devastating disappointment to lose a beautiful ten-foot bear because you used the wrong bullet. I had a guy do exactly that about five years ago. He did two things wrong: He wanted to use a bullet we'd had poor experience with over the years, and he didn't want anybody to do a follow-up shot for him. He hit the bear well, but we looked for days and never found it, one of the very few wounded bears we've ever lost. I think the bullet just went zinging right through the bear and never opened up.

Gary "Butch" King: I like the heaviest bullet a given rifle shoots well, either 250- or 300-grain. As for construction, I like the Swift A-Frame.

Mike Munsey: I recommend any of the premium bullets on the market today, such as Trophy Bonded Bear Claw, Nosler Partition, and Barnes X-Bullet. I also recommend as heavy a bullet as possible.

Scott Newman: I think the hunter should use the biggest bullet available for the caliber. The most important thing is that you put the bullet in the right spot so it can do its job. My personal favorite is the Swift A-Frame, and I recommend it over any other. Some people like the Barnes Triple-Shock, and it's a phenomenal bullet, too.

Alisha "Mutts" Rosenbruch-Decker: The heaviest, softest bullet for the caliber of choice is the best for brown bears. We always attempt to approach within one hundred to one hundred fifty yards of the chosen bear, and this relatively short range eliminates any ballistics issues with heavy, softnose bullets.

I think Nosler Partitions are an extremely poor choice for brown bear hunting. Really, bears are a rather thin-skinned animal, so a hard bullet simply blows through with no expansion unless it strikes bone. A favorite of mine that has proven itself over the years is the Hornady round-nose lead-core bullet. This one consistently mushrooms to nearly twice its size, and almost without fail it remains inside the skin on the far side of the body without exiting. This ensures that the full energy of the bullet is absorbed by the animal.

Tracy Vrem: I like Partition bullets in 250 to 300 grains.

By far most brownies are taken with a modern firearm. (Photo courtesy of Dennis Harms)

Do you have any tips on shooting techniques in field situations?

Dennis Harms: First of all, we try to get in as close as we can. You don't want to get too close, either—between fifty and a hundred yards is just about right. Unless the bear turns all four legs up immediately, the hunter definitely needs to keep shooting.

Gary "Butch" King: Anytime the shooter can get on some kind of rest, whether it's a pack or shooting sticks or some natural rest, he should do it.

Mike Munsey: I recommend using a scope, preferably set on low power. It's quicker than iron sights and is better in low-light situations. I also always insist the hunter have a rest and not shoot offhand unless absolutely necessary. I prefer not to use shooting sticks. They are OK in ideal situations, but a lot of times the bear doesn't show up where you were expecting it, and with shooting sticks you have to reposition them, and that takes time and makes noise. Usually a good old log or fallen tree works better than anything.

Scott Newman: Once you get in position, you've got to get some kind of rest to have the best chance. There will be times when there's nothing to lean on and the bear's coming through, so the client is forced to shoot offhand. I tell my clients to practice shooting offhand, shooting off their knees sitting down, and in various other positions because they just might end up having to use one of those positions. They should practice shooting offhand as fast as they can out to fifty yards.

Alisha "Mutts" Rosenbruch-Decker: A hunter expecting success on a brown bear hunt needs to be comfortable in and familiar with a few basic shooting positions. Often, hunting in the rain forest will allow the shooter a dead rest on a log or rock. It's a mistake, however, to rely on that position alone. The most-used position is sitting on your backside with knees pulled up and both elbows resting on your knees. This position gives a solid, dead rest in a situation where a prone position drops you too low and a standing position is not feasible. Prone is also a reliable position, though, and the hunter should be comfortable with it. The other main option would be shooting from one knee while in a kneeling position, as you might have to do if a bear is spotted while hunter and guide are walking in a stream.

Tracy Vrem: I stick to the basics. I have my hunter breathe deeply, relax, and squeeze the trigger.

What advice do you give your hunters on shot placement on a brown bear?

Dennis Harms: If you're sideways to the animal, a shot low in the front shoulder is perfect because it anchors the bear so you can finish him off with your second shot. A heart shot is a killing one, of course, but the problem is it usually doesn't anchor the bear and he's off into the alders before you can put in another shot. A brown bear can run a mighty long way with the heart shot out, and then you've got to go into the brush after him, and you don't know if he's dead or not. If the bear is

Jeff Rann used heavy artillery to take this giant Alaska Peninsula brown bear. (Photo courtesy of Gary "Butch" King)

facing toward you, shoot him in the chest just below the head and you'll take out the heart and lungs.

Gary "Butch" King: Three-legged bears will run right over the top of a mountain. Bears with no lungs don't go far. It's obvious where you want to place the shot.

Mike Munsey: Shot placement, of course, depends on the situation. If the bear is broadside, I tell the hunter to shoot him right behind the shoulder. The shoulder itself is also a good target, but there's more meat and bone for the bullet to travel through to get to the vitals. Right behind the shoulder, especially if the bear is angled slightly away, is the ultimate shot. If the bear is facing away from you, then it's best to wait for him to turn around. Never take a rear-end shot. A bear facing you directly can be shot in the chest, but I try to stay away from head shots. The neck is a good shot for a finisher at close range. It's also an effective first shot from longer range, but before I'd recommend it, I would want to make sure the hunter is an excellent shot and that this shot is his only option.

Scott Newman: Primarily it depends on the shot angle, but you've got to get the lungs. The heart is very low in the chest and is easy to miss. If you get a good shot through the lungs, you've got the bear.

Most hunters grew up shooting deer or elk—nondangerous game—and have trained themselves to shoot so as to ruin a minimal amount of meat. Something happens to people when you put them in front of a bear. They revert to old habits and tend to shoot to ruin as little meat as possible. The problem is that if they aim behind the shoulder and pull the shot just a little, they hit too far back and all of a sudden you've got a gut-shot bear on your hands. I have them shade the shot a little more to the front so they don't miss the kill zone. If the bear is angling toward them, they should shoot in front of the near shoulder; if it's angling away, they should shoot behind the near shoulder. I try to have them visualize the position of the opposite shoulder so they think three-dimensionally. I often remind them of exactly where to aim just as they're getting ready to shoot—just to keep them on track mentally—and they generally do it pretty well.

Alisha "Mutts" Rosenbruch-Decker: In the rain forest of Southeast Alaska, shot placement is of paramount importance. On a perfectly broadside shot, do not hold behind the front leg! Brown bears, with long hair and loose skin, show very little body definition. This factor, combined with frequent low-light conditions, persuades a hunter to center on the mass of the animal. This placement results in both a gut-shot bear that may well be unrecoverable and a hunter who has filled his brown bear tag in a most unfulfilling way. On a bear standing perfectly broadside, the hunter should aim at a spot a third of the way up the body from the bottom of the chest directly up to the center of the front leg. With an animal quartering either toward or away from the hunter, the shot should be aimed at a location between the front legs, low in the chest, which will likely get the heart. A heart-shot bear will typically travel no farther than fifty to a hundred yards.

Tracy Vrem: I send out charts to my hunters on shot placement. I like a broadside lower-shoulder shot that breaks the leg bone and takes out the heart.

How many of your first-time Alaskan brown bear hunters are intimidated by the prospect of seeking a dangerous animal? Describe some typical reactions.

Dennis Harms: A hunter who has gone through the process of researching the hunt and booking it has probably prepared pretty well for what he's getting into, so we haven't particularly had a problem with it. There are some, though, who are irrationally afraid of going into the brush, but I can't think of a specific incident where it caused a problem.

Gary "Butch" King: Brown bears are indeed intimidating, and people do have a tendency to be afraid of them. It helps to remember that you're packing a big rifle and so is your guide. What's most important is to get up close and personal. There's nothing better than having a fifty-yard shot at a big bear, because first of all it's exhilarating, and secondly it's highly effective in bringing that bear down.

I can remember one spring hunt when we had located a big bear in a thick brush patch, and it was in there all day long. We waited so long I finally figured there was no way we were going to get him except to go in after him. The hunter, a European, and I had a bit of a language barrier, but I had him following me close. I started crawling through the brush. Finally I got within about twenty-five yards of the bear, and could see he was sleeping in there. I turned around to motion to my hunter—and found I was in there with the bear all by myself! I had to figure out how to back out without waking the creature. I found the hunter standing outside the brush smoking cigarettes one after another!

Mike Munsey: I would say most first-time hunters are more intimidated by the hunt itself—the climbing, the glassing, the prospect of nasty weather—than the danger posed by the game. I'm sure some are apprehensive at the beginning, but they quickly get into the routine of the hunt and settle down. A

The rifle and the hunter together aren't as long as this monster bear hide. (Photo courtesy of Gary "Butch" King)

lot of hunters, first-timers or not, are under the impression that a wounded bear will attack every time. In reality, a wounded bear is usually just trying to get away, and that's why it's important to start pursuing it immediately.

Scott Newman: I'm sure every first-time brown bear hunter has some degree of intimidation, though you won't get most of them to admit it. It's a mental thing—here's a hunter who hasn't been in Alaska even twenty-four hours yet and you've got him on a beach with a nine-foot brown bear walking right toward him! It takes most newcomers a while to become mentally prepared for the hunt, and their eyes can become huge when a bear is approaching!

Alisha "Mutts" Rosenbruch-Decker: Brown bears are highly publicized animals that are often portrayed as vicious and aggressive. Many first-time bear hunters come with a near-irrational fear of how these animals will react to them in the field. The truth is that if a bear wanted to, it could get you almost any time you go into the field, because these creatures are silent, agile, alert, and extremely smart. However, brown bears are

Jeff and Dustin Neal with another ten-footer taken with a modern rifle. (Photo courtesy of Tracy Vrem)

neither vicious nor aggressive. Generally, after a few days in the field it's possible to show a hunter these attributes.

The plain fact is that many hunters and most non-hunters are extremely uncomfortable being close to these giants. An extreme example involved a non-hunting wife who remained in the skiff while we made a final stalk. I anchored the skiff out in the bay to accommodate the falling tide. When her husband and I returned after the stalk, the wife was standing in the skiff, still anchored out in the bay, banging an oar on the aluminum sides to make sure no bears swam out to get her.

Tracy Vrem: Most hunters are not overtly intimidated, in my opinion. However, I sometimes see that change the closer a given hunter gets to the bear during the stalk. I've had a few hunters quit the hunt and want to go home at that point.

Does it help to prepare a person mentally if he or she has already hunted black bears successfully?

Dennis Harms: I'd say the more hunting experience they have, whether it's black bears or whatever kind of game, the less apt they are to get buck fever. I don't know that there's any particular advantage in having hunted black bears as opposed to hunting other game, especially the way most black bear hunts are conducted these days.

Gary "Butch" King: I think it does. Typically, today's black bear hunts are done from tree stands over a barrel of day-old doughnuts, and maybe that sort of hunt isn't as valuable. If a hunter goes on a genuine spot-and-stalk hunt, though, it does help. You have to remember that being in the Alaska wilderness isn't all about the animal. It's about other things, like being left alone in this vast, wild country after the sound of the airplane has faded away. I think you've got to prepare yourself mentally for that as much as for the animal.

Mike Munsey: I don't believe so, mainly because the two types of hunting are so different.

Scott Newman: I don't know. I had one guy who had shot all kinds of dangerous African game, including a couple of lions, and his encounter with a brown bear left him kind of panicked. However, I would say that experience is generally a good teacher.

Alisha "Mutts" Rosenbruch-Decker: That is an interesting question. Realistically, I would say yes, especially because our black bears are often the size of a grizzly bear, the hunt conditions and hunt procedures are exactly the same, and black bears are actually often harder to dispatch. The last part of that statement has to do with the fact that brown and black bears have different personalities. Browns typically react to a shot by spinning and biting back at themselves while black bears immediately head for the woods like a rocket. These tendencies often afford a reasonable second shot on a brown bear while a black bear simply disappears.

However, the question is interesting because it centers on the average hunter's attitude. A hunter may feel that a black bear is no big deal and would contribute nothing to helping him hunt brown bears. Sadly, black bears sometimes have almost vermin status: "Oh, I've shot seventeen black bears—they're easy to kill." Almost invariably, such a hunter ends up wounding and losing his brown bear trophy. So, in a nutshell, I believe that a hunter with the right attitude would be well served to have successfully killed a black bear.

Tracy Vrem: That depends on the type of black bear hunt they've been on. It's not much help if all they've done was sit in a tree stand over bait.

How do you prepare for and handle overpowering excitement in a hunter/client?

Dennis Harms: There can be quite a rush when you're really close to the largest carnivore in the world. Some hunters become so excited they have trouble holding their gun steady. It helps a lot to have a rifle rest of some kind, such as shooting sticks. You just do everything you can to calm them down, and try to give them some confidence by getting them a good rest.

Gary "Butch" King: You've got to get clients in a zone where they feel safe. They've got to be insulated from whatever perceived danger might be bothering them. That danger could be from the bear or from the sense of being alone in a big wilderness, but you've got to explain to them that you as the guide have the situation under control and that the danger is mainly perceived and not real. If they're trying to shoot and start shaking, the guide has to pull them off and go into the mode of just watching the animal. If it's a situation where you've got time, such as a bear feeding on berries or in a salmon stream, you can wait for the hunter to calm down and then try again.

Mike Munsey: If a hunter comes into camp excited about his hunt, that's great. But if he comes in so excited he can't settle down, then usually a short climb up the mountain on the first day of hunting will have a calming effect and get him into the routine of the hunt. Often a day of glassing will tire him out, and from then on he's fine.

Scott Newman: It can be difficult. I remember one gentleman from Mexico. . . . We had several things working against us, including a language barrier. Around the dinner table we talked about various situations in detail, and I probably covered more things in more detail with that particular client than I had with any other. Later, in the field, when it came down to the point where we were about to shoot a bear, I looked away from him to get a better look at the animal, and before

Mike Cuppetilli proves you can take a huge bear with a bow. (Photo courtesy of Tracy Vrem)

I realized it I had moved some distance away from my client. If you're not right next to your client, you are out of control! That was a mistake on my part. So the way to handle overpowering excitement is to be right there next to your hunter and be talking to him all the time.

Alisha "Mutts" Rosenbruch-Decker: It's important for a hunter to experience excitement and to be enthused about a hunt. After all, isn't that passion what drives us to hunt? However, overpowering excitement can compromise what takes place on the final stalk, setup, and shot placement. A hunter will not get lucky with a poorly placed shot. The first shot is worth more than whatever else happens after that, so a hunter has got to make the first one count. Often, simply talking the person through a shot sequence is sufficient to calm and reassure him. Sometimes a physical hand on the shoulder with eye contact to convey confidence is important as well. I have personally found that confidence builds confidence.

Tracy Vrem: Any guide worth his salt hopes to have enough time with the hunter in the field to get some idea of his personality traits. I always tell my guides that the real apprenticeship in

Handling weapons in a skiff requires an extra big measure of caution. (Photo courtesy of Alisha "Mutts" Rosenbruch-Decker)

becoming a bear guide is to get a college degree in psychology! The hardest part of our job is to make sure we can handle any personality type so as to ensure a fair, safe, and hopefully successful hunt. Communication is the most important part of handling any situation. Those hours spent glassing for bears are the perfect time to go over expectations and cover different scenarios that might develop. Discussing ahead of time what you and the client will do on the actual stalk and shot goes a long way toward preventing problems.

Do you have any wise words on bowhunting? Black-powder hunting?

Dennis Harms: I don't take bow hunters or black-powder hunters. There's an outfitter on Dead Man Bay who takes quite a few bow hunters, and I refer them to him. Unless an archer or black-powder shooter would be satisfied to take a smaller bear, he'd better be prepared to go on several hunts. It's tough enough to take a really big brown bear with a rifle; with bowhunting everything has to line up just right. If a bow hunter simply wants to take a bear, there are plenty of opportunities—we see between seventy-five and a hundred fifty bears on an average hunt.

Gary "Butch" King: In my younger years I did take both kinds of non-rifle hunters, but now I don't. The statistics I've built over the years show clearly that the average number of rifle shots fired at the brown bears we've taken has been four and a half. Why bring a one-shot weapon to a four-shot event? For that reason I take out only rifle hunters. I don't have anything to prove, but I appreciate the hunter who does. Way back when, I took out dozens of bow hunters, and only one of those hunts turned out really well. They almost always ended up with a bang, something the bow hunter doesn't like to hear. But it's our policy that when a wounded bear is leaving the arena, we shoot our backup weapons. A bow hunter can make a beautiful shot and still that bear is going to try to leave the arena most of the time. We've got to do it the way we do because there's not much future in going into the brush after wounded bears.

Mike Munsey: I encourage hunters to use heavy bullets and heavy calibers to make sure the kill is as quick and clean as possible. I believe we owe it to the animal, and to me both bowhunting and black-powder hunting go against that belief. That's not to say we won't take bow hunters or black-powder hunters, but we make it clear to them ahead of time that if a bear is hit and getting away, your guide will shoot. Not only is it the right thing to do, but it's the law in Alaska. That policy tends to turn off some bow hunters and black-powder hunters.

Scott Newman: I've done some bow hunts, but I have absolutely zero experience with black-powder hunting. I took out one bow hunter just four and a half months or so after I got mauled. I could barely walk and was probably in the worst condition mentally I'd ever been in, but I took him anyway. On the fifth day he shot a really nice bear that squared nine feet.

The best thing about bowhunting is that you can see where the arrow goes. You shoot a brown bear in the big toe with a .458, and he'll disappear and you'll have no idea what sort of situation you're dealing with. But when you shoot that arrow, you know what kind of damage you did. If you hit a bear a little too far back, the best thing to do is back off for about twenty-four hours; the bear will likely move about forty yards and lie down. The next day you'll find him dead. It's really important not to push a bear in a situation like that.

Alisha "Mutts" Rosenbruch-Decker: Bowhunting and black-powder hunting both require a different approach. Only hand-selected bow hunters or black-powder users are allowed to hunt with us. The rain forest of Southeast Alaska provides an added challenge: Bears are very difficult to track in this environment. Shot placement by hunters with either weapon must be very good, with little or no room for error.

Tracy Vrem: Nonrifle users must know their limitations and that their odds for success are reduced. It's necessary to have clear and concise communication with your guide about backup: When, where, and why.

Do you take any special precautions when guiding bow hunters or black-powder hunters?

Dennis Harms: The question doesn't apply, since I don't take either.

Gary "Butch" King: As I said, we don't take them at all on our hunts. Let some of those young guides who have something to prove do it. I enjoy keeping all my boys safe, hunters and guides, and I like them to keep all their fingers and toes.

Mike Munsey: Because of our backup policy, we don't have many bowmen or black-powder hunters.

Scott Newman: I make sure the hunter shoots every day so he's good to go. I insist that he use a six-bladed broadhead, too.

Alisha "Mutts" Rosenbruch-Decker: Few things place such a pall of gloom on a hunter's outlook and the overall hunt experience as a wounded animal that cannot be found. Hunters with a weapon that increases the need for a perfectly placed shot will not have as many opportunities as a hunter with a conventional firearm. We carefully screen any hunters wishing to hunt with a bow or muzzleloader. We take only that special hunter who is willing to accept the reduced opportunity level and has the discipline to wait for that perfect shot.

Tracy Vrem: There is just a natural extra sense of caution when you set up for a stalk with either of those weapons. Obviously, shooting distances are considerably shorter, so sight lines are very important. If possible I like to gain a height advantage or interpose some type of obstacle between hunter and quarry to slow the bear down should he decide to charge after the shot.

Chapter 5

HUNTING BROWN BEARS IN ALASKA

Is there anything special about hunting brown bears in Alaska that is particularly significant (i. e., sets it apart from other kinds of hunting)?

Dennis Harms: Many people have told me that going after Kodiak bears is truly the greatest of all hunts, and many of these are guys who have hunted all over the world for every conceivable type of game. Why this ranking? It's because of the fair-chase aspect of the hunt, the number of bears you see, the fact that it takes place in true wilderness, and that when you get a big bear it's so spectacular. I think that everything just comes together to make it a truly special experience.

Gary "Butch" King: Some of the logistical things come to mind. To hunt brown bears you've got to go live in the bear's bailiwick, unlike most other hunts where you can just visit it for the day. You're living in the country favored by the biggest carnivore that walks the earth, and nothing can kill you quicker than a brown bear. That in itself is particularly significant!

Mike Munsey: I guess I'm biased, but personally I think the Alaskan brown bear is the most magnificent trophy in North America. That, and the style of hunting required—meaning spot-and-stalk and lots of hard work—makes it the premier hunt on our continent.

Scott Newman: It's a hunt for a truly dangerous beast, sure, but it's also wonderful just being out there. That's especially true in the springtime, with so much going on—nature is on the move, moose are calving, and birds are all around. It's just interesting and I love it.

Alisha "Mutts" Rosenbruch-Decker: Alaskan brown bear hunting is almost a religion to me, almost a spiritual experience.

Mutts with a fine Southeast Alaskan brown bear. (Photo courtesy of Alisha "Mutts" Rosenbruch-Decker)

Perhaps this feeling is due partly to the fact that I was born and raised near these amazing animals and was destined to hunt them. Perhaps it has even more to do with the fact that brown bears are among the most magnificent creatures that have ever walked the planet. To see a giant old boar gliding shadowlike down a secluded trail beneath an eight-hundred-year-old Sitka spruce is an experience beyond describing. To successfully hunt brown bears, you must immerse yourself in their world.

Tracy Vrem: There is definitely an added element of danger. Knowing that at some point you could find yourself the one being hunted raises the stakes significantly.

Give us your perspective on hunting Alaskan brown bears as a game-management tool.

Dennis Harms: It's a very important tool. Before about 1960, the game department allowed a very liberal take of brown bears. About the time I started guiding, the department adopted a much more conservative approach, even though we had pretty darned good hunting even back then. It's just gotten better and better, proving that you can hunt the bears and have a population that's healthier than if they weren't hunted at all. Over the last thirty-eight years the hunting on Kodiak has improved every year. Of course, today they're trying to manage moose in grizzly areas by liberalizing the grizzly take, and I disagree with this approach. This is in response mainly to the pro-wolf crowd, which goes bananas every time the game department mentions wolf control. What's needed isn't taking more grizzlies but instead a quality wolf-control program, if they really want to help the moose.

So far the grizzly hasn't become the poster child of the antihunting groups, but that could easily happen. The reason taking more grizzlies isn't as effective is that wolves kill moose every day of the year, while grizzlies do so mainly when the moose are calving. When moose numbers are down, it's usually because wolf numbers—not grizzly numbers—are up. They need to do more wolf control and less bear control.

Gary "Butch" King: Thirty years ago we had an area biologist, Jim Farrell, who preceded Dick Sellers. Our moose in those days were in dire straits, and we proposed liberalizing brown bear hunting to help the moose population. His reply made a lot of sense. He said that there were moose from the Alaska Peninsula all the way east to Nova Scotia, but right here is the only place we've got these giant brown bears. He said that what we manage on the Alaska Peninsula is brown bears, and it's done primarily for their welfare and not that of other species.

Since I came to the Alaska Peninsula in 1969, and even before that, the whole area has been managed to produce big brown bears. The seasons are short to limit opportunities, and that's for a reason—limiting the take allows these bears to attain their potential. Another way to do it would be to put bear hunting on a permit system, which is an absolute disaster for outfitters. The Alaska Peninsula has proved the success of the system used, and I've seen the population and quality of bears increase dramatically over the years through good management. We keep excellent records, and what they show is a very steady improvement in the size of bears we're taking. Since 1990 we've taken four bears with skulls measuring over thirty inches, something we never thought possible years ago. Only a dozen such bears have ever been taken, and four of them have come from our area. For that you can't give credit to anything except excellent management. What we *don't* need is "ballot-box biology," and unfortunately that's how our wolf population is being managed, and it's killing our moose and caribou herds.

Mike Munsey: The brown bear population on Kodiak Island has actually increased in the last twenty years, to an all-time high of 3,500 animals. That, and the fact we are taking more big bears than ever before, indicates to me that the management system here on Kodiak is working. When the permit system was implemented here back in the '70s, we had to deal with a reduction in the number of hunters and had to tighten our belts somewhat, but today hunting is better than ever, so it's hard to complain. We are taking fewer hunters than we did when my dad was operating, but producing nicer bears and happier hunters, albeit at higher prices.

Scott Newman: That's kind of a big one. In Southeast Alaska brown bears are managed by the 4 percent harvest-level guideline, with a 1½ percent female component built into it. It ties in well with my ideas of trophy hunting. We shoot a big bear or nothing, because we don't intentionally shoot small bears or females. If a client doesn't see a bear that meets our expectations, he just goes home without a bear. The reason is that adult males are the most expendable portion of the population. Biologists say that by the time a large male reaches the end of his natural lifespan he has killed thirty to forty cubs. By taking out such an animal, you're saving a lot of younger animals. It's a natural function of a bear population, but still it's helpful to the population to harvest older males.

Alisha "Mutts" Rosenbruch-Decker: The state of Alaska, over approximately the last ten years, has adhered to a strict 4 percent harvest objective on the ABC Islands. This harvest cap has yielded an incredible result in that we have more and larger bears. I have personally seen an increase not only in the number of bears spotted but also in their size and quality.

Additionally, recent years have seen a reduction in habitat destruction, making a marked improvement in overall brown bear population health. Brown bears are extremely sensitive to human encroachment and to habitat destruction such as clear-cut logging.

Mutts glassing for brown bears, with bear dog "Braveheart" standing by. (Photo courtesy of Alisha "Mutts" Rosenbruch-Decker)

Tracy Vrem: I think the management concept is correct, but often the implementation is too late. I have seen instances where a moose population is adversely affected by too much predation by brown bears. Once the problem is recognized by area biologists and corrective measures are implemented by the Board of Game, however, often it's too late to do any good. The balance of predator versus ungulate has turned in favor of the predators.

We live in such a huge state that the Alaska Department of Fish and Game is often understaffed and underfunded. Because of these deficiencies, it is difficult to implement effective proactive game-management measures. My experience is that the Board of Game is more reactionary than proactive. Unfortunately, not a lot of weight is given to input from guides in the decision-making process there. I think there is an erroneous perception that guides are only concerned about making money, no matter the consequences to the resource. In most cases nothing could be further from the truth, because to maintain our businesses we've got to have a sustainable yield of all species. Game management is a complex and difficult task, but if you throw in politics and emotions, rather than knowledgeable information and scientific studies, at some point it becomes impossible.

What is the most common mistake made by guided Alaskan brown bear hunters?

Dennis Harms: The biggest mistake is the guy who can't judge bear size and he's out guiding hunters. Usually that's because the Master Guide hasn't done his job in educating his assistant guides. An awful lot of the bears shot each year suffer tremendous ground shrinkage.

Gary "Butch" King: On the actual hunt itself, that would be doing too much walking. Brown bears have a tremendous sense of smell, and the more scent you lay down, the fewer bears you'll have in your area. You might not even see them, but if they're there and you're walking all over the area, they'll leave. They can also hide so you never see them, but if they come across your scent, they'll leave the area. You should walk only from your camp to your lookout; then just sit on that lookout and glass. If you figure out where the bears are eating and sleeping, you're going to get one.

Mike Munsey: Hunters have a tendency to panic as the hunt wears on and want to settle for a smaller or rubbed bear. We take more bears in the later part of a hunt, especially after about the seventh or eighth day, so hunters need to realize that it's a twelve-day hunt for a reason, and their chances of getting a nice bear are just as good on the hunt's last day as on any other day.

Scott Newman: It comes back to not listening to the guide. If the client will listen to the guide and actually do what he says, that's the number one element of success. Another big mistake is not preparing adequately for the hunt. Before he flies, the hunter needs to be thinking about the hunt, calling the outfitter when he has a question, and just basically getting mentally prepared. If he is prepared in this way, he's in a much better position to follow instructions from his guide.

Alisha "Mutts" Rosenbruch-Decker: I feel the most common mistake made by guided hunters is to mistrust and not listen to their guide. Second-guessing your guide is not only counterproductive but can also become a stumbling block that

A typical Alaska Peninsula spike camp. (Photo courtesy of Tracy Vrem)

creates problems throughout the hunt. Bear hunters invest a substantial amount of both money and time. If a hunter will allow himself to relax and enjoy the hunt, and trust that the guide will do everything in his power to bring success, so much more can be accomplished. Some incomprehensible law of the "bear gods" dictates that it simply does not work to push too hard to kill the perfect bear. Clearly, hard work and dedication are absolutely necessary, but it's nearly impossible to get a hunter onto a bear if he emits a lot of nervous or anxious energy. It is a concept that is difficult to explain, but those of us who have experienced it will vouch for its truth.

Tracy Vrem: The most common mistake hunters make is not doing their homework before they even arrive for the hunt. The hunter needs to check references, ask questions, and then be committed enough to stay the entire duration of the hunt. Once hunters are in the field, they often turn down respectable bears in the hope of killing a monster. Later, as the hunt begins to wind down, a sense of urgency sets in and can force them to accept any legal bear. In my opinion a hunter should do some soul-searching before the hunt to establish a baseline size below which they will refuse to shoot. By making that choice, they might not go home with a bear, but they can come again—and it's the right choice. Or they might agree to take a respectable bear early in the hunt—the point being that a decent bear in hand is better than a runt bear on the last day or a monster that doesn't happen. It's better to go home without a bear than to settle for an immature one.

What factor would most improve a guided hunter's chances of taking game [patience, physical fitness, mental preparation, equipment, practice with choice of weapon, other]?

Dennis Harms: The number one thing is to go to a good area and go at the right time. In some areas the bears are more active in the spring and thus hunter success is higher; in other areas fall is the best time. So timing of the hunt is the second most important thing. The third most important factor is going with a guide who has the patience to glass hour after hour to find the right bear, and then the ability to judge whether it's a big one or not. The factors you list are all important, but the most essential one of them is to have a good rifle the client can shoot well, and a bullet with good construction to do the job.

Gary "Butch" King: Patience and staying put are paramount. Mental preparation is important because you're going to be isolated in the great unknown for a time. You've also got to get along with your guide. In addition, you've got to keep your camp organized and stay dry so you can endure. If you get wet the first couple of days, you'll have to return to the lodge and reorganize. If you don't have a lodge to go back to, you've got a problem.

Mike Munsey: Patience is probably the most important factor. There's long-term patience to endure the whole hunt, plus patience to sit and glass for long hours each day. Most hunters tell me the toughest part of their hunt is the mental stamina required to sit and glass the mountains for hours, especially when the hunting is slow. Running a close second would be physical

Jeff Chaulk's monster Alaska Peninsula brown bear. (Photo courtesy of Tracy Vrem)

fitness and the ability to climb the mountains and follow your guide wherever he feels you need to go.

Scott Newman: Before the hunt, clients should call me whenever they have a question so that when they get here they know what to expect. I know what I can provide in Alaska, and the client might be thinking otherwise. The more we communicate, the better we understand our obligations and the better he knows what he'll be facing.

Alisha "Mutts" Rosenbruch-Decker: The most important single thing a guided hunter can do to improve his chances is to relax and trust that the guide will do everything he can to get them that perfect trophy. A hunter who's there to fully enjoy the adventure will find that the guide will actually push harder for success and covet that perfect old ten-foot boar even more than the hunter.

Tracy Vrem: All of the above apply. The mental aspect is very important. The hunter should be prepared to spend all day behind his binoculars while keeping a positive attitude.

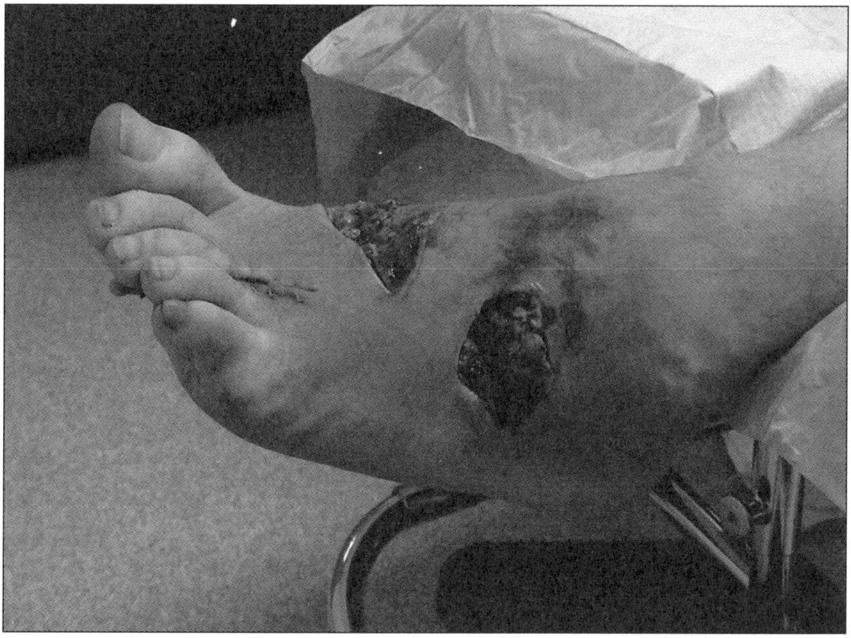

Be careful you don't get bit—these monsters can inflict a lot of damage fast! (Photo courtesy of Scott Newman)

Besides the weapon, what kind of equipment should every hunter carry, and what is the most important single piece of that equipment?

Dennis Harms: Good raingear is tops on my list, and it's the most important item besides the weapon, too.

Gary "Butch" King: Good raingear is the answer to the question, and second is good footwear. A GPS is a great advantage today, too. You also need flashlights or headlamps with plenty of batteries. Another vital item is one of those plastic water purifiers. We fly all the drinking water into our camps, but in case you get caught out and need water, this item lets you filter it yourself.

Mike Munsey: Besides good, warm clothing, reliable, clear binoculars are the most important piece of equipment.

Scott Newman: In this part of the world, you've got to get out of the skiff with absolutely everything you need. For me, the number one thing is my hand-held marine VHF radio. I usually have my cell phone on me, too, though coverage up here isn't very good. When you get out of your skiff in Alaska, you just might never see it again! Now, that's never happened to me, but it could get away from you for a whole host of reasons. If you don't have a radio, you're in big trouble. With the radio, sending for an assistant guide to come pick you up is a piece of cake. When I got mauled by a bear, I had my radio in my pocket. Within seconds of getting away from that bear, I put in a call to the Coast Guard, and all of a sudden the whole world knew I was in trouble. I also carry a personal locator beacon all the time.

Alisha "Mutts" Rosenbruch-Decker: High-quality binoculars can make the hunt more enjoyable by allowing participation in spotting the game and enjoying the beauty of the animal once it's found. Also, it's always a good idea to carry a good-quality camera, preferably a small one. I always carry a camera in the field, and over the years I've captured some amazing images.

Tracy Vrem: If your guide does not carry a satellite phone or an emergency locator beacon, I'd recommend you take one yourself. A daypack, too, is very helpful. A hunter should carry a pocketknife, matches or lighter, a small flashlight, an extra pair of dry socks, and Gore-Tex socks. Finally, the hunter needs to have a warm hat and gloves, water, and a small amount of food or candy bars.

Are there any common items of equipment that you believe are unnecessary, redundant, or just plain worthless for hunting Alaskan brown bears?

Dennis Harms: Quite often you get a guy who wants to bring a pistol, and on a brown bear hunt it's just a worthless piece of steel, just a bunch of extra weight to carry around.

Gary "Butch" King: We give our hunters a pretty elaborate list, and they pretty much follow it, so we don't have much of a problem with that. Trying to bring too much stuff is a problem, because we've got to fly it around. I hate those gigantic Cabela's bags that will hold a ton—you can't even get them in a Super Cub. I think those may be the bags that Super Cubs came in!

A beautiful Southeast Alaska brownie taken along a salmon stream. (Photo courtesy of Scott Newman)

Mike Munsey: Side arms are the most common unnecessary item. They just add weight and really serve no purpose. Spotting scopes are a necessary item but are usually redundant for a client because our guides each carry one. Unless a hunter likes to spend hours looking through a spotting scope, they aren't necessary.

Scott Newman: I hate to say this, but most of the time I spot the bear. Binoculars are handy sometimes, but as soon as we spot a bear, they're nothing but in the way. It's important for me to have binoculars but not so much so for the client.

Alisha "Mutts" Rosenbruch-Decker: Not really, but let me elaborate a little more on what's truly necessary. Superior gear is essential in hunting brown bears. High-quality, quiet, and absolutely waterproof raingear is a must. Wool or polar fleece clothing is highly recommended as opposed to cotton clothing. Hip-length boots are also a must item. Either ankle-fit or stocking-foot waders requiring a wading shoe are functional. A waterproof bag for extra clothing and a waterproof gun bag are also items of great worth.

Tracy Vrem: Cotton clothing is absolutely worthless and should be left at the main camp. Handguns and too many clothes are other items that are not necessary and shouldn't be brought along.

Tell us your method of field-judging the size of Alaskan brown bears.

Dennis Harms: Well, you're getting into my secrets here, but I'll tell you. The very first thing you do is determine the sex of the bear. I've seen critters with a belly dragging the ground and a big hump on the back, and it looks like a big old boar but is really a twenty-year-old sow. That's the major secret to taking big bears—simply deciding whether it's a male or female. On Kodiak Island, once you've decided it's a male and it's an adult, you're already looking at a nine-foot bear, minimum. If it's a boar and you're absolutely certain, plus it has a big hump and a sway back, then you're looking at a ten-foot bear.

Some guides out there consistently take small bears, and I don't know if it's because they're lazy or maybe they just haven't been able to put anything together on this question. More importantly, they haven't been able to pass the information on to their assistants so they can put it into practice.

Gary "Butch" King: Before we start a hunt we review a video put out by the Alaska Department of Fish and Game called *Take a Closer Look*. The guides, too, see it before any clients even arrive. It shows the different things to look at, such as ear size and how far apart they are, how broad the bear is in the chest, how thick through the withers, what the face looks like, whether the belly is hanging down or whether he's just a little butterball.

Everybody realizes that a bear doesn't have a full curl or a sixty-inch antler spread. A bear is the hardest animal in the world to judge for size. What we like to do is make this a learning process for the clients so they can also judge in the field. We want the

Packing out a big hide can be a tough job! (Photo courtesy of Scott Newman)

hunter and the guide to agree, when the big bear shows up, that this is the one. You've got to be sure because it's not like a salmon that you can throw back because it's too small. You can quote me on this one: A tape measure will make a liar out of every guide. You want that to be a good bear, but my guides won't give you an estimated measurement. In our country, we only have three sizes of bears: Small, medium, and large. A small bear you let walk. A medium bear, you check your blisters, the weather, and how many days you have left. A large bear, get ready!

Mike Munsey: This is a tough question because it's hard to explain to someone how to judge bear size. It comes from experience, and as I said before, either you have it or you don't. That being said, I will try to explain some of my methods. First impressions are important. As I'm glassing, I have an idea in my mind of how large a bear should look at that distance. If he surprises me by how large or how small he looks at first, then that impression is usually correct. After first spotting a bear, I always check him out in the spotting scope and look for things like head shape, body shape, length of neck, length of stride, and generally how the bear acts. A large bear is very deliberate in his actions, whereas a smaller bear might run around more and be curious about things in his path.

Scott Newman: Ninety percent of it is looking at the head. There's no exact way to take everything into consideration. It's a whole spectrum of things that tells you it's a big bear. You even consider where the bear is located, what time of day it is, and the general movement of the animal. A big bear walks very purposefully. I look also at the angle of the head, the hide, everything. I try to put the whole picture together to make a decision. The ears are pretty important. A bear's ears don't grow like the rest of the body; they become smaller in relation to the head as the animal gets bigger, and they move farther apart and farther down on the side of the head. Too, there are some very subtle geometric things and some things about the hair that help you know it's a big bear.

Alisha "Mutts" Rosenbruch-Decker: Judging bears is a challenging task since there are no horns or antlers to define

A typical Kodiak spike camp. (Photo courtesy of Dennis Harms)

sex and size. Size is judged by a number of factors and not any single thing. Look at the age shown in the face of the bear; the overall body configuration and mass; the bear's length, height, and width; plus the width of the front paws in relation to the legs. Also consider the size and shape of the nose pad and the position and size of the ears in relation to the size of the head.

Tracy Vrem: The first thing I try to judge is the length of the body nose to tail. I look at the shape of the face—boars generally have a long nose with ears far apart when relaxed. Boars also have a long neck and a small head compared to the rest of the body. A large rear end is also a good indicator. A large brown bear is built a lot like a large polar bear. It has a large rear-end section, a long body, a long neck, and a small-looking head and front shoulders.

What is the most reliable way to determine sex when no cubs are present? Give us some other methods as well.

Dennis Harms: This is the first step in determining the size of the bear as well. You can imagine how many bears I've seen in guiding for more than forty years, and I've also had fishing camps for a lot of those years. I must have looked at twenty thousand bears in my lifetime. Now here's the best method I've found: the relative length of the neck compared to the body. A

A huge Alaska Peninsula brownie is the reward for lots of hard work. (Photo courtesy of Gary "Butch" King)

mature boar has a long, tapering neck that's big around. You can sometimes tell it's a big boar from three or four miles away through the spotting scope using the neck configuration alone.

There are several other methods we use, but they aren't quite as accurate. The front shoulders of a boar are usually much bigger, while the sows tend to have a bigger rear end. They're a little like people in this respect, and the same is true of horses. Another thing is that female bears have a relatively short, pointed nose. Now, some ugly sows out there have a really big old nose, so it's not as reliable as the neck dimensions, but it's still a good indicator. An older boar will have a big nose. You can get a feel for this by looking at dogs—it's entirely the same thing. A female Labrador retriever will have a smaller nose than a male. Still, you've got to look at everything, because it's easy to get fooled no matter how hard you try.

Gary "Butch" King: Sex is very difficult. One analogy is to put a Labrador retriever out there a hundred fifty yards and tell me whether it's a male of female. Then put two of them out there, a male and a female. With both of them, you've got a lot better chance of telling which is the male and which the female. When there's only one, it's the hardest thing in the world to judge. Anybody who says they're always 100 percent right is 100 percent wrong. About 80 percent of the bears we take are males. We categorize them as small, medium, and large, and small and medium bears tend to be females. Lighter-colored bears tend to be females, too, but the No. 1 SCI bear we took was a giant male with a 30½-inch skull and he was butter-yellow! You can't go by color, but most females are typically light on the back with chocolate legs. Nobody should be disappointed with a female bear, however; a huge dry sow is a major trophy, and we've had quite a few such bears go over nine feet.

Mike Munsey: Size is the most reliable method. A large bear is almost always a boar. Also, body shape and head size are good indicators, but they can still fool you. To be safe, just stick with the large bears.

Scott Newman: That's a pretty difficult thing to determine sometimes. One thing many hunters don't realize is that the big boars usually leave the salmon streams by September, and all you might see there after that is a lot of sows. Sows have a pear-shaped body that's generally shorter than a boar's. The diameter of the muzzle when they're looking straight at you is a lot smaller than that of a boar. Their hair is different, too, more fluffy in appearance. Their ears are fluffy, too, even jagged. Still, these differences are very subtle, and you've got to see a lot of bears if you're to make the right call most of the time.

Alisha "Mutts" Rosenbruch-Decker: The most positive and reliable way to determine the sex of a lone bear is to view either a penis sheath or a scrotum. Sows also have a pronounced "pear" shape, heavier in the back end with a more compact, tapered front end. When viewed from the front, a sow will appear "tapered." This means you can see the hindquarters in addition to the front shoulders. A boar is often so heavy and square on the front end that the hindquarters are obscured when he's viewed from the front. Color can sometimes play a factor in judging the size and sex of a bear. Boars tend to be dark-colored, and sows are often lighter. Viewed at a distance, the profile is also a factor. Often a bear with a very pronounced hump is either a sow or an adolescent animal. Boars have a very long, flat back with a rather square dropoff at the back end; sows and young bears often slope at a 45-degree angle before the vertical dropoff. Successful judging requires looking at a lot of bears over a long period of time.

Tracy Vrem: Face shape is a good indicator. Faces on sow bears are shorter, with an attenuated nose and a more pointed snout. Sows also tend to be not as long of neck as a big boar. I have to say, however, that it is very difficult to distinguish an eight-foot boar from an eight-foot sow.

How do you normally follow up after a shot at an Alaskan brown bear?

Dennis Harms: Most of the time I slap the hunter on the back a few times! No, if the bear has just been shot, we want a follow-up shot right away, because a bear can be back on its feet and gone in a split second, even if you knock it down with the first shot. Too often the hunter sees the bear go down and thinks he's got a dead animal, so he doesn't get another shot in it right away. You can't afford to take even five seconds to congratulate yourself on a good shot. Then, after the shooting is over, we stand there a few minutes to make sure it's going to stay down. In the unfortunate situation where you hit it a couple of times but it still gets into the brush, you've got a really dirty, tough job on your hands.

Gary "Butch" King: Keep him in the arena, that's the most important thing. A lot of our bears are one-shot kills, and we keep records of that, but almost always it's because the animal got out of the arena so fast there wasn't time for follow-up shots, and when we tracked him we found him dead. If he's not dead, you might get eight- to ten-shot bears.

Mike Munsey: I have already addressed this issue, but I will go over it again. I and my guides will not shoot unless necessary. We will tell the hunter to keep shooting until the bear is obviously dead and we have told him to quit shooting. If the bear appears to be wounded and yet is on its feet either running

Super Cub access is essential in many areas to harvest brownies successfully. (Photo courtesy of Gary "Butch" King)

or walking, we will shoot. There is a law in Alaska that requires a guide to do everything in his power to make sure a wounded bear is bagged, and that means the guide must shoot if he feels the bear is getting away wounded. There is also a law stating that if a hunter wounds a bear, he must punch his tag and thus his hunt is over, so it is in the hunter's best interest to have the guide assist if the bear is wounded.

Scott Newman: Do you mean before I got mauled or after I got mauled? Before I was mauled, I would proceed right in after the bear. My area is a rain forest and everything can be washed away if you wait until the next day. Now that I've been mauled, I do it differently. I'm much more cautious, I carry my .458, and I don't run right in after a wounded bear.

Alisha "Mutts" Rosenbruch-Decker: A backup shot is a very interesting concept. As a guide, I have a few milliseconds to view that animal through the scope, determine if and where that animal is hit, and whether a backup shot is necessary at all. During that moment in time a responsible decision must be made. I always use a backup shot as a last resort. I avoid shooting if at all possible to allow the hunter a chance to finish the animal alone.

Tracy Vrem: I tell my hunters to plan on emptying their rifle. I've witnessed the following scenario on several occasions: The hunter shoots and the bear goes down; we tell the hunter to put another round in the bear, which for some reason he doesn't do. There is no second shot, and the bear gets up and starts running! My policy is to have the hunter empty his rifle, make sure the bear has been hit, and if the bear looks like it might escape, then I start shooting.

What procedure do you follow in tracking a wounded brown bear?

Dennis Harms: The first thing we do is have the hunter take off his rifle sling, because it's just going to be in the way in the thick stuff. We also make sure he's got his riflescope set on the lowest power. Whether you want the hunter to go in there with you depends entirely on the situation. You first assess how much blood you find and what kind of blood it is so you have some idea of where the animal was hit. A brown bear sometimes can produce a tremendous amount of blood and still not be fatally wounded. We may wait some period of time if we feel the bear will expire or stiffen up some, but that depends a lot on whether it's raining and what time of day it is and so on. Ideally, you've got the guide and packer plus the hunter, and one tries to stay on the track while the two others stay to one side or the other. We carefully keep track of each other so we don't accidentally shoot one another in the process.

I remember one time a few years ago when a hunter hit a bear pretty good right at dark and there was no way to track it until the next day. We worked our way along the track, and that bear charged us at really close range. The assistant guide shot the bear three times and stopped the charge, but still it was moving around and I had to put a couple of shots in to finish it. Tracking a wounded bear can be a really dangerous situation.

Gary "Butch" King: You've got to give the wounded bear plenty of time, although it depends a lot on the topography. If you've seen him cross a ridge a half-mile away, it's time to get moving. But if he just went into a brushpile across the way, you're

A little lady with a very large Kodiak bear skin. (Photo courtesy of Dennis Harms)

better off sitting and watching to see that he doesn't slither out on you instead of pushing through there right away.

Mike Munsey: It's important to start tracking the bear as soon as possible. Generally there is an immediate blood trail to get you going in the right direction, but depending on how badly the bear is wounded, that blood trail can disappear after a distance. If there's snow the job is easier, but following an intermittent blood trail in brush or grass can be very difficult, so you want to get moving as soon as possible. Generally the guide will start tracking and have the hunter watch for any movement out ahead of the guide. It is the hunter's and guide's moral and legal obligation to find that bear, regardless of the amount of time spent. Sometimes that means coming back the next day and picking up the blood trail again. We are fortunate in that we do not have many wounded bears, and I think our backup policy has helped in that regard.

Scott Newman: I keep my eyes open and follow the action very carefully. I never let my guard down.

Alisha "Mutts" Rosenbruch-Decker: We start by waiting twenty to thirty minutes before going into the woods. If daylight allows, at that point the hunter remains in the open and I go in alone, carefully following the sign, and especially blood if it is present. By going in alone, I don't disturb the sign and I can listen more carefully for any noise that may indicate the bear's whereabouts. Most often the hunter is uncomfortable with these large bears to begin with, and it can be worrisome to me if he is in the woods with me. If the shot is made close to darkness, as is often the case, I'll take a quiet, cursory look into the fringe cover with a flashlight, and then we'll leave the area until morning. Under those circumstances, all our guides generally return together to the scene along with our Jack Russell terrier, named Braveheart, to search for the animal.

Tracy Vrem: Every circumstance is different. We consider how many shots were fired, where in the body the bullets likely struck, and how the bear reacted. But the major factor is the kind of cover into which the bear escaped. Did he disappear into heavy alders? Run up a snow-covered valley? If the cover is tight with very limited visibility, you need to wait at least an hour before starting to follow the blood trail. After you mark the bear's last known location, if possible you need to get some elevation and glass while waiting for the hour to go by.

Stalking a wounded bear in heavy cover is terrifying at best. A very slow and methodical tracking of the blood trail is in order. Unfortunately, bears have a way of bleeding less and less the farther they travel, to the point that they quit bleeding altogether—basically because fat plugs the wound. If the bleeding stops altogether, the odds are you have a lost bear.

I was guiding a dentist from Arkansas one fall, and we found a 9½-foot boar and put four .375 H&H bullets into him. The bear was sorely wounded and there was blood everywhere. Even so, the animal rolled a couple of times and took off running. The cover in that creek bottom was not tremendously thick, and we saw the bear run several hundred yards upstream before we lost sight of him. I took off running after him. I could see him from time to time and was slowly gaining on him. The bear was obviously hit very well, but he was nevertheless on the verge of getting away. After about a half-mile he left the creek and started to climb the side of the mountain. I continued along his blood trail at a brisk trot in hopes of getting a shot, but the blood started to dry up. Luckily, because the bear was headed uphill, I could catch a glimpse of him every now and then. The hill was practically a mountain and had a series of folds and small valleys. After about forty-five minutes and nearly two miles, I closed enough on the bear to kill him. Had I waited for the standard hour on this bear, as is often recommended, I believe we might never have found him.

Chapter 6

SPECIFIC GUIDING AREAS FOR HUNTING BROWN BEARS IN ALASKA

Describe your home guiding area and any distinctions that set it apart.

Dennis Harms: I've got three guiding areas on Kodiak, and they're all quite different. On the southwest side, we hunt the Alitak Peninsula, an area of rolling mountains that average about two thousand feet high. The very bottoms of the canyons have a lot of brush, but the terrain up on the sides of the mountains is fairly open. The southwestern sector is what I'd call rolling hills about five hundred feet high, and it's fairly open. The bears lay up in what brush is there, but when they move they're not hard to see. We use large Zodiac boats to travel from place to place on the ocean to access different parts of the area. As I mentioned earlier, the bears in this particular area tend to have larger skulls but bodies that aren't quite as big as in some other places.

Our next area is Frazier Lake, which is seven miles long itself, and the surrounding hunting area varies between fifteen and twenty miles long. We do spike-camp there in canyons that are too remote to go in and out in one day. We do some hunting on the lake from boats as well, going from one spot to another and glassing all day long. That area has a moderate amount of brush but lots of open areas, too.

The final place we hunt is farther north on the island, on the south arm of Uganik Bay. We hunt from the salt water inland for about twelve miles. There is a lot of brush here, especially in the first mile or so from the ocean. After that you get to some open areas. The bears are a lot tougher to hunt here because of the terrain and vegetation, and it takes a lot of patience. Even after you spot one, it's sometimes very hard to keep track of him long enough to get a shot because of all the brush. The big positive is that some huge

This gigantic Alaska Peninsula bear was taken by Adam Gregory. (Photo courtesy of Gary "Butch" King)

bears live here and get very old because they survive in that country year after year. This particular area is physically challenging, so I only take hunters in there who are in good shape.

Gary "Butch" King: We've got one of the highest peaks on the Alaska Peninsula, Mount Aniakchak, right in our backyard. That high mountain tends to make the rivers short, but they're rivers that pack a lot of fish and that's good for the bears. The Peninsula itself has a flat coastal plain on the northwest side, but the Pacific side tends to be steeper and have even shorter rivers. Often on the Pacific side you're hunting tight little bays and such, and the weather there is a little warmer. Most of our camps are on the north side, so if you're on the Pacific side you're farther from the support of the base camp. Our satellite phones are very important.

Mike Munsey: We operate in Uyak and Spiridon Bay on Kodiak Island, on land divided into three guiding areas: North Uyak, South Uyak, and South Spiridon. We have guided in this same area for

Incredible scenery can be found in the Alaskan wilderness. (Photo courtesy of Alisha "Mutts" Rosenbruch-Decker)

the past fifty-two years, since my dad started Munsey's Bear Camp back in 1956. These bays are long and deep, with mountains on each side, so the primary method of hunting is spot-and-stalk. Most days you sit on one side of the bay or on an island in the middle of the bay and glass the mountains. There are also river valleys in each of our areas, and some days are spent walking up the valleys and hunting the rivers themselves or the mountains lining the valleys. The mountains are half covered with alders, which the bears love. They find most of their food in the alders and like the protection the brushy trees afford them. In addition to several salmon spawning streams in each area, there is also a plentiful supply of salmonberries and alderberries, which the bears love to eat in the fall. Because of this bountiful food source, Uyak and Spiridon Bays boast some of the highest bear concentrations on Kodiak Island.

Scott Newman: Admiralty Island is one of the most beautiful and diverse places in the world. It's a tremendously entertaining place to hunt, and it's a treat to even come here. We do our hunting from a fine boat with excellent, comfortable accommodations, so you don't have to worry about sleeping in a wet place in the woods.

Alisha "Mutts" Rosenbruch-Decker: Hunting brown bears in Southeast Alaska is a unique experience. Base camp is a custom-built yacht equipped with two sixteen-foot and two eighteen-foot skiffs that are used to access individual hunting areas; hunters return to the vessel each night.

Spring hunts are spot-and-stalk affairs, with bears emerging from their dens and coming to the shoreline to forage for new grass, small crabs, and kelp. Early spring finds bears traveling in search of food, while later in the spring the rut begins, prompting all the boars to move around in search of sows. Fall hunts are centered around small streams where bears congregate to feed on salmon in preparation for winter hibernation. Skiffs launched from the mother vessel are used to access the mouth of these small river systems, and from there a walk-then-sit style of hunting is employed as fresh sign is encountered. The spring and fall hunts are very different from each other, but each has its advantages.

The grandeur of the country is beyond description. Old-growth rain forest carpets mountains that fall into a beautiful ocean rich in sea life. It is very common to see humpback whales, orcas, sea lions, seals, bald eagles, Sitka black-tailed deer, land otters, mink, marten, and myriad bird life. There is always something of beauty to enjoy.

Tracy Vrem: My main guiding area is on the northern part of the Alaska Peninsula, and my base camp is some sixty miles south of King Salmon, Alaska. My area takes in what's known as the Island Arm of Becharof Lake, second largest lake in the state. It has one of the largest runs of red salmon of any lake in the state, over a million. The majority of the salmon spawning streams in that area are in the Island Arm of Becharof, and that's smack in the center of my guiding area. Over the last forty years or so the state has done a great job of maintaining the salmon runs. The food sources are so good for brown bears that I'm continually seeing sows with at least three and sometimes four cubs. They reproduce so well because of the constant food source provided by salmon runs.

How much of a role do food sources play in hunting bears in your area?

Dennis Harms: In the fall the bears definitely congregate on the salmon streams. In the spring you find them in their favorite areas to hibernate. They like to go high to hibernate, and I believe they do that to keep from getting wet, since it rains a lot in winter at the lower elevations, but up high there's snow and everything's frozen. When they first get out of hibernation, they move long distances to find food, so they're much more scattered in springtime.

Gary "Butch" King: For the spring season, food sources make very little difference. You could find a bear on a carcass washed up on the beach, but that's unusual. In the fall it's very important to be on a salmon stream.

Mike Munsey: Food is more important in the fall than in spring. In the fall we mainly hunt the river valleys where the

This big brownie was taken in Southeast Alaska. (Photo courtesy of Alisha "Mutts" Rosenbruch-Decker)

bears concentrate to feed on salmon. In the spring they are more vegetarian and their food sources are everywhere, so the bears can be found practically anywhere.

Scott Newman: In the springtime you have several different scenarios. In early spring the first bears coming to the beaches are the animals highest on the hierarchy ladder; they show up early for that new grass along the shore. You'll usually kill the biggest bears that first week. By the end of May or the first of June, all you're going to see on the beaches is smaller bears. However, if you hunt enough, you'll eventually find a big bear with a sow. What happens is the bigger bears follow the green-up of grass as it moves inland and upward in elevation, which allows access to the beaches for the next bears in the hierarchy.

Alisha "Mutts" Rosenbruch-Decker: Clearly, food sources are a draw factor that brings these secretive animals into places where they may be accessed by hunters. The food sources in springtime include fresh grass, seaweed, and small crustaceans. In the fall it's salmon. Again, the draw of spawning salmon helps to congregate the bears in areas where they are accessible.

Tracy Vrem: Food sources play a big part. Through the 1960s, '70s, and '80s there was a huge commercial harvest of silver salmon. After that, the market for them kind of collapsed, so the silver salmon runs have gotten larger and larger over the last fifteen years or so. Silvers are the last species of salmon to run in Alaska, going even into October, and I'm now seeing salmon in the streams later and later in the year. In the past there would be only an escapement of a few hundred silvers in some streams, but now we're seeing five or six thousand fish there. What that's doing is holding more bears longer on the streams. Prior to this development, when the red salmon run was over much earlier, the bears would go to berries and ground squirrels, but now they keep right on eating fish. They do still eat lots of berries, because we have a huge crop of them, besides the ground squirrels, caribou, and moose that are available.

How many of your bears are taken incidentally [as opposed to being the primary species sought]?

Dennis Harms: We never take an incidental brown bear. Sometimes in the fall we will take a Sitka black-tailed deer as an incidental species while we're hunting brown bears. On Kodiak a lot is involved in getting the permits to hunt brown bears, so there's nothing incidental about it.

Gary "Butch" King: Our seasons for other species don't coincide at all with bear season, so any incidental taking would be actually an accidental taking. It's no accident that the seasons don't coincide, either. It's because the Alaska Peninsula is managed for trophy brown bears. As part of that strategy, officials keep bear season closed during moose season, because every time there's a moose kill, there's a bear on the remains within a few days. If the seasons coincided and you killed your moose on day six of a ten-day hunt, you'd have a bear on the moose remains with only a day or two to go. You'd be tempted to kill whatever bear showed up, even if it was only a seven-footer. That goes against all good brown bear management principles, so in really good brown bear areas the moose season never coincides with the brown bear season.

Some of the wonderful scenery isn't composed of water, mountains, and sky. (Photo courtesy of Scott Newman)

Mike Munsey: None. Because of the permit system, each of our bears is taken by a hunter specifically targeting a bear. Sometimes deer are taken incidentally, but never bears.

Scott Newman: In general our hunts are dedicated to brown bears, so we take very few while incidentally doing something else.

Alisha "Mutts" Rosenbruch-Decker: Our brown bears are always the primary species on a hunt. We never encounter an incidental take of a brown bear.

Tracy Vrem: None. All our hunts are dedicated to hunting just bears. You can take an incidental wolf on a spring hunt, but you're on a bear hunt.

What kind of terrain is ideal for hunting Alaskan brown bears?

Dennis Harms: You've got to have mountains so you can see the bears. It's pretty hard to hunt bears in flat country because you can't see them. Basically, high terrain massively expands the amount of country visible to you.

Gary "Butch" King: You've got to get on a high spot and see as much country as you can.

An awesome Alaska sunset, which is often the best time to hunt brown bears. (Photo courtesy of Scott Newman)

Mike Munsey: Mountainous areas with lots of alder cover are best here on Kodiak. Also, any valleys that afford seclusion to older boars are prime, assuming they offer a good food source.

Scott Newman: I look for places where bears can have some privacy and solitude and feel secure. Until you see one in such a place, you can't move in on it. I've killed lots of brown bears just by knowing when they're going to be in a certain place, and I'm there waiting when they step out. I know what they're looking for, and I know how they think. There are certain little places bears like to frequent, and it takes time to learn those places.

Alisha "Mutts" Rosenbruch-Decker: As described above, ideal terrain depends on whether it's the spring or fall season. In spring the bears are down along the shoreline, and as the season progresses they move into grass flats. With the arrival of fall, bears use various river systems to gain access to spawning salmon. Typically, very small systems with shallow water tend to hold bears if larger drainage systems are flooding.

Tracy Vrem: In the fall we're definitely keying on salmon streams of various sizes, from a major river to a tiny sliver of a stream. Wherever there are silver salmon, you should look for a bear. You also need to find a place with some elevation so you can glass a long way. In the fall we also try to keep an eye on good areas of berry production, because the bears eat a lot of them. In the spring we're not focusing on the streams, obviously—we're hunting everywhere. We go into some of our spike camps and set up so we can glass 360 degrees from the mountaintops to the lake bottoms. Bears can show up anywhere, but there's more bear activity up higher, usually between one and three thousand feet.

Describe your typical camp setup and camp routine.

Dennis Harms: All of our camps are in the Kodiak National Wildlife Refuge, so we have to boat in or fly in all our camps and pull them out when we're done, along with every gum wrapper and everything else. We set up a base camp with wall tents heated by fuel oil in most cases so you can dry out in the evenings. We sometimes use advance camps with fairly large tents that we leave at the head of a bay or somewhere for two or three days. In those camps we use some type of dome tent with a smaller stove. The third type of camp is the spike, and the setup is much like a Dall sheep camp, with mountain-type tents and a backpack kind of setup. We use spike camps to access more remote areas that aren't accessible any other way. We've taken a lot of big bears that way. Most hunting is in the Kodiak National Wildlife Refuge, where you can't build a cabin because there's no private land.

Getting camps in and out costs a lot, and that's one reason Kodiak bear hunting is expensive compared to other kinds of bear hunts. Also, the Alaska Department of Fish and Game decided it would charge us $1,000 per year for each cabin we had. Well, you could only use them every other year, meaning $2,000 of your hunt fee went to pay for the cabin. All the outfitters thus burned the cabins down instead of paying the outrageous fee. We went to high-quality tents that are 10x10 feet in size, and we can put cots and a stove in there. We have our guys get up each day, have breakfast, fix a lunch, and walk to their glassing place. They keep doing that until they see the right bear.

Mike Munsey: We have three different camps from which we hunt. Our base-camp hunt is the most comfortable. There is a nice log cabin for clients, with bed linens plus bathrooms with hot and cold running water and showers. Our other camps are either cabins or tent frames. All have wooden floors with kerosene heaters, but no running water or bathrooms. Boats are used in all our camps except the Spiridon location in the fall, when we camp in a river valley since this is a walking hunt. We use the boats to get around the hunting area, but we do not generally hunt out of the boats. Most hunting is done from shore, glassing the mountains or walking up the valleys.

Scott Newman: We hunt from a good boat, which gives us the ability to move somewhere else if things aren't going well. That's a huge advantage. It's also a very relaxing way to go, because when you're not out in the skiff, you can have your housecoat and slippers on and be enjoying a drink or whatever. We've also got all the comforts of home, and you can brush your teeth and take a shower whenever you want. In the springtime all the hunting is in the afternoon and evening. In May each day gets ten minutes longer.

Alisha "Mutts" Rosenbruch-Decker: Our yacht is a tremendously expensive base camp, with all queen suites and private baths. We stay there every night while we're hunting, and it's extremely comfortable.

Tracy Vrem: Our hunters all come first to the main camp, where we get them squared away with their gear and get their licenses and paperwork in order; then we take them to our range and make sure their rifle and scope are doing the job. From there I fly them out into the field with the guide, sometimes in one load if it's one of my bigger Cessnas, or the guide first and then the hunter if it's a Super Cub. The spike camp consists of a big Eureka Bomb Shelter tent or a heavy-duty Cabela's tent, and inside we have cots to get the hunters up off the ground. We have a food box with a stove on it, and we do all our cooking and eating in the tent. I try to locate the spike camp as close

A quiet bay on Kodiak sets the mood for an evening of bear hunting. (Photo courtesy of Dennis Harms)

as I can to the glassing place so the people aren't spreading their scent all over the country. We can usually get them within a quarter-mile, and sometimes as close as two hundred yards or so. We make it a practice to feed our clients well so nobody can complain about the food. We have a cooked breakfast of bacon and eggs, pack some type of lunch, stay at the glassing hill all day long, and at day's end we have a good cooked meal with some kind of fresh meat. In a word, though, the routine is glassing and more glassing.

What is your success rate on trophy animals?

Dennis Harms: You can do 100 percent on Kodiak if you aren't too particular. We're particular, though, and we get a lot of guys who want a ten-footer or nothing, and you can't be 100 percent on ten-footers. We run about 94 percent most years. Our goal is at least a nine-foot bear for every hunter.

Gary "Butch" King: On our last fall hunt we were fifteen out of sixteen at Cinder River Lodge. I'd say our spring hunts run in

The legendary Kodiak bear is a creature that many outdoorsmen crave to hunt. (Photo courtesy of Dennis Harms)

the 80 percent range. We have a higher success on the fall hunts because the bears are more predictable. On spring hunts we tend to have more success on the real giants in the ten-foot class. Early or late is of no consequence because the season is so short.

Mike Munsey: Our size average over the past ten years has been a hide squaring over nine feet, and we usually take one or two ten-footers a year. Our success rate runs about 85 percent. Generally speaking, if a hunter is in good physical shape and is able to devote the time and effort necessary, his chances of taking a nine-foot-plus bear approach 100 percent.

Scott Newman: I'd estimate 80 to 85 percent, year in and year out. If we get a really late spring, it sure affects our success adversely.

Alisha "Mutts" Rosenbruch-Decker: Success on trophy brown bears in our operation is very high. Our goal and advice to hunters is to never shoot a bear under nine feet square, and we always try to harvest boars. It is rare for us to harvest a sow. Skin quality is important as well, and hunters are given every chance to decide if they like what they see "on the hoof." It is extremely rare when a hunter does not get a chance at a trophy bear. This doesn't mean that the hunter always pulls the trigger, but the opportunity usually presents. Hunting brown bears is not an exact science, and a hunter may spend ten days in the field for a single five-second window at that trophy boar. If a hunter is prepared for that opportunity, then a trophy animal should be harvested. If that hunter is not ready, he still retains that memory of a close encounter with a phenomenal animal.

Tracy Vrem: Our trophy bears average over nine feet. Generally we get at least two a year that square over ten feet, and every year we take one or two that will make Boone and Crockett. We have some huge bears that don't make twenty-eight inches, though. We killed two bears recently—one squared ten feet two inches but was aged at only eight years, and the other was almost ten feet but only six years old. Imagine how big these guys would have been if they'd been around a few more years! Our success rate on all bears runs about 85 percent in both spring and fall.

Describe your usual hunting method and any common variations.

Dennis Harms: Normally on a fall hunt we get up around 6:30 A.M., have a good breakfast, and then get out into the field about 7:30. It's not as important to be up early in the spring, because the bears usually don't get active until it warms up a little. The big thing you have to look at is which way the wind is blowing; that determines to a great degree how you'll hunt that day. You basically never get a bear that's coming from downwind. If you want to hunt a canyon and the wind is coming out of it, you can hunt there. If it's blowing up the canyon, you've just got to change locations. The wind is the number one thing to watch. Generally, we go to the highest promontory that's well-located and we sit there and glass all day.

Another thing we've started doing is to carry along a 10x12-foot nylon waterproof fly. If the day looks like it's going to be wet, we set this thing up so we can keep ourselves and our gear dry. The deal is you can hunt much longer if you're dry than if you're wet. On a typical day when we use that fly, we've got food and coffee and we see a lot of bears. We see five or more bears every day, but most of them we don't go after. We hunt long hours, and afterward we go back to base camp and have a good meal before going to bed.

Gary "Butch" King: It's glass and watch, and when opportunity knocks, we answer the door.

Mike Munsey: Since all our bear hunting is spot-and-stalk, we spend most of the day glassing. We might go to a spot on the beach where we can see the opposite mountainside well and sit there and glass for half a day. As the sun moves in the sky, we might switch sides of the bay or change positions in the afternoon. Or we might walk up a river drainage or a mountain valley, glassing as we go. This method is especially effective if we have seen a bear in that valley earlier, and we'll go in and spend the day looking for him.

Scott Newman: In the spring we have a leisurely morning, pack a lunch around noon, and head out to hunt. In the fall we hunt both morning and evening, though I prefer mornings. If the wind is good, as it usually is, you can walk up a stream or get way up a hill with the wind in your face. Around 10:30 in the morning the wind shifts and starts blowing upstream, so you can hunt back down again with the wind still in your face. It really works well.

Alisha "Mutts" Rosenbruch-Decker: A common day in the field during the spring season is primarily an afternoon and evening hunt. Twilight in the spring extends until close to midnight. A typical spring hunt involves leaving the yacht with a sack lunch and a guide to cruise promising stretches of shoreline, drift in the skiff, or sit in a likely place and watch a wide area. The hunt usually lasts as long as light allows, because very often larger boars venture forth as darkness approaches. We seldom return to the vessel before midnight or 1:00 A.M. Dinner is served shortly thereafter, and then, after reviewing the day's events, all retire. Breakfast is rarely early the next morning.

A typical fall hunt also involves leaving the vessel in a skiff, generally with a sack lunch and a guide. However, rather than cruising the shoreline, the skiff is used only to access various river systems. We'll anchor the skiff at the mouth of a stream and then begin the hunt on foot. We move as silently as possible up the rivers, and when fresh sign is encountered, there is a fair amount of sitting and waiting. In these small river systems the average shot is generally twenty to fifty yards, though a few stretches of river allow a longer shot up to a hundred yards or so. Hunting techniques are always adjusted to individual situations, using natural cover, wind, and instinct to maximize the overall experience.

Tracy Vrem: It's basically all spot-and-stalk. The guide and hunter are the only ones in the area, so there's no competition for the bears. If things are slow in a spike camp for half the hunt and the hunters aren't seeing much, sometimes I'll move them to another location. It's not usually that I think the first place won't produce, but the client needs to feel we're doing all we can to get him a bear. Also, a change of scenery is sometimes refreshing and rekindles optimism in the client. Other times I insist the hunter stay put, and most of the time it works out (and it makes me look like I know what I'm doing)! I just want my clients to know that I want them to get a bear just as much as they do.

Tell us your method of getting close enough to a bear for a shot.

Dennis Harms: Again, the most important thing is the wind. You just can't get up on a bear if the wind isn't in your favor. A lot has been written about how poorly bears see. Well, they don't see as well as a deer or other ungulates, but they see a lot better than most writers give them credit for. In fact, they probably see a lot of things we don't know they see, but they aren't intimidated and don't react like a deer to what they see. With these things in mind, we basically sneak in there and keep track of the bear while staying as quiet as possible. But keeping the wind in your favor is by far the most important factor.

Sterling Whitaker's bear is tagged and bagged on the Alaska Peninsula. (Photo courtesy of Tracy Vrem)

Gary "Butch" King: You've got to get in front of a bear and ambush him. Sometimes you can hunker down and the bear will feed right by you. Another thing that gives away a bear is the birds—a lot of times you'll see birds flying before you see the bear.

Mike Munsey: Because of a bear's acute sense of smell, wind direction is the most important factor when making a stalk. This can be difficult because the wind can be blowing in an entirely different direction on the mountain or in a valley compared to out on the bay. Once we have established wind direction, we then try to get to a place on the mountain where we can see the area we last saw the bear. It can take up to several hours to climb these mountains and the bear may have moved some distance in that time, so it's important to have a good vantage point from which to find the bear again. It's also important to keep quiet as we are climbing, since a bear's hearing is excellent, too.

Once we spot the bear again and are ready to make the final stalk, noise level becomes even more important, especially if there aren't any barriers, such as hills, between us and the bear. If the bear is working toward us, our job is that much easier. If not, then it's just a matter of moving quietly and trying to get within shooting range, preferably above the bear, but that's not totally necessary. We find a good area from which to shoot, a place where we can see the bear clearly with no brush in the way. If he's within range, preferably a hundred yards or less, the hunter usually has time to make the kill before the bear moves out of sight again.

Scott Newman: The one thing I've figured out in this part of the world is that these big bears are educated and they know the game. One way they ensure their comfort level is they don't stay out in the open for very long. When we spot our bear, I try to get there as fast as I can because he may not be out but five or ten minutes. Sometimes we get him right then and there. If I can't get there in time, I know he'll come back out again. It's usually about 6:00 or 6:30 in the evening when I get my hunter set up in good position, and very, very often the bear will come right back out and we'll get him.

Alisha "Mutts" Rosenbruch-Decker: Stalking a brown bear is an incredible challenge. As often as not, bears travel with the wind, and this can present an ideal situation. If you know the local features of the area and the bear's habits, you can often get ahead of that animal and have him walk to you. This is the best way to get close enough for a good shot. However, this prime opportunity is not always possible. A personal favorite technique of mine is to remove my boots and stalk in socks. This method has helped my hunters take an incredible number of trophies. By moving through the woods in soft wool socks and quiet clothing, I have a very acute feeling of what is under me, eliminating many common noises that can ruin even the most perfect stalk. The slightest swish or the smallest crack of a stick will announce your presence to a bear. Since bears are very wary and are never more than a few steps from the edge of the woods, the animal will simply vanish into the timber without the slightest sign of curiosity or aggression.

Tracy Vrem: I get pretty aggressive when we spot the bear we want. The number one consideration is scent, and you've got to keep the wind in your favor in planning your approach. If you've got that worked out, you can get pretty brazen about approaching—until you get a few hundred yards from the bear. After that he might see you, so you've got to keep something between you and the bear.

Do you have both a spring and a fall season in your area?

Dennis Harms: Yes, we have both on Kodiak.

Gary "Butch" King: In even years we have a spring season, and in odd years we have a fall season here on the Alaska Peninsula.

Mike Munsey: Yes, our spring hunts on Kodiak run 21 April through 2 May and 4 May through 15 May. Our fall hunts are 25 October through 6 November.

Scott Newman: Yes.

Alisha "Mutts" Rosenbruch-Decker: Yes, we have both a spring and a fall season every year in Southeast Alaska.

Tracy Vrem: Odd years have fall seasons and even years have spring seasons on the Peninsula. That's good for the bears but bad for outfitters. After we have a spring hunt, we then have an eighteen-month layoff when we can't hunt at all.

Which season (spring or fall) offers the best hunting in your area? Early or late in either season?

Dennis Harms: I only run hunts that I think are good hunts! In the fall on Kodiak, the season is so late that a lot of bears have gone into hibernation, particularly on the north end of the island. At that time it's pretty important to hunt over a food source such as a salmon stream, and there are usually some fish even that late. On spring hunts—and I actually like these best—it's light from early morning until 10:00 P.M., so you have a long day to hunt. In the fall the days are very short, which reduces dramatically the time you can be in the field. If you can find a good salmon stream that nobody is bothering, a hunt there in the fall can be very, very effective. Because the fall hunt is so late on Kodiak, beginning 25 October and running into November, fall hides are superb.

Big boys grow even bigger in the alder tangles of Kodiak Island (Photo courtesy of Mike Munsey)

Gary "Butch" King: It's higher in the fall overall, but slightly more really big bears are taken on the spring hunts.

Mike Munsey: Generally speaking, the spring season is a little better than fall. The advantages of a spring season are better weather, longer days (more daylight hours), and generally more bears moving around. The disadvantage to the spring is that you might have to look over some bears with rubbed pelts. If it's an early spring and the bears have been out of hibernation a while, they might start rubbing their fur in warm weather, so you have to watch out for that. Because of rubbing later on, the early spring is probably our best all-round hunt. The advantages of the fall season are that the hides are in prime condition and you are able to hunt deer in addition to bear. The primary disadvantage of a fall hunt is weather. It can be cold and miserable on Kodiak in late October and November.

Scott Newman: Most of our hunts are in the spring, but I take a couple in the fall, too. Early spring is best, as I've mentioned before, and that's probably my favorite hunt. Later you see more bears, but this means wading through a lot of sows and immature bears. It's really hard to keep from shooting a sow at that time of year.

Alisha "Mutts" Rosenbruch-Decker: Comparing spring and fall hunts is like comparing apples and oranges: Both are tasty fruit, but they are very different. I have already described some of the differences pretty well under another question, I think. With the state setting quite a long season, we have chosen the best dates for hunter success. We begin brown bear hunting on 23 April and continue right through to the end of the season on 20 May. In the fall we begin when the season opens on 15 September. However, we finish up our fall brown bear hunts long before the season closes, to eliminate as many weather challenges as possible. Both spring and fall hunts are highly successful, and each yields large trophies.

Tracy Vrem: Strictly from a hunting perspective, spring and fall are about the same, with similar success rates. In the fall we see more bears, but a lot of them are sows and cubs. In the spring we see more of the bigger bears, and we have more daylight in which to make longer stalks. From an aesthetic standpoint, though, I really like a fall hunt because the bull moose and caribou have antlers, you can hunt ptarmigan, you can fish, and you have the fall colors. Spring is pretty drab and boring as far as scenery goes, although taking a wolf is a possibility then.

Are badly rubbed hides a problem in your area? What's the best time of year to avoid this problem?

Dennis Harms: Particularly on the southwest end of the island, we encounter quite a few rubbed bears in spring. We look them over carefully before considering taking one. We don't have this problem on our fall hunts.

Gary "Butch" King: The Alaska Peninsula is one of the most scrutinized, managed areas in the whole world. The season is only sixteen days long. It is set up to coincide with when the bears are coming out of hibernation, but it closes before they get a chance to rub. You've still got to watch for them, but generally rubbed hides are never a problem.

Mike Munsey: This is not usually a problem, but it can be, given a very warm spring. Even when there's an early spring, we generally do not have any trouble picking through the rubbed bears and finding well-furred ones. Rubbed bears are very obvious from a distance, so it's easy to spot the problem and avoid shooting them.

Scott Newman: It depends on the season, but generally you do get a lot more rubbed bears on Admiralty Island than anywhere else. However, there are enough bears here that you can just keep looking if you see a rubbed one.

Alisha "Mutts" Rosenbruch-Decker: Rubbed bears are no more prominent in Southeast Alaska than they are in other portions of their range. Rubbing is an interesting behavior commonly thought to be mainly a shedding process. I don't believe this is really the case; I think it depends on the individual bear and its personality and tendencies. It is possible to see a bear very early in the spring that is rubbed nearly bald, even with deep snow on the ground. In the same year, late in the season, another bear may boast a thick, lush winter hide when the temperature is 65 during the day. It simply depends on the individual bear. The good news is that rubs are visible on the live animal, and during the judging process that element can be discussed as well. Fall bears, having shed out completely over the summer months, are in the process of growing new hair, so consequently they typically have no bad rubs.

Tracy Vrem: I've seen it happen, worse in some years than others. Generally, it's not a problem. I think spring and fall are about the same, as far as incidence of rubs goes. You just have to look the bear over well, and usually it's pretty easy to pick out a bad rub. If the bear is in a stream and is wet, though, it gets a lot tougher. There's no question the hide is thicker on a spring bear, especially after it goes through the tanning process. You can often tell where the stitching is located on the mount of a fall bear.

How much does weather influence your hunting success and methods?

Dennis Harms: It's a major factor in the spring. Bears will be quite active if the weather is nice then, but if you get a lot of rain, wind, and snow, they just lie down wherever they are and might not move for days. In the fall on the salmon streams on the north end of Kodiak, the bears head for hibernation about the same time the season opens. On the south side of the island they're still in feeding mode, and they'll sneak down to the stream and grab a salmon and head for a brush patch again. In the spring on a nice day, you'll probably see five to eight bears. If it's a really crappy day and the rain is blowing horizontally, you're lucky to see even a couple.

Gary "Butch" King: Weather can certainly be a limiting factor, especially cold and wind, but I must say we've taken a lot of bears on cold, wet, windy days. Reduced visibility has some negative impact, especially in the spring, when there are no leaves on the brush and you can see a bear three miles away if it's clear. Weather is something you have to take as it comes, but the bears were there before the weather came in and they're still there when it's bad.

Look at the giant head on this bear!

Mike Munsey: Weather is a very important factor in hunting success, especially during the fall season. If we get an early snow, that can be helpful for tracking an animal. But if it gets cold early with lots of snow, that can drive the bears up the mountain and even into their dens early. On the spring hunt, warm weather, in addition to causing them to rub, can also bring an early crop of green shoots, a major food source. This can bring the bears down the mountain to feed on them. However, extremely warm weather can cause the alders to leaf out early, making it difficult to see bears low on the mountains.

Scott Newman: The type of spring you're having has a lot to do with how it goes. If it stays cold, you just don't see many bears. When it warms up, they're everywhere.

Alisha "Mutts" Rosenbruch-Decker: When hunting in a free-range situation, weather typically plays a significant role. Southeast Alaska is no different. Weather clearly affects how the animals move and how hunters can get around in the area. Storms and wind can have the direct effect of reducing the overall area hunters can access. We choose our hunt dates carefully to allow plenty of time to work around storm systems. If the wind is blowing and seas are high outside of a protected bay, we hunt that day within the bay. Safety is always of paramount importance. Generally storms don't last too long, and within a day or two hunters are able to get into more exposed areas again.

Tracy Vrem: Weather's biggest influence is on visibility. Fog and rain make it very difficult to glass any distance. High wind is a tough situation because you need to be looking into the wind, and the tendency is to look away from the wind toward where your scent is blowing. If you actually spot a bear, bad weather can in fact be a plus, and help you make the approach. The weather can get so bad that you're pretty much stuck in your tent. However, on an average ten-day hunt, a hunter usually loses only a day and a half to adverse weather.

Section II

HUNTING GRIZZLY BEARS IN COASTAL BRITISH COLUMBIA

Chapter 7
SELECTING AN OUTFITTER

What should a hunter look for in a coastal grizzly bear outfitter/guide?

Guy Anttila: A long span of years in the business is definitely a positive. This usually indicates the outfitter is stable and able to handle financial and logistical challenges.

Peter Klaui: The area to be hunted is one important thing to check out. It should have a good record of producing trophy bears. The outfitter should be capable of taking a client on a good hunt, and you have to ask a lot of questions to determine this.

What are [a] the most important single characteristic and [b] the worst possible deficiency in a coastal grizzly bear guide?

Guy Anttila: The most important trait should be that the guide is comfortable at what he's doing. He should also be

Some outfitters offer a very comfortable base from which to hunt coastal grizzlies. (Photo courtesy of Peter Klaui)

A big coastal grizzly taken amid spectacular scenery. (Photo courtesy of Guy Anttila)

knowledgeable about what will attract bears to certain locations, such as understanding the different salmon runs, berry crops, and other types of foods that attract bears to certain places at particular times of year. Not knowing such important details would be the worst characteristic.

Peter Klaui: Any guide must be willing to do his utmost to get his hunter what he's seeking. He also needs to be amicable and able to get along with people. The worst deficiency would be the guide who isn't safe and takes unnecessary risks that can turn into disasters. Inexperience is a major factor in both these shortcomings.

Is there any exceptional qualification for being a coastal grizzly bear guide that may not apply to other types of guiding?

Guy Anttila: We have all heard that bears have a good nose, and a good guide constantly keeps this unavoidable fact

Harry Leggett took this all-time Boone and Crockett record grizzly. (Photo courtesy of Peter Klaui)

in mind. I hunted bears for many years without realizing what an unbelievable sense of smell these animals possess. The reason for my slowness to appreciate this fact is that many small and average-size bears get your scent but still go on doing whatever they're doing. Big boars of trophy quality, bears that may be older than twenty years of age, become extremely experienced as well as cautious.

At one time a hunter and I were wading through a stream with rubber boots. At one place we crossed a gravel bar, reentered the water, and continued on to a vantage point where we sat for the rest of the day. We saw a sow and cub come up the creek, walk over the gravel bar, and continue up the creek. They finally passed us, the sow catching a fish now and again, and eventually disappeared. The reason we had chosen this particular spot was that we had seen a huge grizzly track earlier that morning that looked like it might be a day or so old. I was thinking that maybe this was his fishing hole, so we decided to invest the day waiting, knowing that this bear would be a terrific trophy if we could connect. The day crept by, with the hunter and me watching mainly fish and mergansers. Four and a half hours later the big bear appeared out of the forest, moving very methodically, as virtually all the big guys do. He was heading across the gravel bar, apparently to catch a fish, when his nose went down into the gravel. He looked up and took a long time to study things to the right and to the left. With no hesitation he slowly walked back into the forest from where he had appeared. It was obvious that the bear had smelled our tracks. He probably didn't smell human scent, but smelling rubber particles left behind when we crossed the bar meant the same thing to him—danger! I expect the sow that had come by earlier also smelled our track at the same place, but it didn't seem important to her.

Peter Klaui: Judging bears well is the first thing that comes to mind. All these bears look big at first glance. Good judgment and good eyes are absolutely essential in hunting coastal grizzlies. In addition, a guide should be safety-minded in a special way, even more so than with any other type of guiding, and must keep his client's experience in mind. The hunter may never have hunted anything except white-tailed deer.

Does your area boast a really good source of protein to help bears grow big (salmon streams, plentiful ungulates, large ground-squirrel population, etc.)?

Guy Anttila: We definitely have big bears. The abundance of moose, mountain goats, mountain caribou, and black bears—in addition to the food sources mentioned above—and a relatively short time in the den ensure big bears.

Peter Klaui: Yes, we have plenty of salmon streams, and the area has a long record of producing trophy bears. The world record was taken in my area in 1981, and I believe it's still No. 4 in the Boone and Crockett listings. Since I purchased the area, eight or nine bears taken here have made Boone and Crockett, and the rest have made the Safari Club International book. It's a good trophy area.

What does a good coastal grizzly guide do to ensure his clients' safety?

Guy Anttila: We pay particular attention to firearms safety. The hunter poses more of a threat to life and limb than the bear. We coach our clients in good, steady shot placement so that we can avoid, as much as possible, the need to plunge into thick brush after a wounded grizzly.

Peter Klaui: The only sensory advantage we have over the bear is our eyesight, so I advise my guides to stay out of the brush so they can see and maintain good separation between them and the bear. We generally set up in a good area that has adequate visibility so we can see the bear before he sees us. We don't do any walking up the creeks in hip boots in places where you can only see five or ten yards ahead. Visibility is your most important ally. If you try to work your way up a river, you not only lose visibility but you can't hear anything because of the flowing water—and you can't even smell a bear in the fall because of all the dead fish. You've got to stay out in the open on a sandbar or some other place where you can see. We use four-wheel-drive pickups in some places, and we can drive to some good streams and park very near good glassing areas. It's all spot-and-stalk, and it takes a lot of time behind the binoculars.

Chapter 8

COASTAL BRITISH COLUMBIA GRIZZLY GUIDES EVALUATE THE HUNTER

What is your favorite type of hunter (personality, physical abilities, experience level, socioeconomic status, etc.)?

Guy Anttila: The most fun to be around is the enthusiastic character who is willing to do his best even under circumstances that can sometimes be difficult.

Peter Klaui: My favorite is the guy who's a real hunter, and who is there for all aspects of the hunt. There's always lady luck and other factors we can't control, but the hunter who doesn't quit is a guy I really admire. Patience is probably the most outstanding attribute I like to see in a hunter. Physical

Fishing is good all along the B.C. and Alaska coasts while hunting fall bears. (Photo courtesy of Alisha "Mutts" Rosenbruch-Decker)

Persistent hunters who glass a lot are more likely to be successful. (Photo courtesy of Alisha "Mutts" Rosenbruch-Decker)

ability is a low to average requirement, and as for experience, all a hunter needs is to be able to shoot. This hunting here is not like some hunts where you need to be able to call in an elk or do something else specialized. Finding a big bear just takes patience and the knowledge that you're in a good area.

How important is it for the hunter to be in top physical shape?

Guy Anttila: It is always easier for a hunter to accomplish his goals if he is in reasonably good physical condition. This is particularly true during spring hunts, when the bears' favorite food may be up on a mountainside—a two-hour climb to reach a feeding bear is not uncommon.

Peter Klaui: It's just not important in our area. Hunters are either out in a boat with a guide or they're being driven around in a four-wheel-drive vehicle, so they only need to be alive and relatively well.

Should inexperienced and/or physically challenged hunters go after coastal grizzly bears? Why or why not?

Guy Anttila: Why not? We can handle inexperienced hunters—in fact, they tend to listen to the guide better. Whether we can take a person with a disability depends on the degree of the problem.

Peter Klaui: With the proper guide, the inexperienced hunter is no problem. Sometimes he's a pleasure because he listens better. The guy who's shot fifty animals in Africa thinks he can come in and chase grizzlies around and tell you how you should hunt them, but he can't. Physically handicapped hunters can be problematic, but if we prepare ahead, we can sometimes accommodate them, depending on the degree and kind of disability they have.

Is there any particular characteristic in a hunter that would make you refuse to guide him?

Guy Anttila: The only type of hunter I would not encourage to book a hunt with me is the individual who thinks he knows everything about bears and bear hunting and can't stop telling me about it.

Peter Klaui: That's a tough one because it's pretty much impossible to evaluate a hunter before he shows up. I have never had a hunter I had to send home. There's the odd hunter we'd not like to see return, but usually it's a personality problem. Ninety-nine percent of the time everything works out and there are few clashes.

What is the most dangerous thing a client can do while hunting coastal grizzly bears? Can you share an instance where a client placed himself [or the guide] in danger?

Guy Anttila: Poor shot placement is definitely hazardous. For example, one year we put a stalk on a grizzly feeding on a mountainside. Everything was going well, and an hour later we reached the boulder we had chosen to be our benchrest. The

Hunter Robert Clancy is a happy camper as he is congratulated by guide Mike Klaui. (Photo courtesy of Peter Klaui)

bear had hardly moved and was eighty yards from us broadside, feeding and unaware of our presence—making our job seem easy. The hunter rested his .375 H&H on top of the boulder for what should have been a chip shot. As soon as he touched the trigger the grizzly was airborne and heading our way. I threw up my .375 and fired, reloaded and shot again, and the hunter, too, shot a second time. The bear was still coming at us at full speed and by this time had covered about three-quarters of the distance separating us. I worked the bolt for my third shot and fired. The bear piled into the dirt only yards from our feet.

We skinned the animal with interest to determine entry and exit wounds. The hunter's first shot did not connect with bone or the shoulder; instead he had instinctively aimed behind the front leg, as a deer hunter would do. He hit exactly where he aimed, making a double lung shot on the bear. My first shot entered the right side of the neck and exited just before the left hip, but my second shot missed, as did the hunter's second shot. My third shot, to our amazement, hit the bear in the left hind knee. Picture the bear on the fly toward you; as it happened, the bear's left

Mike Adams takes a tremendous B.C. coastal grizzly. Note the incredible claws! (Photo courtesy of Guy Anttila)

hind foot was higher than his knee and my shot was slightly low, most likely between the front legs and under the belly, catching the knee on the way out and totally removing it from the rest of the body. This shot dumped the bear, which skidded to a halt in front of us. The first two hits were both killing shots, but since only soft tissue was damaged, the bear's adrenaline enabled him to cover seventy-five yards in just a few seconds.

Peter Klaui: British Columbia law says the guide must stay within normal talking range of the client while guiding. Because of this, we don't have very many problems with clients doing anything dangerous. The most dangerous situation would be if they ignored the guide's instructions or wandered off on their own. We keep very close tabs on them, though, so this is unlikely.

Chapter 9

COASTAL BRITISH COLUMBIA GRIZZLY GUIDES EVALUATE HUNTING ARMS

What is your favorite rifle caliber for coastal grizzlies, and do you recommend this caliber to clients?

Guy Anttila: I like the big calibers. My personal favorite is the .375 H&H with 300-grain bullets, and I recommend it for clients.

Peter Klaui: I like either a .338 or a .375, either of which is excellent for our bears.

What is your choice as a backup weapon?

Guy Anttila: The .375 H&H.

Peter Klaui: Again, I like the .375, which is our standard. I have an 8mm, too, that's good. But the .375 is what we normally use.

What is your advice on bullet weight? Bullet construction?

Guy Anttila: I recommend the biggest bullet your weapon will shoot accurately. I'm not into types of bullets and the nuances of ballistics, so I have no strong opinions there.

Peter Klaui: The heavier the bullet, the better. As for construction, I like the coppers such as the Barnes-X or the Trophy Bonded Bear Claw. I sure don't like most of the so-called bonded bullets, because they tend to come apart on impact. You need something that retains its weight and is 250 grains or more.

Do you have any tips on shooting techniques in field situations?

Guy Anttila: Get a rest whenever possible, but be able to shoot offhand if the situation requires it.

Scott Nelson used a modern firearm to take this huge coastal B.C. grizzly. (Photo courtesy of Peter Klaui)

Peter Klaui: You've got to be able to acquire your target quickly in our area, because you're usually dealing with moving bears. The hunter should be able to shoot from a natural rest of some kind, or from a sitting or kneeling position. I think shooting sticks just get in the way. The big thing is the time element—here you're not sitting in a tree stand where you've got all day.

What advice do you give your hunters on shot placement on a coastal grizzly?

Guy Anttila: It's already been said many times, but I'll say it again: Break the bear down and you'll have plenty of time to kill him. It's best to have a broadside shot or have the bear slightly quartering toward you. Take out the shoulder when the lungs are lined up; or, quartering away, take him through the lungs, lining up the far leg or shoulder. Always think about where the exit wound will be, and mentally line up the bullet's likely path through the body. Should the bear be on a flat-out charge, my choice is to place the bullet on either side of his neck—that puts the bulk of the body directly behind.

All of these angles will accomplish the same thing: A shoulder or a leg will be busted, and the bear will go down. His next move will be to try to get on all fours again, which can't be done since you took out one of the legs and you have him anchored. You now have plenty of time to kill him.

Peter Klaui: We prefer lung shots, because a good lung hit tells us we've got a dead bear. I don't believe in the shoulder thing because if you try that, you can miss the vitals and a very bad situation can develop.

How many of your first-time hunters are intimidated by the prospect of hunting a dangerous animal? Describe some typical reactions.

Guy Anttila: Most hunters feel threatened to some degree if they've never before hunted dangerous game. On the light side, I sometimes say that a head-on shot at a charging grizzly is easy because the animal is the size of an oil drum, and if you're not sure of yourself, just wait a couple more seconds and the target will be that much bigger.

Peter Klaui: I think most hunters are intimidated to some degree when they see a griz for the first time, mainly because of the critter's size. Still, it's not often you see a grizzly doing something ferocious. Hunting grizzlies really isn't any more dangerous than hunting any other animal, unless you make a mistake that causes it to become dangerous. That's why you try always to shoot from a place where you've got the advantage. I don't even like to mention what a bad shot can do to a hunt, and besides, we don't allow bad shots in our operation!

Use enough gun on a grizzly this size! (Photo courtesy of Guy Anttila)

Does it help to prepare a person mentally if he has already hunted black bears successfully?

Guy Anttila: I believe it is helpful, but black bears are an entirely different creature from grizzlies.

Peter Klaui: I think so. It's much better than having experience only with deer and turkeys. It's a natural progression to go from black bears to hunting the bigger bears.

The claws on a big bear don't come much better than the ones found on this coastal grizzly. (Photo courtesy of Guy Anttila)

How do you prepare for and handle overpowering excitement in a hunter/client?

Guy Anttila: I slow the person down and try to talk him through the situation. If a hunter is really shaking, I make him hold off on the shot, even if we lose an opportunity. It's a disaster to make a poor shot on a grizzly, so we just can't risk it.

Peter Klaui: Again, it's important to have clients in a place where they have an obvious advantage that can help keep them calm. Most of the time there's no huge hurry, so the hunter has time to collect himself before shooting. If necessary I tell him to calm down because we've got all day and there's no hurry. Communication is the key to keeping your hunter from coming unglued.

Do you have any wise words on bowhunting? Black-powder hunting?

Guy Anttila: I have seen a grizzly die with an arrow through both lungs after a short burst of speed for about thirty yards. But if you don't have the proper angle for a double lung shot, simply don't release that arrow. The success rate in finding a bear that is not arrowed through both lungs is not very good. As for muzzleloaders, the bigger the slug the better I like it.

Peter Klaui: I've taken some black-powder hunters but no bow hunters. We have a problem with bow hunters. If you have to use the backup weapon, they're not happy and you can be sure you're going to have to go into the brush after the bear. If we have to finish it off, as is so often the case, that nullifies its Pope and Young status and the hunter isn't pleased. It's just too much trouble and there are too many potential problems. Now, black-powder hunters we do take, because most of today's black-powder guns are actually modern weapons and are pretty efficient.

Do you take any special precautions when hunting with bow hunters or black-powder hunters?

Guy Anttila: Not really. We try not to let them shoot until things are just right, and that minimizes the need for special precautions.

Peter Klaui: We do get them as close as possible, but we do that with our modern firearm hunters, too. All our hunters have to prove they can shoot, so the first thing we do is spend an hour on the range with them until we're satisfied. We do that with black-powder hunters, too, of course. If a client's gun is a problem, we can supply him one that we know shoots straight.

Chapter 10

HUNTING GRIZZLY BEARS IN COASTAL BRITISH COLUMBIA

Is there anything special about coastal grizzly hunting that sets it apart from other types of hunting?

Guy Anttila: While hunting coastal grizzlies, it's hard to avoid being periodically reminded that we are after dangerous game. Fortunately, most of the bears want no part of us, but if you spend enough time in grizzly country you will be tested by some individual bear that wonders whether he is number one—or you are.

Peter Klaui: They're among the largest carnivores in North America, and it's a thrill to outsmart one of them. It's a true hunting situation, not like many hunts we read about or see on television where basically all they're doing is entrapping an animal. The spot-and-stalk type of hunting we do is unique. You don't call grizzlies in, you don't generally sit in trees and wait for them to show up, and many of the ones you see in our area are trophy animals. You may not see as many as you see in some photos, like in the bear-viewing areas of Alaska, where you may see thirty bears in a quarter-mile of river. Hunting these coastal grizzlies, in my opinion, is the world's ultimate carnivore hunt.

Give us your perspective on coastal grizzly hunting as a game-management tool.

Guy Anttila: In the season just past I had five grizzly hunters because the computer in some remote biologist's office spit out that number as the desired quota for my area. It seems that biologists are more than willing to ignore two hundred-plus bear sightings a year in my area and that the boars our hunters kill are often over twenty years of age. It isn't really management these days; it's degenerated into politically correct guessing.

Rugged mist-shrouded mountains are part of the challenge of hunting on the northwest coast of North America. (Photo courtesy of Alisha Rosenbruch-Decker)

Peter Klaui: It's a real conservation tool when you eliminate older, trophy-class male grizzly bears. These bears are the arch-enemies of sows and cubs, and when you take one, there's no telling how many cubs you save. We've noticed in our area that when we take a big trophy bear or two from a drainage, the next year the place is crawling with sows and cubs and juveniles. Usually another big guy shows up, too. We basically hunt right on the coast, but inland from that coast we have some two hundred miles of roadless wilderness, and the bears just keep coming out of that wilderness down to the coast. There is zero resident pressure, no weekend warriors, and no other hunters anywhere.

What is the most common mistake made by guided coastal grizzly hunters?

Guy Anttila: The most common serious mistake is automatically aiming for the lungs or behind the leg, as most clients have habitually done with other game, and this comes naturally because of their experience with deer and elk. Many stories about the results of such bullet placement could be told, and the outcome is sometimes not good.

Peter Klaui: We don't run into many mistakes because we supply good instructions, a guide who hangs close with the hunter, and a good equipment list. I don't think there's a common mistake made by our hunters, but if there is anything, it would be deficient shooting ability.

What can a guided hunter do that would most improve the chances of taking game [patience, physical fitness, mental preparation, equipment, practice with choice of weapon, other]?

Guy Anttila: The client should do as much research as possible on bear hunting in his chosen area. Keep phoning the outfitter from time to time as you come up with new questions. The better prepared you are mentally, as well as physically, the easier it is to handle those dry days when you can't find a bear no matter what.

Peter Klaui: It sure pays to be as familiar with your firearm as possible; practice shooting, loading while you're moving, unloading, etc. Patience is another big factor. All the equipment and other things we can work around. What our hunters really need are good binoculars, a gun, and a load of patience.

Besides the weapon, what kind of equipment should every hunter carry and which item is the most important?

Guy Anttila: Every person entering our woods should be equipped to start a fire. A little piece of fire starter can make a world of difference if everything is damp. You could be in a situation where you have major problems, and your cell phone probably won't do you any good where you are grizzly hunting. Wood is always available, though, so if you build a fire big enough, you will be found.

Hunter Joe Cedarland with a monstrous coastal B.C. grizzly. (Photo courtesy of Peter Klaui)

Peter Klaui: High-quality, waterproof, fog-proof binoculars and riflescope are both equally necessary and important. Hunters also need good waterproof boots and topnotch raingear. Beyond that, it still comes back to the firearm and the ability to use it.

Are there any common items of equipment that you feel are unnecessary, redundant, or just plain worthless?

Guy Anttila: Two items that I often find to be hindrances to the hunter are bipods and shooting sticks. In our type of terrain there is almost always something that can be used for a rest, but I find that people who carry shooting sticks forget to look around for a natural rest. A bipod is excellent in open country where you have plenty of time to set up, but here a bipod is just extra weight to drag up a mountain and it often puts the rifle out of balance when you swing it up to your shoulder.

Peter Klaui: We get the odd guy who comes with a whole bag full of unnecessary stuff, and I have no idea why. I assume he bought the stuff specially for this trip and is determined to have it whether he needs it or not.

Tell us your method of field-judging the size of coastal grizzlies.

Guy Anttila: It is not easy to explain in words how to determine a grizzly's size, but anyone meeting up with a big bear knows it. When glassing bears at a distance, the smaller, lighter-colored bears seem like kids on a playground. They constantly scurry around wasting energy and not necessarily accomplishing much. Smaller bears also tend to be leggy. Where I've hunted grizzlies, the really big boars are always dark in color. They may be born with lighter colors like blond and yellow mixed with brown. The light colors tend to fade with age, but sometimes the tips of the guard hairs remain light-colored, causing people to refer to such animals as "silvertips." If you watch a very heavy bear on a mountainside, you can actually see the weight shifting when he takes a step. Big bears sport bellies that hang close to the ground. It's tremendously helpful to look at tracks if possible. A rule of thumb is that if the front pad leaves a print seven inches wide, it was made by a bear of about eight feet. Guides will watch for many variables, and often we will spend some time looking through a spotting scope before expressing an opinion of a bear's size.

Peter Klaui: You're talking about how far away they are, too, of course. You compare that animal to a log or a stump of known size nearby. Body size is far easier to judge than skull size. If it's a big male, in our area you know he's going to have a skull measurement of 23-plus inches, and more likely over 24 inches. I don't believe guys who say they can judge a trophy bear within a sixteenth of an inch. I can't do that, and I've been at this a long, long time. If we judge an animal by stride, body

Another great coastal grizzly taken in British Columbia. (Photo courtesy of Guy Anttila)

size, how square it appears, and the way it walks, and say it's a big bear—then it's a big bear. A really big bear will lock the back knee joint in order to carry his weight better, and you can actually see them doing this.

As I said, trophies also look square; they're as big in the front shoulders as they are in the back, and sometimes the front shoulders are even bigger than the back. Everyone looks at the width between the ears, and I guess that's a good thing to check, but we find in our area that length of the skull is where you really win on a grizzly. All mature male grizzlies are eight to nine inches wide in the skull, or very slightly wider, and most are within a quarter-inch of the same measurement. However, the length of the skull is what determines how well it will score. If you're looking for something truly exceptional, it should have a long spread between the nose tip and the ears, a spread that can vary by up to two inches on a trophy bear, as opposed to only a quarter-inch of variation in width.

What is the most reliable way to determine sex when no cubs are present? Give us some other methods as well.

Guy Anttila: If the bear is "pretty," leave it alone because it's a female. A bear with pretty colors is not likely to be a trophy bear. During mating season in the spring, when you see a male and a female together, it is quite easy to see which is the male, because he is likely to be 20 to 25 percent larger and much darker. The boars tend to carry their heads lower, too.

Peter Klaui: We call the sows Aunt Jemimas! They've got a really big rear end. They're small in the shoulders and somewhat pear-shaped as viewed from the side. A mature sow and a mature boar are fairly easy to distinguish, although on juveniles it's much harder. The facial characteristics of a sow are distinctive, too. Their eyes are closer together, the head is small (making the ears look bigger), and usually the snout is more pointed.

How do you normally follow up after a shot at a coastal grizzly?

Guy Anttila: When my hunter shoots and I can see that it was a good hit, there is no need for me to help out. In that case I will not shoot—after all, it is the hunter's bear, and I'm sure he feels better about it if the guide doesn't have to put a hole in it as well. On the other hand, we always stand ready should the first shot not be a good one, because obviously tracking wounded grizzlies is not a lot of fun.

Peter Klaui: Our guides are instructed by me to take a follow-up shot if they're certain a client made a bad shot. Some hunters have a big problem with that, but that's just too bad. If we see a bear improperly hit in the shoulder and it's basically limping away and the hunter doesn't recycle and shoot quickly

New world record SCI grizzly, taken by hunter Gabriel Perez-Maura with Peter Klaui in 2008. (Photo courtesy of Peter Klaui)

like he should, we shoot. That aspect of our handling of the situation after the shot is always a problem for hunters, but we really can't afford to do it any other way.

What procedure do you follow in tracking a wounded coastal grizzly?

Guy Anttila: When there is an obvious blood trail where he disappeared, we usually leave him alone for a while, even sometimes overnight, before we begin tracking. Often an extra guide will go along, and the process is slow. Grizzlies do seem to expect you to follow, and they usually make figure-sixes on the hillside so they place themselves uphill of their backtrail. This is their instinctive way of creating a situation that will allow them to charge downhill at you. A well-trained dog can be very useful in a follow-up because the wounded bear will pay attention to the barking dog, an invaluable distraction that permits the guides to move in from the side to finish off the bear.

Peter Klaui: We leave him alone for a long time without following, at least an hour or so. We evaluate the situation and do everything possible to recover that bear, but given the virtually impenetrable vegetation in our area, we've got a pretty limited chance of finding the animal without a dog. That's why our guides don't hesitate to put in a follow-up shot. We don't keep dogs for following bears, though we have called in dogs in a few instances. Knock on wood, we've never lost a wounded bear. That's a tribute to the way we set up the shot and the way we coach the hunter to make a good shot. And sometimes, fortunately or unfortunately, it's a tribute to a timely follow-up shot by one of our guides.

Chapter 11

SPECIFIC GUIDING AREAS FOR HUNTING GRIZZLY BEARS IN COASTAL BRITISH COLUMBIA

Describe your home guiding area and any distinctions that set it apart.

Guy Anttila: Our guiding area is a gorgeous, expansive piece of wilderness just south of the Yukon border. It is bounded on the west by Alaska for over a hundred miles. When Elsie and I purchased this fantastic area, we were thrilled with its beauty and diversity. There are many high mountains, and it has sheep, moose, mountain goats, and of course grizzlies in abundance. Elsie has been my partner and companion throughout it all, and we're extremely proud of our area.

Peter Klaui: Our guiding area is close to eight thousand square miles, of which we hunt only 10 percent or so because the rest is inaccessible. What we have is a unique piece of land in which there is no human influence at all. There are no settlements, no roads, just nothing. It's similar to some places in Alaska, but it's almost unique in British Columbia. We do have a lot of islands along our coast, and on these we hunt mainly black bears, although there are also grizzlies there. However, on most of them grizzly hunting isn't open. We've seen a lot of grizzlies out on islands, which was never the case twenty years ago.

I think our area is one of the best places in the world to hunt grizzly bears. It has the genes, the habitat, the history of producing big grizzlies, and it produced the largest grizzly ever taken in British Columbia. We've got rivers with spawning salmon, and alpine meadows for the bears in the summer where heavy logging in the past hundred years has left ideal conditions for tremendous berry crops. Logging really helps the habitat—it doesn't decrease it. Logging is essentially habitat construction, not habitat destruction as some antihunters maintain. The places humans can't reach

Some monster grizzlies live near the salmon streams of coastal British Columbia. (Photo courtesy of Peter Klaui)

must number in the thousands, and it's from these areas that the bears travel to the coast where we hunt them. We've got a lot of other wildlife, too, besides bears, including black-tailed deer, wolf, cougar, the odd wolverine, sea ducks, and a whole host of migratory birds. It's just a great, scenic area.

How much of a role do food sources play in hunting bears in your area?

Guy Anttila: They play a big role, mainly because of the salmon runs. The weather determines when spring arrives, and bears don't check how calendars and ocean currents affect salmon runs, of course. That's just part of the uncertainty factor in hunting what some people say is the greatest trophy animal in North America.

Peter Klaui: Our bears eat a lot of salmon, but they aren't big carnivores in the sense of catching and eating other game. They eat fish in the fall, and the rest of the time they're mostly vegetarians, eating everything from roots to skunk cabbage to berries. For our bears to grow so big there must be excellent food sources.

How many of your bears are taken incidentally (as opposed to being the primary species sought)?

Guy Anttila: All our spring bears are the primary animal sought; other seasons are generally closed then. In the fall we do some dedicated grizzly hunting, but we do take some incidental bears when a guy has tags for other species as well.

Peter Klaui: None at all. All of our bear hunts are directed specifically at either grizzlies or black bears.

What kind of terrain is ideal for hunting coastal grizzly bears?

Guy Anttila: Open country is ideal, especially in the spring when there are no salmon in the streams. In the fall a stream with a good run of salmon is ideal.

Peter Klaui: There are two things. In the springtime you're looking for grassy estuaries at the heads of inlets where there's greenery, as well as beach areas, creek mouths, etc., where vegetation is sprouting. Bears also pick up some protein on the beach, such as mussels and other sea creatures. In the fall the ideal terrain is a big sandbar on an active salmon stream where you can see a long way.

Describe your typical camp setup and camp routine.

Guy Anttila: Our bear camps tend to vary a lot. We have pretty fancy base camps with showers and cooks, but it can get down to the two-man tent with an open fire for heat and cooking. We make our hunters as comfortable as possible, but if your goal is to have the best chance of going home with a big grizzly, then you need to be flexible. You make sure the outfitter knows what you want and then let him plan it. Your success is his success! In the spring we go out and do a lot of glassing, and in the fall we watch salmon streams where a big boar has been fishing.

Peter Klaui: Our base camp is a sixty-foot yacht. It's a very mobile camp, and our hunters live like kings, eat like kings, and sleep like kings. They can watch hockey games at night on satellite television if they want. We anchor our boat close to an access point to a stream or a road system in the fall, head out in a large skiff or jump in a four-wheel-drive Suburban, and go hunting for the day. In the springtime we use smaller eighteen-foot skiffs and cruise the beaches and river estuaries.

What is your success rate on trophy animals?

Guy Anttila: It would be very unusual for a client not to have an opportunity to kill a good trophy boar since it is common to see ten to thirty grizzlies during a hunt. Out of that number you should see one to three large boars that may be in the eight- to nine-and-a-half-foot class. Not everyone kills a bear, but most people have their opportunity.

Peter Klaui: That changes from year to year and hunter to hunter. Last year we were five for five and the year before that two for two, so I guess you could say we were 100 percent for two years. The year before that we had a couple of guys who didn't get a bear, including one who never even saw a bear. The weather plays a big role in our success rate. Overall, I'd say we're 50 to 75 percent, and the overall success of nonresident tags in British Columbia is only 11 percent. It's even lower for British Columbia residents. That's a fact that a lot of hunters don't know. With us, if you get a grizzly, it will truly be a trophy, and that's one of the real strong points of our operation. For example, this past year we were five for five with three Boone and Crockett bears and two SCI bears. Two of those hunts have been nominated for exceptional-hunt awards from the Guide-Outfitters Association of British Columbia, so that's pretty special. Weather has a lot to do with it, but so does Lady Luck.

Describe your usual hunting method and any common variations.

Guy Anttila: We usually head out in the morning to get to one or more vantage spots from which to glass. In the spring we want

Spectacular seaside scenery is almost routine when hunting bears on the coast. (Photo courtesy of Alisha "Mutts" Rosenbruch-Decker)

to be glassing the south or southwest slopes of the mountains. These slopes get a maximum amount of sunshine and therefore the first greens appear there. Although grizzlies will take every opportunity to find avalanche-killed meat—snow-covered moose and mountain goats and the like—they also do their share of killing. That's particularly true at calving time, but since that time doesn't last very long, the bears' main diet in the spring tends to be grasses and roots. We hunt these food sources diligently. In the fall salmon streams are a major focus.

Peter Klaui: In the spring our smaller skiffs cruise to where the guide and hunter can spot and glass. When we locate a good bear, we plan a stalk or wait for a bear that's coming in our direction. You always use your vision as your primary advantage. In the fall you can even sit in the truck and watch a salmon stream. We don't like to do a lot of walking around because you just stink the place up and spook the bears out of there. You need to be able to see a large area where bears might be traveling along the rivers, or where there are sandbars and you can see a bear when it comes out to fish. We do not walk miles and miles trying to shake a bear out; we wait for them to come to us.

Tell us your method of getting close enough for a shot.

Guy Anttila: I do not like long-distance shots at grizzlies. Most of the problems with wounded animals have occurred because someone shot without closing to a respectable distance—a hundred yards or so. If a bear is more than two hundred yards away, you can usually get closer. If I could place the bear at the ideal distance from the gun barrel, it would be about eighty to one hundred yards. At that distance it is rare to have problems.

Peter Klaui: It's a conventional stalk situation. You stay downwind from the bear, try to get inside two hundred yards, and then wait until the proper shot presents.

Do you have both a spring and a fall season in your area?

Guy Anttila: Yes.
Peter Klaui: Yes.

Which one offers the best hunting in your area? Early or late in either season?

Guy Anttila: The two seasons are entirely different. During fall hunts we find ourselves in closer quarters with the bears because we sit on salmon spawning channels that are often heavily brushed in. When a bear appears, he may be fifty yards away and sometimes even closer. Heavy vegetation totally changes our style of hunting, whether it is salmon or berries or other vegetation in the valley meadows. Even there we are often within shooting range when we see the bear.

Peter Klaui: I think fall is best for quality bears because the big guys are coming down out of the high country to feed on fish. In the spring there are lots of bears, but they're very

Guy and Elsie Anttila with the trophy of a lifetime taken in their British Columbia area. (Photo courtesy of Guy Anttila)

scattered out and can be hard to find, though you can run into them anywhere.

Are badly rubbed hides a problem in your area? When is it best to hunt to avoid this problem?

Guy Anttila: Fortunately, where we hunt, which is mainly along the east slopes of the Coast Range, we do not see a lot of rubbed bears during the hunting season.

Peter Klaui: Fall is the best time to avoid rubbed hides—you never see them then. You do see one occasionally in the spring. Also, in spring the fur gets back-combed and looks irregular, so I prefer fall hides over spring hides. I realize that may not be the case in places like Alaska, where the guides are probably up there on snowshoes shaking the bears out of their dens. Rubbing is probably worse here on the coast because of warmer temperatures and the "instant spring" sort of thing.

How much does weather influence hunting success and how you hunt in your area?

Guy Anttila: The weather always will have a strong influence on our success rates. If we have fog, we can't fly and hunters on the ground can't even glass the mountainsides. On such days we may find ourselves by a fire waiting for the weather to lift and probably hunting some less desirable spots in the valleys.

Peter Klaui: It influences both things an awful lot. Cold, rainy weather with hurricane-force winds is the worst-case scenario, and it can happen in either spring or fall. The bears just hole up and don't move around at all.

Section III

HUNTING GRIZZLY BEARS IN INTERIOR ALASKA

Chapter 12
SELECTING AN OUTFITTER

What should a hunter look for in an interior Alaska grizzly bear outfitter/guide?

Dave Leonard: If I were the hunter, I'd be looking for an outfitter with a good area and a history of producing good bears. You can research that through a number of references, such as the record books of Safari Club International and the Boone and Crockett Club. You can also get such biological data from the Alaska Department of Fish and Game.

As for the outfitter himself, I'd place a lot of emphasis on attitude and enthusiasm. There are a lot of guides and outfitters who've been doing this work a long time, and it's easy to lose those qualities after a while. I've always promised myself that I'd get out if it ever became a chore instead of something that I enjoy doing. It's hard work, but it's fulfilling, too.

I'd look for someone who treats every single client like I'd want to be treated on a guided hunt, and we certainly try our level best to do exactly that in our operation. Longevity in the business is a grand thing, but be careful not to book with someone who's burned out and has lost all his enthusiasm.

Joe Mott: In my opinion one of the best things a hunter can do is to check references on the guide. One thing somewhat unique that Stoney River Lodge does is to send every prospective hunter a list of all its past hunters, not just the successful ones. When the hunter calls people on that list, he gets a pretty clear picture of what he's dealing with at Stoney River Lodge.

Larry Rivers: The hunter should first seek out an outfitter whose hunting style matches what the hunter enjoys. Some guys come to camp and the first thing they want to know is where the Jack Daniels is located. Such a hunter ought to look for a guide that brings in a lot of Jack Daniels. One of our primary rules was that you don't mix gunpowder and alcohol, so someone like that who came into one of my camps probably wasn't very happy. Some hunting camps are pretty rough and everyone has a can of beer in hand and they're telling bawdy stories. Others, more dedicated to the hunt, try to get to bed at a reasonable hour and get up early. I think in the final analysis you've got to talk to the outfitter and his clients and see if you have a meeting of the minds. It really does pay to be kindred spirits with your outfitter/guide.

Hide of a really big interior grizzly hanging at Stoney River Lodge. (Photo courtesy of Joe Mott)

Also important are what kind of game is available and the style of hunting that will be done. Some people want to be back in a nice hunting lodge every night, so they'd best pick an outfitter who offers that. Then you've got the hunter who wants to sit on a horse all day—and isn't going to fly if he can help it. Some outfitters let you shoot at a bear at two hundred yards while others, me included, want you below fifty yards. I liked to get my hunter in really close because it made him remember the hunt and gave him a better chance to make a good shot. My wife always wanted to know why we'd take a shot at a sheep at six or seven hundred yards, but when we were hunting something as dangerous as a grizzly, we wanted to be within fifty yards. Some guys want a nice lodge and a Scotch in hand at day's end, while the next guy wants to be out in the wilderness unshaven and dirty and after the biggest animal he can find.

In the final analysis, some hunters think we're selling dead animals, but we're not. We're selling an experience, and the hunter needs to be sure he's buying the experience he wants. If

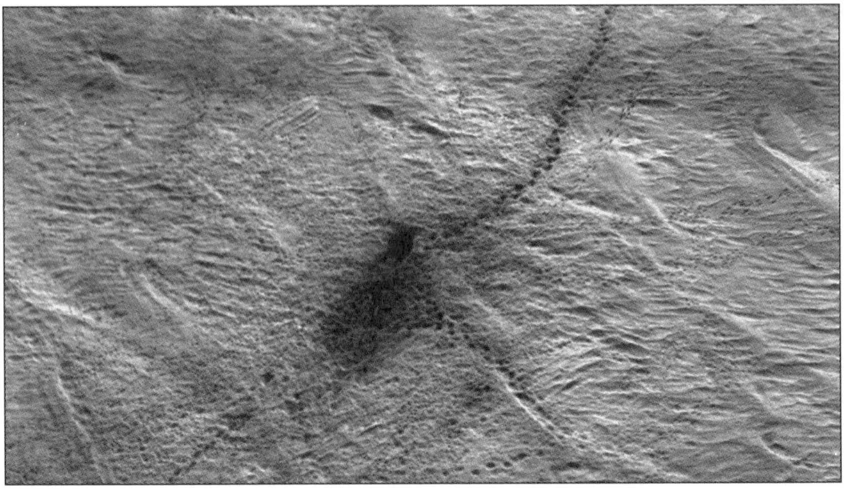

The kind of evidence you're seeking: A grizzly den at 4,500 feet in the western Arctic. (Photo courtesy of Dave Leonard)

a customer isn't looking for what we're selling, we have a moral responsibility not to sell it to him.

What are [a] the most important single characteristic and [b] the worst possible deficiency in an interior Alaska grizzly guide?

Dave Leonard: I'd say the single most important guide characteristic is being tightly focused on the job at hand. The worst deficiency would be indecisiveness and the inability to make quick, effective decisions.

Joe Mott: I've always joked that a guide has to be part psychologist, part gunsmith, part photographer, and just a little bit of everything else. Still, his most important quality is the ability to get along with all types of hunters and all kinds of personalities. There's nothing worse than being in camp with a hunter who has an overbearing personality and being unable to deal with it.

The worst deficiency in a guide would be overconfidence. Guiding is a constant growing process, and if you think you know it all, that's a joke. If I run into a guide who insists he knows it all, I'd have to question that attitude. I've seen such a blustery attitude in some guides, and it isn't pleasing to me; it also isn't truthful.

Larry Rivers: The best possible thing would be a guide who's not afraid of grizzly bears, and an awful lot of them are. Even if it's just in his mind, that kind of guide is going to resent being out there with the bears, and that's not what you want. It's somewhat paradoxical, but a guide's worst possible deficiency is an all-consuming love of hunting—to the point that he lives and breathes it. Such guys get just as excited as the client, and they make terrible guides. In a guide you want someone who's a clinical professional. When there's a decision to be made, he's not making it based on adrenaline or a macho image, he's evaluating the situation calmly and doing what's best for all concerned. Your best guides are pure, clinical killers who don't let their emotions become a big drag on their ability to make good decisions. In those decisions they consider the weather, the terrain, the client, and so on. If the client goes against recommendations and brings leather boots instead of waders, his guide has to tell him to get in the river with him and wade anyway. If you get a guide who's too polite and worries about such things, you'll likely lose your chance at a bear.

Another necessary element in a guide is patience—the willingness to sit on his butt for days on end because that's what it takes most of the time. If you really want to be successful hunting grizzlies, you've got to get above the timberline where the berry patches are located. Sometimes you have to hunt the bears down in the creek bottoms, where you can't see (we call that "stumble hunting"). You might bump into a bear, and even if the guide can't tell whether it's a trophy, you'd better shoot it because you're not going to see another one there.

Is there any exceptional qualification for being an interior Alaska grizzly guide that may not apply to other types of guiding?

Dave Leonard: It's especially important that the guide have a really good instinct about grizzlies. It takes almost a sixth sense to be a top bear guide. You need the ability to think like a bear. This think-like-the-quarry quality isn't quite as important when you're talking about hunting sheep or moose, but it's certainly paramount in guiding for bears. You must have that instinct to consistently be successful. I've had clients comment on that intangible aspect after we've conducted a long, hard stalk or followed tracks around in circles for a long time, and it's really hard to explain how we do it. But without that instinct, a grizzly guide is at a distinct disadvantage. Obviously, you can't always guess right about what a bear's going to do, but sometimes you just have to follow your gut instinct, and so often it turns out to be right and you get the bear.

Joe Mott: A grizzly guide has to have respect for the creature he's hunting, probably more so than a guide for any other animal. He also can't have what could be called fear of the grizzly. He's got to understand and respect the grizzly's capabilities, and then balance his approach with this knowledge yet without any big element of anxiety about guiding a hunter to the animal. You just don't barge in to confront a grizzly because you're carrying the biggest gun in the world. You have to respect these animals, not only because they're dangerous but also because they're truly magnificent.

Larry Rivers: The griz guide must have good equipment, starting with optics—no cheapo binoculars.

Does your area boast a really good source of protein to help bears grow big (salmon streams, plentiful ungulates, large ground-squirrel population, etc.)?

Dave Leonard: We have plenty of food for our bears. The Noatak River system has perhaps the most northerly run of salmon in the world, and these chum salmon really help our bears. Usually it's a great summer run, but our season runs right onto the tail end of it. There are plenty of moose in the area, too, and the bears certainly become proficient at hunting them. There are also caribou, and the grizzlies kill a lot of them, too. In addition, our area also supports a really major population of Arctic ground squirrels, and you often find bears digging for them. In addition to animal protein, there are the usual grasses and sedges, plus

Guide Dave Leonard watched this bear kill and bury the moose—then he got his hunter in position. (Photo courtesy of Dave Leonard)

berries and plentiful willow root. I can honestly say we've got it all when it comes to bear food.

Joe Mott: We have river drainages with salmon runs, even in our interior grizzly area. There are also quite a few ungulates such as moose and caribou, and the grizzlies feed on these when they can. Still, I think the majority of the interior grizzly's diet is grasses and berries. We've got a tremendous blueberry crop all over our area, and to me that's the ideal bear food; berry patches are the ideal place to hunt bears in the fall. At that time the berries are ripe and the grizzlies keep their noses to the bushes and really chow down.

Larry Rivers: I've seen grizzlies up in the Arctic where there are no salmon, and occasionally they'll push ten feet. Some people say the coastal bears get iodine from the fish, and that stimulates the thyroid and makes them grow. As far as I know, it's all speculation. In general, I'd say grizzly growth has a lot to do with salmon sources, but the bears of Southeast Alaska get plenty of salmon and yet don't average nearly as big. On Kodiak the outstanding feature of the bears is their skull size, not the size of the hide. There are some big-bodied bears there, don't get me wrong, but those bears just genetically have bigger skulls for some reason.

As an aside, people up here used to wear buffalo robes, but some richer people wanted something better than the common

The timeless Super Cub, a necessary part of many hunts for an interior Alaska grizzly. (Photo courtesy of Larry Rivers)

man had, so most got a bear robe. There were three companies that traded in bear robes, the Kodiak Brown Bear Company, the Alaska Peninsula Bear Company, and the Kamchatka Brown Bear Company. The Kodiak people were a lot more successful in promoting their bears as the best and biggest. We still live today with that legacy of Kodiak's supposed superiority.

What does a good interior Alaska grizzly guide do to ensure safety while hunting North America's most dangerous game?

Dave Leonard: I've thought about that question a great deal. We try to actively communicate safety to each new client, and instill it in our guides as well. We brief clients thoroughly on hunter behavior and make it clear what's acceptable and what's not. We don't allow any drinking in conjunction with handling firearms, for example.

Another really important element is that we make sure each hunter understands not to chamber a round before the guide instructs him to do so. I've almost had my head taken off a couple of times over the years, so we're pretty emphatic on this point. An experienced hunter knows he should chamber a round when he sees a bear coming down on them, but I'm talking about the hunter who has this terrible fetish for walking around in the boonies with a round in the chamber. That's the biggest danger on any bear hunt: You never know what might happen when you're working through the brush with a round in the ready position and the guide doesn't even know it. So we emphasize that point with our clients. You've got to trust your guide's experience and chamber a round only when he tells you to do so.

Joe Mott: One of the best safety measures is to keep a clean camp. Where you set up camp is also fairly important, too. You need to stay out of heavy timber close to a river, because that's where the bears are going to be traveling. I like to keep our camps out in the open so we can see. While we're actually hunting, everyone really needs to keep their eyes open. I even keep a close watch behind me, just in case. With grizzlies, you just never know. If we're going to cross an area of timber, I spend a little time glassing the area to avoid bumping into a sow and cubs or even a big boar. I'm not against going down into the timber after a bear, but if there's an alternative I'll take it. Staying where you can see well is a lot safer than bumping into them in the brush.

Larry Rivers: The guide's got to pray a lot! The whole thing about bears being out to get you by charging is really just a promotion to make the hunt a little more adventuresome. Up in the high country, where it's open, you can see a bear coming literally miles away, so safety isn't a big issue up there. You're not stalking sows and cubs, so you won't get tangled up with a protective mother bear.

I don't think it's a very risky hunt, unless you get in there close with some Nimrod who can't shoot, which happens too often. Most Americans think they're a crack shot because they're American or because they've shot a thousand rounds off a bench. I have yet to see a single guide carrying around a bench for his client to use in the field. All a bench does is to prove the rifle—not the hunter—can shoot straight. I made my clients practice prone, and sometimes they had no idea how to do it. We also didn't hang meat around the camp—a sure way to attract bears—and we did all the cooking right there in the tents.

Chapter 13

INTERIOR ALASKA GRIZZLY GUIDES EVALUATE THE HUNTER

What is your favorite type of hunter [personality, physical abilities, experience level, socioeconomic status, etc.]?

Dave Leonard: We get all types, but my favorite is the easygoing hunter. Patience, too, is certainly a virtue because we're often fighting an uphill battle with Mother Nature and other things beyond our control. Physical ability isn't as important as endurance, and endurance so often comes from the lifestyle a person lives. A guy can be in top physical condition but lack the drive and determination to go that extra mile to get a bear. I really appreciate it when I see these characteristics in a hunter.

A moderate to high level of experience is definitely a desirable quality as well. I get some guys who haven't hunted very much, not even deer as a young person, but they decide, sort of as a macho kind of thing, that they want to go shoot a bear. I respect that desire, but I don't hesitate to question them closely about their goals and expectations. If they've only hunted deer and small game in their life, I try to get them to book a hunt for caribou or moose so they get some more experience before taking on a grizzly. That gets them into bear country so they're around these daunting animals a little before they actually go hunt them.

Another virtue I really like is a willingness to listen well to instructions. A lot of professional people we guide are extremely wealthy and capable, but if one of them won't listen to the guide, it's a real hardship. I highly value the characteristic of listening. If the hunter doesn't agree with something, he ought to be willing to at least listen to the guide's point of view about why he's doing things the way he does.

Joe Mott: As for personality, I like someone who's easygoing and likable. Physical ability, too, is definitely a plus because bear

Are you man enough to hang in there and hunt bears in the brutal Alaska weather? (Photo courtesy of Joe Mott)

hunting in Alaska isn't easy, especially for interior grizzlies. In the spring especially, when some hunters are trying on snowshoes for the first time in their life, it can seem like they've never had any exercise. I asked them, "Good grief, what have you been doing at home for exercise?" Those devices don't have a motor, but if you want to hunt grizzlies in the spring, you've got to strap them on and go. If a guy can't go, we try to hunt around the lodge and stay in the easier places, while still doing our best to give the client a chance to take a bear. If I were hunting alone, there are a lot of things I would do differently, but I'm limited by the capabilities of my hunters. I fully realize that most hunters don't have a whole lot of experience with this kind of hunting and that I need to help them along as much as possible.

Socioeconomic status doesn't matter at all to me. I've had some really nice rich hunters and some really nice poor hunters, and also the opposite in both. Some think that people with a lot of money are really full of themselves, but that's not necessarily so. I can probably count on the fingers of one hand the ones over the years who were in that category. Most of our clients are really fine people.

Larry Rivers: In my camps I didn't want a guy who was in the bottle. I wanted a serious hunter who was there to hunt and could put together a good shot group at a hundred yards. I like a light-hearted hunter, someone who's not too serious for his own good. As to physical ability, a bear seeker has to be able to walk, especially when a bear is sighted. If a customer is so badly out of shape he can't bring his leg up because it bounces off his belly, he shouldn't even be out there. Those tundra tussocks we fight all the time don't grow on sidewalks. A guy has to be patient, too. On a ten-day hunt, for example, he's got to be willing to sit there ten full days. The way to shoot a big bear on the last day is to pass up small ones on the earlier days. If you shoot a small bear, you're never going to shoot a big one.

How important is it for the hunter to be in top physical shape?

Dave Leonard: I've wrestled a little with that question, but I'd say it never hurt anyone to be in good physical shape. It isn't necessarily a top item on our list of ideal-client characteristics, because bear hunters really don't usually need to be in "sheep shape" like our high-mountain hunters do. Typically, if a hunter has a good measure of patience and can sit and glass and then do one big push to get to a bear, he or she can get the job done. That patience attribute is far superior to having a guy who runs marathons and feels like he's got to be continually on the move, because all he'll do is spread a lot of scent around and run all the bears over the mountain. It's far better to let your optics do your walking and wait for the right situation. Then it becomes more like a chess game in which you plan every move carefully and come out a winner.

Joe Mott: It sure helps a lot. The better shape the hunter is in, the higher his odds on taking a bear.

Larry Rivers: It's not important at all—up until the actual stalk. It doesn't take much in the way of conditioning to sit and drink coffee and glass. After you spot the bear, though, the physical demand may go up. It depends on a lot of things: How far away is the bear? How rough is the country you'll have to cross? How much muskeg is there? Many other obstacles, too, may require physical stamina. I've never seen someone in good shape who didn't get his bear. How physically fit a bear hunter should be is like asking how long a string is. It's absolutely impossible to say in advance what will be required of the hunter.

Should inexperienced or physically challenged hunters hunt interior Alaska grizzly bears? Why or why not?

Dave Leonard: I'd discourage the lightly experienced hunter. I think a person needs to get some experience before taking on an animal as challenging as a grizzly. With an inexperienced hunter, I'm most concerned about him doing something that causes a disaster; you just don't know what a neophyte is going to do. I've had them eject all their shells when it came time to shoot and never fire a round. I've also had them walk around all day with the rifle pointing at their guide, and we find out there's been a live round in the chamber all that time. Of course, we've all been inexperienced at some point, but I don't think you should take on a serious bear hunt until you have at least a moderate amount of experience.

The physically challenged hunter? Well, I try never to turn those guys down if I can help it. I understand their situation, and I want to help whenever I can. However, we're just not set up to give a guy with a truly major handicap, such as being wheelchair-bound, a safe and high-quality experience. The reason, of course, is the extreme difficulty and remoteness of the terrain. I try really hard to help disabled persons, and if I feel I don't have the situation for them, I try hard to find someone who can take them out, maybe in a boat or from a comfortable main lodge—that way they can have a quality bear hunt as much as their abilities allow. There are definitely some good situations in which a truly handicapped hunter can take a bear, but unfortunately my operation can offer only so much help.

Joe Mott: I've taken a lot of inexperienced people on their first bear hunt. A lot of the burden in that case falls on the guide; he has to be competent enough to overcome the inexperience and get the job done right. I've had only one or two hunters over the years who just weren't up to it when it came time to close in on the bear. They got more nervous and afraid the closer we got, to the point that I had to back off. One guy was simply terrified. If the hunter will listen to the guide and do what he asks, inexperience isn't a big factor.

The worst physical challenge I've had was a fall hunt involving a hunter who required a cane to walk. He got a moose on his first hunt with us, and he came back again and took a bear. We haven't really had much experience with hunters with major handicaps, like being confined to a wheelchair. In the places we have to hunt, we just can't get them around.

Larry Rivers: Why not? They're not market hunting—they're going for the enjoyment of being out there. Hunting is a great excuse just to be in the great outdoors. We've taken guys with plastic arteries who couldn't walk a hundred and fifty yards, and they did OK. We've even taken people in wheelchairs. Some of them came back year after year, and sometimes their condition didn't allow them ever to actually shoot a bear. But they were out there like any other hunter, having the greatest outdoor experience a person can have.

I had one guy who kept rebooking well into his nineties! When he finally died, he left instructions for me to spread his ashes up here, half over bear camp and half over sheep camp, and I was more than glad to comply. Just because a person can't walk, does that mean I shouldn't take him? Well, he's out there in camp right now and I'm not! They should have a chance to do this if they really want to. We would do everything we could to make them successful, and if they didn't take a bear, they still had a great hunt.

Is there any particular characteristic in a hunter that would make you refuse to guide him for an interior Alaska grizzly?

Dave Leonard: Well, being a concessionaire on government land, I don't like the word "refuse," but I certainly avoid certain types. There have been people who have approached me about a hunt but left me feeling uncomfortable about them. Part of my feeling came from their very arrogant, know-it-all attitude—you could tell they weren't willing to listen to me or my guide. Some of them came across as being willing to do unethical or illegal things, and apparently expected me to go along. I just couldn't take a person like that.

Joe Mott: I hate to see arrogance and a know-it-all attitude in hunters, and I've had a couple over the years. I wouldn't want to see them come back unless their attitude changed. Once, on a moose hunt, I had a hunter tell me that the area we were hunting was obviously a migration route and none of the animals was sticking around. While he's rambling on about this, I'm looking at three sets of moose antlers sticking up out of the brush that he can't see! We got him a nice moose. That particular fellow was obviously not strong-willed enough just to stomp away mad.

Larry Rivers: There are a few. I wouldn't guide a guy who wanted to live in his bottle. Then there's the hunter who can't talk about anything but size—it has to square ten feet, make Boone and Crockett, etc. I wouldn't take such a person out, even if I thought I could get him that quality of bear. Another turn-off is a guy who walks up to my booth at a show and says he's saved all his life for this hunt and expects the biggest bear in Alaska. I would realize right away that I just couldn't live up to his expectations—he wouldn't enjoy the hunt and was sure

Snowshoe hunting for Arctic grizzlies is as physically demanding as it gets, but the reward of a bear that squares over nine feet makes it all worthwhile! (Photo courtesy of Dave Leonard)

to go home miserable. There are a few exceptions, and we may have disappointed a few people who should have been happy, but you can't always recognize that kind of person.

What is the most dangerous thing a client can do while hunting interior Alaska grizzlies? Can you share an incident in which a client placed himself or the guide in danger?

Dave Leonard: Other than carrying his rifle with a round chambered, a client's most dangerous act is to totally freeze up. I've had that happen, and so has one of my assistant guides. My assistant and his hunter had seen a big bear go back into a den, and they waited around for the better part of two days, hoping he would show again. Finally they went over to the den, holding the higher ground, and eventually worked their way down to the opening in the hillside. The guide yelled a couple of times but nothing happened, so he threw a snowball in the hole. His hunter, whom the guide thought was pretty accomplished, was standing by with his rifle. The guide glanced over at the hunter, and as he did he caught a flicker of movement out of the corner of his eye: That bear was coming out as if shot out of a cannon and was just thirty feet away! The hunter completely froze up and couldn't get his wits about him enough to get off a shot. The guide yelled loudly and the bear turned 90 degrees, barely missing him. Finally the hunter gathered himself together enough to get off a shot. The guide also shot and they did get the bear. Afterward they rehearsed all this, the guy admitted he had a round chambered when they approached the den, but he froze up and forgot to take the safety off. Luckily nobody got hurt, but it was a close call.

Joe Mott: In all the many years I've been doing this, I've never had a bad encounter with a bear. Once a hunter and I tried to sneak up on a bear, but we were wearing snowshoes and it sounded like we were walking on cornflakes. When we reached the riverbank, we could see the bear lying on a moose he had killed, and you could tell he was starting to get interested in the noise we were making. What then happened was that he ran toward us to the riverbank, stomping and woofing, obviously thinking we were another bear and a threat to his meat. That one turned out all right when we shot the bear.

Another dangerous thing is to try to take a bear with one shot. Some hunters think they can do this, and I'm right there saying repeatedly, "Shoot him again!" I've had hunters refuse to shoot again, insisting the bear was down for good, and the bear suddenly jumps up and gets away!

Larry Rivers: There are a lot of dangerous things clients can do. The most dangerous hunters are Germans, who for some reason put a round in the chamber when they walk out of camp. It isn't only Germans, of course, but they seem to be among the worst. The hunter walking behind you is by far the biggest danger a guide faces. As a rule, I would unload their gun three times, and the fourth time I would unload it and throw the ammo away!

Alaska's tangled alder thickets hold some really good grizzlies. (Photo courtesy of Larry Rivers)

Sometimes it takes such a drastic step to get their attention. You put up your binoculars to look at a bear, and they throw up their rifle and shoot! They're right behind you and you get all that magnum muzzle blast. You can lose most of your hearing that way in a flash. They don't listen and they get excited, so you have little chance to plan how you're going to approach the situation safely and without taking that blast in the ear. It's certainly not that way with all hunters, of course—some are cool and experienced and willing to do exactly the right, safe thing. But I would watch all of them until I was sure about them.

Chapter 14

INTERIOR ALASKA GRIZZLY GUIDES EVALUATE HUNTING ARMS

What is your favorite rifle caliber for hunting grizzly bears in interior Alaska, and do you recommend it to clients?

Dave Leonard: What I recommend for clients is not necessarily what I recommend as a backup weapon. One of my all-time favorites for grizzlies is the .338 Winchester Magnum. With a variety of bullet weights available, it shoots quite flatly, so if necessary you could make a 200-yard shot. Of course we do try to get closer than that to grizzlies, but in some instances a longer shot is necessary. If you can get within thirty or forty yards, as we usually try to do, it's got great knockdown power as well.

Joe Mott: I've had clients take big bears with a .30-06, but I prefer something larger. It really comes down to a recommendation that the client shoot the largest caliber he's comfortable shooting. I like to see at least a .300 Winchester Magnum, because then you're starting to get into some real penetration power. I've had hunters bring to camp a brand-new .300 out of the box, and they just can't shoot it well!

Larry Rivers: They need to bring a rifle they can shoot straight. But it needs to be a .270 or better, and not one of the .17 or .223 miniatures. That kind of hunter generally does very, very well. If a man brings a .375 but is so afraid of recoil that he can't shoot it without flinching, I'd rather he use a smaller caliber. A big gun a hunter can't handle is a terrible choice of weapon. We would always take clients to the range first, partly to see if their gun was on and partly to see how they shot, but also to see if they had a flinch—if so, they couldn't blame a miss on us. We would work the bolt and hand the rifle to the man on safety and let him fire. Then we'd work the bolt again and hand it to him on safety, but this time there would be no round in the chamber and he didn't know it. When he yanked that trigger and pulled the barrel six inches to the side, he surely recognized that he had a flinch. Until that light went on, however, he would almost uniformly deny that he had one. If we and the hunter all knew he had a flinch, we could generally work it right out of the man. I've had hunters bring an expensive .375 and then, on the range, literally close their eyes and turn their head sideways before they pulled the trigger. That's not a good thing.

What is your choice as a backup weapon for hunting interior Alaska grizzlies?

Dave Leonard: The .375 H&H is hard to beat. I also own a .416 Remington Magnum, though I tend to reserve it mainly as a backup weapon on brown bears rather than grizzlies.

Joe Mott: I carry a .375 H&H Magnum as a backup weapon. As I said before, bigger is better if you can shoot straight with it.

Larry Rivers: I carried a .375. I've got gun cases full of rifles, but the .375 is the one that will really knock a bear down. The .300 won't do it. The .338 won't do it. But the bear knows it when he's hit well with a .375—it always knocks him down. That gives you time to reload and give it to him again. Those really big calibers, like a .416 or a .458, have great knockdown power, too, but a lot of times when the client shoots, the bear is fast heading the other way and sometimes it takes a pretty long shot to stop him. The really big calibers don't reach out well enough to kill a fleeing bear because they just don't shoot flat enough. The .375 is just right, and I kept mine sighted so that if I could see the bear, I didn't have to do any math at all (I usually didn't have time anyway). I just put the gun on him and fired, and it was really effective even out past three hundred yards.

What is your advice on bullet weight and construction?

Dave Leonard: In my .375 H&H I shoot both 275- and 300-grain bullets. I use the larger bullet if we're going in on a wounded bear, since it's likely to be up close and personal and a larger bullet is less likely to be deflected by brush. If it's a more open situation where I might have to take a longer shot, the 275-grain bullet has proved to be more than adequate. As for construction, I like the Swift A-Frame and any kind of good partition bullets. Some of the newer innovations, like the Barnes Triple-Shock X-Bullets, are also proving to be deadly.

A bipod is often useful as a rest when hunting grizzlies in Alaska's interior—no matter the size of the hunter! (Photo courtesy of Larry Rivers)

We went through a period when some of our clients had been hunting thick-skinned game in Africa and showed up with solids. But you really don't want to poke a hole through a bear. You want that bullet to stay in there and do maximum damage and, ideally, not even exit, so the bear absorbs every ounce of energy from the round. You don't really have to worry so much about making a bear bleed, because they don't really do much bleeding in any case. Most of them have a lot of fat, so wounds tend to seal back up and quit bleeding quickly. I always recommend a bullet that's constructed to expand and do maximum damage inside the animal.

Joe Mott: I don't have any strong prejudices on this. I like a heavyweight bullet that has good expansion characteristics. To this day I still hunt with a Nosler Partition. I realize that many other controlled-expansion bullets have emerged over the past twenty years, and they're probably all good.

Larry Rivers: My personal preference after years of experience in the field is the Barnes X-Bullet. You couldn't get me to shoot a Nosler on a bet. The partition part means loss of the front end, and this round also sometimes loses about 25 percent of the back end, too. The Barnes bullets may lose some tenths of a grain, but they keep most of their weight. Now, if you want to recover meat, don't ever use a Barnes X-Bullet, because it destroys tremendous amounts of flesh. The Winchester Fail-Safe does the same thing, so don't use these on your caribou or elk.

One other reason not to use Barnes bullets is that you've got to handload them. I never let one of my guides use handloads, because once in a while you get a misfire. I couldn't afford that, so we required factory loads in all our backup rifles. It's tremendously more cost-effective to let Winchester or Federal or Remington carry the liability instead of me. I do really like the Federal Safari Grade. Most heavy bullets aren't designed to be accurate out to long distances.

Do you have any tips on shooting techniques in field situations?

Dave Leonard: We've started recommending that guys bring along two walking sticks, which can also be used as shooting sticks. I supply the snowshoes, but most guys aren't used to them and a pair of walking sticks helps them a lot. You can punch your walking sticks down into the snow and make a pretty good rest out of a pair of them.

Another thing we often do when we're on snowshoes—if we've got the time—is take them off and make a really good rest out of them. You've got to watch the muzzle so you don't end up clipping the tundra or snow and ruining your shot. The hunter also needs to practice shooting off one knee, shooting offhand, shooting kneeling, and the like because the situation could present where you need to make such a shot. I'm mildly impressed by a guy who shoots a group off the bench in which every bullet is touching, but if he can make consistently good shots in field situations, now, *that* is impressive. I want a guy who can shoot straight when I need him to shoot straight.

Joe Mott: Most hunters want to lie down and get a good rest, or find a tree limb or something. That's a good thing to do, but I like my hunters to be able to shoot well offhand, too. Where we hunt bears it's very brushy, and sometimes the only way you can get a shot is to stand up and shoot. Hunters signed up with us would be well advised to practice shooting offhand.

Larry Rivers: I'm pretty opinionated on everything, and if you want two opinions I can give you both of them! My tip is to shoot prone with a bipod. The scope has to be mounted vertically over the action, with no slight tip at all. It's impossible to shoot accurately at all ranges if the scope is mounted at an angle. A lot of physics is involved here, but suffice it to say there are many distances where you just aren't accurate, especially when shooting at acute up or down angles. Get that scope mounted vertically, even if you have to use a vise to get it there.

One more thing: Most American hunters are trained to squeeze the trigger with the index finger, which in a right-handed person pulls the bullet off to the right every single time. We taught our hunters to use the "eye-dropper squeeze": You put your index finger on the trigger, but not past the first joint. The thumb wraps right up the back of the stock behind the trigger, and you essentially try to squeeze the thumb and index finger together as if trying to get a drop out of an eye dropper. That way you can't anticipate the shot and you're unlikely to pull it off to one side. It's the same technique used by biathlon shooters. If you're right-handed, you need to put your right elbow straight outward so you can get that eye-dropper type of squeeze. Another variety of this technique is to get a thumb-hold on the stock, and think of squeezing the thumb and forefinger together. Your accuracy will go up dramatically.

What advice do you give your hunters on shot placement when hunting grizzlies in interior Alaska?

Dave Leonard: I'm partial to shoulder shots so you break the bear down. If you can angle the bullet into the shoulder and get it into the heart-lung area as well, you can usually knock the bear down and get that all-important second shot into him. At our briefings, before we ever start hunting, we advise that the hunter should never pause to admire his first shot if the bear piles up. If the shooter does that, the bear can be up and gone

Even after being skinned, this is an impressive silvertip grizzly. (Photo courtesy of Joe Mott)

in a flash and we can be looking at a bad situation. Make a good, solid first shot, and then get that second shot into the bear to make sure we don't lose him. It's always a really bad idea to stop and admire your first shot just after you make it. Far better to admire it later on when you're skinning the animal.

Joe Mott: I always tell them to make the first shot count, because that's the one that will probably kill the bear. They need to make a good heart–lung shot. After that first shot, they should just try to get some more bullets into him, wherever they may strike.

Larry Rivers: On any bear, you want to break the front shoulder. You could shoot high, just below the hump, and try to shatter the spine. A lot of people think shooting a bear through the shoulder is like shooting a deer or elk, but that's not the point. My personal preference is to go down on the leg, and then go one inch rearward for your aim point. If you miss the leg, you're going to get the heart and lungs. The guy who tells you he shot four times and hit the chest every time, so close together that you could cover the bullet hits with one hand, is an idiot in my unbiased opinion. Once you've blown the heart up with a bullet, you don't need to do it three more times. Go for the liver next, then target a shoulder to break the animal down. Now, that's a sure and secure kill every time.

How many of your first-time clients are intimidated by the prospect of hunting a dangerous animal? Describe some typical reactions.

Dave Leonard: I do get some of that, especially among first-time bear hunters. That's really typical. That's also one reason I recommend making some other hunts before taking on grizzlies, so you're around them some and the intimidation factor goes down. I'd recommend a sheep, caribou, or moose hunt before booking for grizzly. The hunter can then observe the bears a little and learn something about the way they behave before actually hunting them.

Joe Mott: Most of my clients have great respect for the bear, but very few are really intimidated to the point of being afraid. As a rule our hunters are pretty seasoned people who already have a lot of hunting under their belts. They've been around the block once or twice, and are unlikely to get freaked out.

Larry Rivers: Most are intimidated the first time, and some are intimidated every time. Usually it's because they've been reading too many books, can't help but recall the worst-case scenarios, and convince themselves that's the norm. When it comes time to shoot, I've seen guys extract the bolt from the rifle and not know what to do next. I've seen others lever every single bullet through the chamber and never fire a shot. More than one has yanked the trigger and shot the bear in the guts—not a good scene. Everybody gets excited once a bear is spotted, and in some cases all our instructions are out the window.

Does it help prepare a person mentally if he has already hunted black bears successfully?

Dave Leonard: I think it does. For anything you're going to do in life, you've got to get mentally prepared ahead of time, and having taken a black bear or two can be a positive in that regard.

Joe Mott: I think so. Hunting black bears is good seasoning, partly because hunters can take a lot of shots. The main difference, of course, is that black bears are neither as big nor as tough as a grizzly. One problem: Most such hunters have taken their black bear over bait from a tree stand. That's a good way to observe bears, but it's a lot different from spot-and-stalk hunting. Still, overall I think that some black bear experience before you hunt grizzlies makes a tremendous amount of sense.

Larry Rivers: I personally don't think it helps. It can build inappropriate confidence. Some of those guys get to camp and can't wait to get into the field because they think they're mentally ready for a grizzly. I took one very experienced hunter out to camp ahead of the guide, which I didn't usually do, and while I was retrieving the guide a sow and cub walked right through the camp. The man was so freaked out he was hiding when I returned with the guide, and he already wanted to go home.

How do you prepare for and handle overpowering excitement in a hunter/client?

Dave Leonard: That's a tough one. A few times I've found bears on a kill, and the hunter and I stayed put, waiting for the right presentation so we could shoot. When I looked over at the client, I could see him starting to shake. When I see that reaction, I take the hunter back around the side of a hill and have a little talk with him. I ask if he's ever shot a deer before, and the usual reply is, "Yes, I've shot lots of deer." I tell him that we're not shooting a grizzly, we're shooting a deer. All he has to do is put the cross hairs on the shoulder and pull the trigger—just as if he's shooting another deer. I have him take several deep breaths, we walk back to where we can see the bear, and usually the gent calms down and makes a great shot. After it's a done deal, these men can't believe they were so nervous about it!

Joe Mott: I like to tell the hunter that I'm going to get him in a good position so he can make a good shot; I also try to position him well for a second shot, too. However, I want our clients to

This hunter has a scoped rifle and the guide has a rifle with open sights, fairly common when hunting grizzlies. (Photo courtesy Larry Rivers)

realize that as soon as I see the situation going downhill, I'm going to help them kill the bear rather than risk losing a wounded animal. If it's obvious that the hunter's excitement will interfere with his ability to shoot, I just pull him off and don't let him shoot.

Larry Rivers: We wanted them excited! That's why they came here! The theatrics are a part of the experience, and we liked to build that up. We wanted them to remember that hunt a long time. If they're shaking so badly they can't pull the trigger, you can bet they'll never forget that hunt! The uncontrollable excitement that accompanies a hunt for Cape buffalo or lion or leopard—or big bear—is what moves the soul of a dangerous-game hunter. If it weren't for that excitement factor, we'd all just hunt plains game and go home.

Do you have any wise words on bowhunting? Black-powder hunting?

Dave Leonard: I take black-powder hunters, but I'm really particular about taking bow hunters. Hunting bears with a

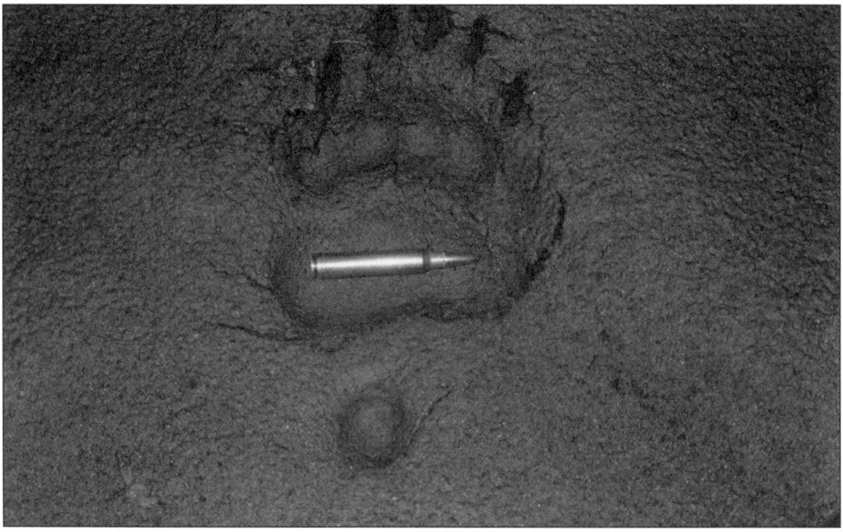

A huge western Arctic grizzly track, as evidenced by the .338 cartridge in it. (Photo courtesy of Dave Leonard)

bow presents problems, most of them involving our moral responsibility to make sure the bear doesn't get away wounded. Bow hunters have such a small margin for error that even a tiny twig, a slight shift in air currents, or a half-step forward by the bear just as the arrow is released can make for a bad shot.

One of my biggest gripes with archery hunting is that the Pope and Young rules don't allow us to take a backup shot; if we do, the bear becomes ineligible for the group's record book. I've taken archery hunters over the years, but it's always a struggle, especially if you don't get on the same page with them ahead of time and discuss all contingencies. I also want to be darn sure they're accomplished and have taken a lot of other animals with that bow before I take them grizzly hunting.

Joe Mott: We take very few bow hunters, and I think we've had only two black-powder hunters over the years. With either, I make it clear to them that if it appears the bear might get away, I'm going to do just like I do with rifle hunters—I'm going to shoot the bear myself with my backup rifle. Bow hunters are kind of a special breed: They like to get in close, put an arrow in the bear, and then let it run off while the arrow does its work. In the thick brush we have, every bear heads for the thickest cover it can find as soon as it's hit. You'd be surprised how far these grizzlies can go with half their lungs or half their heart shot out. If the bear gets into the brush, there's a very good possibility you'll lose it, even if it's dead. So unless that arrow makes an obviously exceptional hit, I have an obligation to keep that bear from reaching the brush. The hunter simply has to understand that necessity up front.

Larry Rivers: I've taken black-powder hunters but not bow hunters. I did take bow hunters for a number of years, during which time my learning curve went up sharply. The problem with a bow hunter in camp is that first off, the person tends to wear a self-righteous halo over his head about how he really gives the animal a chance, and sometimes he really lays it on the rifle hunters. Now, all these hunters come up here to enjoy a good hunt, not to be browbeaten by some self-righteous bow hunter. The truth is that he's simply not being truthful. He says he's giving the animal a better chance, but if that were true, the Pope and Young records wouldn't be needed because bow hunters would enter all their animals in Boone and Crockett. The real truth is that a bow hunter is hunting a different quality of animal—a lower-quality animal, in fact—than the rifle hunter seeks. And yet he's preaching self-righteousness to all the rifle hunters in camp, trying to make them feel inferior, and he can wind up ruining their hunt. I just quit fooling with bow hunters.

Another sore point is that when he goes out there, more often than not he refuses to stay put, instead wandering around and pushing all the bears out of a particular valley, and then he expects you to move him somewhere else. He can ruin three or four valleys for all hunting during a ten-day hunt, if you let him. Maybe some outfitters are willing to put up with that, but I was not. My job was to be sure all my clients enjoyed their hunt.

Do you take any special precautions with bow hunters or black-powder hunters?

Dave Leonard: I'd say the biggest thing is for the guides to bring additional bullets in case we get into a bad situation. Even black-powder hunters often have no chance for a second shot.

For one thing, it takes some time for the smoke to clear after the shot, and even the guide is often in the dark about how effective the shot was. It takes the black-powder hunter a long time to reload, too, relative to a modern firearm hunter, so he's seldom going to get a chance for that critical second shot. I often throw into the kit a satellite phone or the like, just in case we wind up in an emergency situation.

Joe Mott: We tell the hunters who insist on using a bow that they must realize they're cutting their possibility of success in half. That also means it's going to take twice as many stalks to make the hunt work out. It's not every time that you can get within forty yards of a bear, so it's a much more labor-intensive affair, and the hunter has to realize that.

Larry Rivers: I didn't take bow hunters, as I said. I didn't take any special precautions at all with black-powder hunters. We used to try to get all our hunters within fifty yards, and the black-powder hunter throws a really big old piece of lead, so it was never a problem. Most black-powder hunters these days use all that fancy powder and bullets, so their weapon of choice isn't really a primitive weapon at all. It's a real killing device, and it will put a bear down quickly.

Chapter 15

HUNTING GRIZZLY BEARS IN INTERIOR ALASKA

Is there anything about hunting grizzly bears in the interior that is particularly significant to you [i. e., sets it apart from other kinds of hunting]?

Dave Leonard: It's special to me because of how special the grizzly is. I have a level of reverence and respect for grizzlies that transcends the usual game, even though I also respect the sheep and caribou and all the animals we hunt. The grizzly is different, though, and I have a greater measure of admiration for them. We found one trying to cross a creek—he was floundering in the ice and snow and we had him dead to rights. I made the hunter wait until the boar got across the creek and up onto the barren tundra before I'd let him shoot. It just didn't seem fair to take the animal while it was so disadvantaged by terrain it couldn't handle.

Joe Mott: My wife gave me the answer to this one. She told me that obviously this kind of hunting was fun for me or I wouldn't do it. And she's right. There's also the element of danger, which is a challenge that really appeals to me. But most of all I just enjoy pitting myself against an animal that's higher on the intelligence scale than a moose or caribou or most other animals. It's interesting when you're hunting something that also hunts and kills.

Larry Rivers: It pays better for the number of days you spend at it! Now, there's a really good, honest, tight answer! But it's really no different from most other forms of hunting: The wind blows sideways, the grass grows up, stay out of sight, and don't let them smell you. Anybody who tells you differently is pulling your leg. And anybody who sees a bear and tells you he's going to walk over that hill and into that gully and intercept the animal there—in effect pretending he knows exactly what the bear is going to do—is full of beans. That bear doesn't even know what he's going to do when he goes over that hill.

Give us your perspective on hunting grizzly bears in the interior as a game-management tool.

Dave Leonard: It is a very, very important management tool. We target boars (males), and that's very positive for the bear population, as well as for other game in the area. We do take the occasional sow, but I'm always proud of the fact that it's almost always an older sow beyond reproductive years. I was guiding up in the Arctic some years ago and we took a sow that turned out to be thirty-two years old. The grizzly can live a really long life. Still, harvesting boars helps all ungulate populations, and in addition contributes to cub survival.

The management regimen in Alaska is so good that we've got several times more bears in the western Arctic than we did when I first started guiding. In the old days we got seven or eight permits there, but now we get twenty-four. Our taking out the older boars has helped reduce cub mortality by about 48 percent. We've found cubs in the stomachs of older bears we've taken, so it's not just a myth that boars eat cubs. We've even found parts of older bears in their stomachs, too. Harvesting these older boars is a great program, and I only hope we can keep it up, because it's doing a tremendous amount of good. If we left these older boars alone, there's no question we'd have far fewer bears today.

Joe Mott: The bear population is doing really well where our operation is located and, I think, all over Alaska. Our take is about 95 percent big males, and I'm sure that helps the cub crop grow up. At least a couple of times I've taken big boars off dens where they've gone in and killed and eaten the cubs. Right there in a matter of minutes they've killed two or three potential future trophies. Every time we kill a bear, it definitely also helps the moose and caribou calf populations. You can't blame bears completely, though, because our wolf population is way out of control to the point that it's ridiculous, but that's another story.

Larry Rivers: Grizzly bears have got to be managed if you're going to have any other game. They kill a lot of moose calves and a lot of caribou. They also like to kill big bulls of both species, and they do it efficiently, and I don't know why. I've seen brown bears all over Alaska that come out of their den in the spring and lie around that place for several days before they make a move. Grizzlies are different. When they leave the den they get out of there fast and head downhill straight to the calving areas, where they kill an awful lot of calves—as many as the wolves kill.

What is the most common mistake made by guided grizzly hunters in Alaska's interior?

Dave Leonard: I mentioned this before: It's really common—so common it's almost astounding—for a client to admire that first shot and not follow up with a second as quickly as possible. Often a guide has to yell at the hunter to make him snap out of it and get that next shot off. I think hunters lose concentration at that point: There's been so much anticipation up to then, and finally they put a bullet into a bear. They may want to stop there, but they can't—put in another shot! However, none of us is perfect and life is a learning curve.

Another common problem is for the hunter not to listen to the guide's advice. I've had a number of lady hunters over the years, and one quality they have over the guys is that they really listen to the guides. As a result, they're a pleasure to guide.

Joe Mott: Poor bullet placement is the most common mistake. Sometimes it's a costly one, too.

Larry Rivers: They're guided by us, and we never make mistakes! Seriously, the biggest mistake hunters make is thinking the bear is blind, or that he can't smell you. If you've got a 90-degree or better wind, he'll smell you for sure. You've got to have at least a 45-degree wind quartering in your favor, or it's over. Another mistake is thinking you'll catch up with a bear that's walking away from you. The best thing to do is watch and enjoy, because you'll never catch up to him. All you'll do is run up the valley, ruin the area with your human scent, and never catch up.

And speaking of walking in a valley, that's another big mistake hunters make—walking in low spots, especially in the sand along a river. Bears are not brute machines—they're intelligent, discerning animals. Many times I've seen a bear enter a valley where someone has walked in the sand; the animal will put its nose down in the track and immediately get the heck out of there. Bears never look at a caribou track and then head in the wrong direction; instead they look at the track so they know which way to follow the animal. They do the opposite with human footprints—when they see a man's track, they know which way that human is going and they immediately head in the opposite direction.

What can a guided hunter do to improve the chances of taking game (patience, physical fitness, mental preparation, equipment, practice with choice of weapon, other)?

Dave Leonard: All the things listed are important. Follow the recommended equipment list, and if you have a question, call your outfitter and get clarification. That stuff is on the equipment list for a reason, so pay attention to it. Get in the necessary shooting practice, too, including silhouette shooting, so you're proficient. If you're using handloads, be sure that every single bullet will chamber and eject properly.

Getting mentally prepared is very important, especially if you've never hunted grizzlies before. A big help in this area is to talk to hunters who have done it before. Even the outfitter may assume you know what you need to bring and so on, but the hunter who has experienced a first-time grizzly hunt can often offer insights that the outfitter takes for granted.

Joe Mott: All of the above, though I think the most important one is mental preparation. Hunters need to think through the fact they're going on a hunt that's not only physically hard but also involves dangerous game.

Larry Rivers: I'd rate patience as number one. Hunters have to be willing to wear the lenses of their binoculars thin looking through them. They also need to be physically fit so they're up to the task

A fine interior Alaska grizzly taken after a grueling hunt on snowshoes. (Photo courtesy of Joe Mott)

when it's time to move. Bears won't wait for you, so you've got to be able to move fast. Most hunters are a lot tougher physically than they are mentally. They've never pushed themselves hard enough to know how fast they can go, so they sometimes "weenie out" on you.

Another thing is that a hunter has to be willing to stand his ground on the patience issue, even if his guide wants to get up and wander up and down the valley. Stay put! Don't let his inexperience cost you your chance at the bear of a lifetime.

Besides the weapon, what kind of equipment should every hunter carry, and what is the most important single item?

Dave Leonard: I'd say good binoculars are the most important thing besides the weapon. Also, get a really good rifle sling because some of them are really uncomfortable to use.

Ask the Grizzly/Brown Bear Guides

Joe Mott: Almost 100 percent of hunters bring along binoculars, and after a while they seem to tire of using them. Once that happens, only one set of eyes is looking instead of two. Good binoculars are a must, but the hunter has to be determined enough to keep on using them.

I also won't let my hunters leave camp without matches. I like to see a guy who can use a GPS; I tell him to mark the camp's location so that if we should happen to get lost—and it can happen to anybody—we'll be able to find our way back. A compass is a good alternative, and of course hunters should have a sharp, compact knife.

Larry Rivers: The most important single item is good binoculars, followed by ankle-fit hip boots and then a good backpack, raingear, and a good-quality rangefinder.

Are there any items of equipment that you feel are unnecessary, redundant, or plain worthless for hunting interior grizzlies?

Dave Leonard: I love to shoot handguns myself, but on a grizzly hunt they're mostly just an extra piece of dead weight that does the hunter no good whatsoever. A handgun is darned handy if it's in your vehicle and someone tries to rob you, but it has no place on a bear hunt. The hunter can feel free to bring an extra bear rifle but not a handgun. He'll end up packing the short gun all over the place, and will realize that the rifle in his hands is so much more effective and lethal if more firepower is needed. I also worry about a hunter getting shot by the handgun if it hangs up in the brush, or shooting me or one of my guides. Handguns are just an unnecessary hindrance that dramatically increases the danger in the field rather than reducing it. It's pretty rare to stop a charging bear with a handgun, anyway, though I did have a friend put a bullet right between a bear's eyes while he was fishing, and that did the trick.

Joe Mott: A lot of guys bring a pile of worthless gear to camp. I'm sometimes amazed at what comes out of their bags when they arrive. A really huge knife is not necessary unless you're going to cut timber with it. A guy may bring along three or four knives, most of them too big. After two or three days hunters seem to sort things out on their own and stop carrying the things that aren't necessary.

Sometimes guys bring a big-bore sidearm such as a .44 Magnum or bigger, even up to .500. They show it to me and I tell them to carry the thing when they go to the john but not on the hunt. I've had guys come up—especially back when video cameras first came out—carrying a full-size one. You don't see that very much anymore. Back then these guys would waste so much time with their video camera that they didn't have much time to hunt. One fellow had a notion that I was going to carry that big camera for him, but I refused. I told him I had a small camera and so did he and that was enough. If a guy wants a video, that's fine, but don't expect your guide to be the videographer. I'm too much in need of my senses to be doing that while we're hunting.

Larry Rivers: Almost everything hunters bring is useless, except the things I named before. You don't need Rambo knives, stainless-steel Sierra cups, and all the buttons and bells and whistles. When you've stalked to within fifty yards and you're ready for the shot, you can't have some guy say, "Let me pull out my super-duper grizzly gizmo and try it out—I spent three hundred dollars on it." They buy offbeat equipment to drag along and then they want to use it, sometimes at the wrong time. You don't need triple sets of everything, either, because you'll only use one set anyway. Everything you bring should fit in your backpack.

One more useless item is the tape measure. You know what it was invented for? Construction, not to measure your happiness. In our camps we never allowed tape measures. Hunters can measure when they get home. You know the game Monopoly? How many happy players do you have at the end? Only one, right? I can have ten happy hunters in camps—until someone pulls out a tape and measures his animal, and all of a sudden everything changes and I then have only one happy hunter! When that animal gives its life as your trophy, it had better remain a trophy, because you made the decision to pull the trigger.

Tell us your method of field-judging the size of interior Alaska grizzly bears.

Dave Leonard: I could get really long-winded on this one because it's a complicated subject. One thing I look at right off the bat is behavior. A big bear is sure of himself, and you can see that in the way the animal walks. The first physical characteristic I check is the length of the bear's neck as compared to the rest of the body—a big bear has a really long neck. It gets pretty tough when you're trying to determine if the bear is medium-size or truly a giant. I look for space underneath the belly, and I try to evaluate whether the legs show signs of being lanky or not quite filled out yet. It's hard to describe, but the feet and the actual footpads in relation to the legs are much different on a small bear as compared to a really big one.

Even after all the experience I've had, I'm still capable of a mistake in judging size, but I haven't been wrong in a long time. All of my guides have worked for me as packers, and I spend time in the field with them showing them all the subtle differences so that when they start guiding they can put that knowledge to work. I'll go out of my way to show them a bear and ask them to judge it, and then we'll critique how they do. That's especially true if I know the guy is going to be working for me for some time. Most of them catch on pretty well just from seeing more and more bears.

Joe Mott: You're looking for a bear whose body is large in proportion to its head. A cub up to three years old will have a very large head. When that animal is ten, the head looks much smaller. An older bear carries itself at a much slower pace than a rambunctious youngster. The size of the belly is a huge clue—if there's a big old belly that's almost dragging the ground, and maybe he's even a little swaybacked, that's an older and bigger bear.

Larry Rivers: If a hunter has to discuss with the guide whether a bear is big enough, it's really not even big enough to discuss. Dennis Harms wrote a great story on judging bear size, and it's on my Web site. Everybody needs to read it.

What is the most reliable way to determine sex when no cubs are present? Give us some other methods as well.

Dave Leonard: If you see a boar on top breeding another bear, you can be absolutely certain the one on the bottom is a sow. Beyond that, it gets trickier. A little petite nose and its relationship to the brow and bridge of the nose is one subtle hint that triggers a suspicion I'm looking at a sow bear.

I've noticed an interesting little tidbit that I use to distinguish sexes. I described it to Ted Breaker, one of our biologists, and he, too, has observed this and agrees with me. I told him to look at a bear from the rear as it's walking away. A sow looks like an old woman wearing a pair of droopy underwear! You can almost see the same phenomenon in dogs, especially Labrador retrievers after they get a little age on them. Now I train my guides to look for this phenomenon in bears, and it has saved us from making numerous mistakes.

Joe Mott: A single bear is a single bear, and they're all legal to hunt. But bears are a lot like people. Males tend to have the bigger front end and females tend to have the bigger back end. Big bears have big butts anyway, but if you see a bear that looks like he just came out of the gym from lifting weights, you can bet that this is probably a big boar. A big boar should have a wide head, and this trait in combination with other factors tells you what you need to know.

Larry Rivers: There is not really any foolproof way. Send your client up and have him lift the tail!

How do you normally follow up after the shot at an interior Alaska grizzly?

Dave Leonard: Every situation is a little different. Most of the time I like to sit and wait a little while because sometimes you can hear a bear give out a very distinctive death bellow. If we wait and nothing happens, we try to take to the higher ground and do a visual inspection to see if maybe the bear piled up where we can see him. We don't like to wait too long, though, because if the animal isn't hit as hard as you thought, you might have another opportunity for a shot as he crosses an opposite hillside. If we can see the bear lying still, we approach the area from the rear and everybody is chambered up just in case. If the bear still doesn't move, I move to the front and poke it with the gun barrel to make certain it's dead.

It also depends on what type of blood you're seeing, how much of it, whether it's raining or not, and so on. If we shoot a bear right at dark and we can't reach higher ground to try to see it, we might try to follow it. If not, we'll have to wait until the next day and come back and do a more thorough search. If we felt really good about the shot, more often than not we find the bear piled up dead.

Joe Mott: The rule every good guide should follow is: "Have lunch." No, if possible I'll get up on top of the hill and watch to make sure he doesn't come out somewhere. If I think it was a good killing shot, I'll have the hunter stay high to watch the area while I sneak on down there and use my binoculars to search for a little patch of hair somewhere. I don't actually enter the thick brush until I'm sure that enough time has passed.

Here again, though, it depends on the situation. If there's a hill or other vantage point somewhere close, I'll put my hunter up there and I'll go into the bush looking for the bear. I have had hunters follow me into the bush along a blood trail, but I tell them to pay attention—if they hear anything off to one side, check it out immediately because these animals don't make a lot of noise and can be on you before you know it. I always emphasize safety in such situations; I don't want that hunter's gun off safety until he's sighting in on the bear again. I'm the one out front, and I'm more afraid of getting shot by the hunter than mauled by the bear.

Larry Rivers: I would tell the hunter to shoot the bear again. What you do when the client is out of bullets depends on whether the bear is dead or not. In our camps there were no backup shots. Our guides were required to shoot only if the client stopped shooting. When the bear was down, we got downwind and behind it and approached the animal. With a round in the chamber, I would reach out and touch the bear's eyeball with the barrel. If he blinked, I'd pull the trigger. When the confrontation ended like that, we didn't measure the skull. After you make sure he's dead, you shake a lot of hands and take a lot of pictures.

What procedure do you follow in tracking a wounded interior Alaska grizzly?

Dave Leonard: At the start of the season I go over this very question with my guides. The biggest thing is not to get scratched by the bear, so you can't afford to leave safety out of the equation. It's much too easy in a tense situation for the hunter to shoot the guide, or even vice versa.

Situational awareness is a phrase I can't overemphasize. You've got to consider how badly the bear is wounded, how much blood there is, the hunter's condition and disposition, what the wind is doing, and so on. Be aware that a wounded bear might lie in a hole and not even come out until you've walked by, and then all of a sudden you've got a bear charging you from behind. Again, be aware that every situation is different and all contingencies must be considered to prevent someone from getting hurt. That requires keeping all your senses tuned to the maximum, even the sense of smell, because sometimes that's how you'll detect where the bear is.

You have to discuss when and where to chamber a round, and decide whether the hunter goes up on the hill or goes in with you. That usually depends on how calm and cool the hunter is in the situation. Unless he's a pretty experienced hunter, you sure don't want him getting in the way right when you get a shot at the bear.

Joe Mott: I've done plenty of wounded-critter tracking, and it's really amazing how doing that will fine-tune your senses. I've been on my hands and knees in places where you can see only ten or fifteen feet and it's too thick to stand upright. You have to take it really slow, and you never stop looking around. Very, very carefully you follow the blood trail, watching for broken branches or any other sign. If I don't absolutely have to, I won't take the hunter in there. I'll have him stay up high and tell him to yell out if he sees anything.

Larry Rivers: It's really tough. We generally didn't take a client into the alders. We tried really hard not to let that situation happen because there's just no good solution. My job was to go in with the guide on a wounded bear, and we'd make the client stay on the periphery. During September blood is seldom found on a wounded grizzly bear track because you've got all sorts of blueberries and cranberries and bearberries and the leaves are all turning red, so a single spot of blood is nearly impossible to find. When we hunted above timberline, we often saw where a wounded bear was going. If a bear is hit hard, he may run but he won't run far. Part of the guide's job is to make sure the bear is positioned properly before the shot. We would never shoot at a bear that had its head pointed toward the alders, because that's where he'd run every time. Make sure he's pointed away from cover and the body is otherwise positioned properly for the shot.

Chapter 16

SPECIFIC GUIDING AREAS FOR HUNTING GRIZZLY BEARS IN INTERIOR ALASKA

Describe your home guiding area and any distinctions that set it apart.

Dave Leonard: My area is really conducive to hunting grizzlies. For one thing, we've got a tremendous amount of open, bare tundra that allows you to see the bears. We've got some five-thousand-foot mountains, but all around them are lower, rolling foothills. There are lots of small drainages full of willow and cottonwood, and river bottoms with the same vegetation. There's enough cover for the bears, but it's open enough that you can often see them. You can use the terrain to your advantage because of its rolling nature, both to spot the bear and to keep some higher terrain between you and the target while you attempt an approach. Some of the lower parts of my area, down near the Noatak River, are boreal spruce, but it's not very thick like some other places. We have our own airplane, and we pick up our hunters in Kotzebue and fly them out to the hunting area.

Joe Mott: A lot of creeks and major rivers go through our area, with the terrain consisting of hills and plenty of open ground. The best thing about those open hillsides is all the berries that grow there. In the fall, that's where we find the bears. We have a fair amount of mountains around us, and the grizzlies seem to need these for both denning and feeding. You'll see bears going up and down the rivers looking for salmon or a dead moose or something, but when all is said and done you still find the majority of them up on the hillsides eating berries. Our territory is ideal for this. Good vantage points are plentiful, and if you're on one of them, you can see farther than you can hunt.

This great grizzly was taken near the Noatak River in the Alaskan Arctic. (Photo courtesy of Dave Leonard)

Larry Rivers: All guiding areas are different, so ask your outfitter this kind of question. It can vary a lot within a few miles.

How much of a role do food sources play in hunting bears in your area?

Dave Leonard: In the springtime lots of moose will be feeding down in the willows, especially after the buds start to form. The bears come out of hibernation and drop right down into the river bottoms looking for a moose to kill. If they're not successful, they go back up to the snow and may even form a secondary den there while they wait. When conditions get good, they go looking again. When the moose get into a good spot (good for the bears, that is), especially where there's a lot of crusty snow with sugary stuff underneath, the bears ambush them and it's hard for the moose to get away. I've watched them do this quite a few times. Generally a bear will walk down the riverbank, holding the higher ground, and then run right down to the bank and kill a moose by biting it on the end of the nose and getting its claws into the neck. It might take twenty minutes or more, but once the grizzly gets that moose in a death grip, it's essentially all over as the bear wears his victim down. When the moose starts to go down, the bear switches around and bites the neck, and the moose has had it. Bears do this all the time with full-grown moose.

In the fall you've got the chum salmon run, parka squirrels, lots of berries of all kinds, willow roots, sedges and grasses, and so on. All these things play a role in our hunting. The bears may get gorged out on fish and switch to something else as opportunity presents. A lot of times, when it's really late in the season, just before denning time, the bears feast on post-rut moose, some of which are weakened or even injured from fighting. A bear that kills such a moose is at the top of the world—he's heading for the den with his belly full of meat. First thing in the spring, you know where he'll be headed: That moose he killed but didn't finish eating has been frozen and covered with snow all winter, and he heads right back there for his first feeding. Another early spring food source is frozen fish under the ice, where post-spawn salmon have died and started to decompose. In spring you can see where bears have been digging holes in the river to find these frozen fish.

Joe Mott: There's less food for bears in the spring, but more focus on finding food then. I've watched bears in the spring on hillsides eating berries frozen over the winter but still available. Bears have an amazing nose, and they can smell a winter-killed moose five miles away underneath five feet of snow. Obviously you're going to hunt grizzlies where they live, and if it's berries they're eating, that's where you hunt. In the fall you'll surely find a bear on one of our salmon streams. That's especially true when we get an early fall snow and it covers up the berries, because the bears then move down to the rivers looking for something else to eat.

Larry Rivers: Food sources are really everything. Bears don't hang out where there's no food. There are places in the Talkeetnas where you can fly over and look, and if the ground isn't ripe in color, that means a shortage of berries and no bears. I could fly over a valley and decide whether to put a camp in it based solely on the color of the high-country foliage. Now, some years, especially if there's a lot of rain, the berries mature early down in the timber. In that case the bears don't come up to the open hillsides and they can be almost impossible to find. The salmon are always present down in the stream flowing through the timber, of course, and if there are berries there, too, you just won't see a bear. You might have to go "stumble-hunting," as I described before, because you have no other viable choice.

How many of your bears are taken incidentally (as opposed to being the primary species sought)?

Dave Leonard: We take some "incidental" bears in the fall but none in the spring. In the fall hunters have to put in for the permit, but we advise them to buy a grizzly tag. Our hunters are usually on combination hunts, so taking a bear is not purely incidental, but in the fall we do take bears while hunting other species. All spring hunting is dedicated to bears only.

Joe Mott: In the spring, obviously it's 100 percent bear hunting. In the fall, lots of our moose and caribou hunters go ahead and get a bear tag in case they see a good animal. I'd say about 25 percent of the bears we take yearly would be incidental.

Larry Rivers: We didn't do that a lot. The only thing that really combines well with a grizzly hunt is a moose hunt, and I always hated hunting moose. If I booked a ten-day moose hunt and the hunter shot his bull on the second or third day, I had to bring in packers and we spent the whole rest of the time trying to haul the moose out. Incidental bears are unusual if you don't have time to hunt them. If we were hunting grizzly as the primary species, the guide brought the hide out on his back and we very quickly moved on to some other hunt. We did take some incidental bears, though, while hunting Dall sheep.

What kind of terrain is ideal for hunting interior Alaska grizzly bears?

Dave Leonard: Grizzlies like open country with rolling hills but with dense cover in the bottoms. We've got pockets of alders that are ideal for them, but of course they're nothing like the dense tangles you get down on the Alaska Peninsula. Grizzlies need huge amounts of terrain where there is no human presence in the form of developments, mines, and the like. They simply get pushed back from such places, so their habitat shrinks. This may become one of the most critical threats to the grizzly bear as human encroachment in the Arctic becomes more prevalent.

Joe Mott: Open country where you can see is ideal, whether it's spring or fall. In the spring you can often see a bear coming down from the mountains and cut it off. In the fall you can find one miles away feeding on berries and plan a stalk to get to it.

Larry Rivers: Grizzlies live in the mountains and black bears live in the valleys. Grizzlies do not run the black bears out of an area—the two simply live in different habitat. When the berries are thick and ripe, you'll have grizzlies and black bears feeding in the same blueberry patch, and they don't seem to mind each other at all. Grizzlies live the majority of their lives above timberline, so that's where you need to hunt them.

Describe your typical camp setup and camp routine.

Dave Leonard: Like most outfitters, we fly in to our spike camps, landing on gravel bars or ridge tops. We try to set up our tents out of the wind as much as possible. We try to have a good glassing ridge within a half-mile of the camp if possible, because you're going to spend a lot of time up there glassing. There will come a time for a big rush to try to get ahead of your bear, but it just doesn't pay to walk ten or fifteen miles a day looking for a bear. It's much better to let your optics do the walking. With a lot of walking you can wear your hunter out and you're no more likely to see a bear, plus you spread your scent all over the place wherever you walk. If a few days pass with no sightings, I don't hesitate to move a camp to another location.

Joe Mott: The hunters fly in from town and are dropped off at Stoney River Lodge. We bring all our hunters in first to the main camp, which is used primarily by hunters coming and going.

That's where they get their rifles sighted in and sort through their gear. We also entertain the hunters there with fishing and bird hunting, if they have the license for it. Most of the actual hunting is from spike camps, which we access by Super Cub, using mostly skis in the spring and tundra tires in the fall. We do have a Super Cub on floats so we can land on a lake if we find a good spot we can access from there. About half our hunters go on to their spike camp the same day they get to the base camp; the others go the next day.

Our spike camps consist of one guide and one hunter in a Eureka Bomb Shelter tent that can withstand just about any kind of weather. Our hunters are out usually from seven to ten days, and in these amazing Bomb Shelter tents we can stay warm and dry with our Coleman stove and heater, and if we get wet we can dry out if we need to. I've been through some pretty terrible weather in those tents and I've survived. All hunting from there is on foot.

Larry Rivers: I always dropped off my guide with his tent, stove, and food. He'd set up a camp so near the airstrip that I could almost hit him with the wing, and that's pretty close. I'd then bring in the hunter. Nobody was allowed to walk around and spread scent. We used North Face Expedition tents that can handle violent wind and rain, and they warmed up really well with our heaters. I could get both hunter and gear in and out with just two flights, and the same if we had to move them. We found out early that you can't make any money flying canvas around, so we stuck with light stuff that did the job.

What is your success rate on trophy animals?

Dave Leonard: It fluctuates between 50 and 100 percent. On average, we're about 70 percent, I'd estimate.

Joe Mott: Our spring hunts had been 100 percent for a long time, but it can go down some in bad weather. We used to have one early hunt, but over the years we figured out it was just too cold for the bears then. The weather always has a lot to do with the success rate. I'd say 50 to 60 percent of our hunters get a

This huge grizzly was shot on a moose kill in Alaska's western Arctic. (Photo courtesy of Dave Leonard)

trophy bear in the spring. The fall is getting better and better, and it might be as high as 70 percent.

Larry Rivers: It all depended on the client. With our Spanish hunters, success was really low because they wanted the bears to practically come into the tent with them; they didn't want to go out after them. They didn't want to get up in the morning and didn't want to do the walking necessary. In general, up in the Arctic it was usually close to 100 percent. In the Talkeetnas it could range from 90 percent down to 25 percent. There was no way to predict the berry crop and all the other variables a year in advance, so the success rate consequently varied.

Describe your usual hunting method and any common variations.

Dave Leonard: We do a lot of glassing, and that's our primary method.

Ask the Grizzly/Brown Bear Guides

Joe Mott: What we do, either spring or fall, is to go to a high vantage point where we can glass. This requires a lot of mental preparation—a hunter needs to expect many hours of glassing. It can be a letdown for a hunter who plans his big grizzly trip for several years, and then when he gets to spike camp all his guide wants to do is sit up on a hill and spend hour after hour glassing. Hunters need to be mentally prepared for that, because that's what it takes. Sometimes you can move to a different hill and see some different country, but that's not always an advantage. The bottom line is that a big dose of patience is what ultimately will bring a hunter the grizzly he wants.

Larry Rivers: There are no variations. You get up early, have breakfast, and walk to your glassing spot. You stay there until you see your bear, then you plan how to get him. That's it.

Tell us your method of getting close enough to a bear for a shot.

Dave Leonard: We stay out of the bear's sight and watch the wind as we approach. As we're getting close, I have the hunter quietly slide a round into the chamber. Some of our European hunters don't like this, preferring the macho sound of working the bolt vigorously. Such a noise can easily cost you the bear, though. Everything is dependent on the wind, and we check it frequently with a cigarette lighter. At times we've had to remove our waders and even our outer clothes and approach in socked feet to be quiet enough to get really close. When you do get in close, a bear can actually feel your presence. You have to be aware of this and not look so hard at the bear. This awareness is intangible but very real.

Joe Mott: It depends on what the bear is doing. If he's on the move, as they typically are in the spring, I'll watch the bear for a while just to see what he's going to do. Sometimes they'll cut straight across a distant flat and disappear. If he's meandering in a creek bottom or feeding, we plan a stalk to cut him off and get in position to intercept him and get a shot. I don't like to get down in the timber, where I have to rely on the bear coming one specific way. You want to stay in position to adjust your plans in the middle of the stalk if necessary, which happens a lot. You're not really outsmarting the bear—you're anticipating where he'll go and what he'll do.

Larry Rivers: Stay downwind and out of sight, and be willing and able to walk.

Do you have both a spring and a fall season in your area?

Dave Leonard: Yes, we have both.

Joe Mott: Yes.

Larry Rivers: I don't recommend any season, because it varies tremendously from area to area. The hunter should ask his potential outfitter that question, because the answer will vary drastically depending on where you're hunting.

Which season [spring or fall] offers the best hunting in your area? Early or late in either season?

Dave Leonard: Spring is still my favorite time of year. The ideal time in our area in recent years has been from about April 25 to May 10; that's a pretty narrow window of opportunity, but that's when we kill most of our spring bears. Conditions are ideal then, and so are the hides of the bears. Once the rivers start to break up, you just can't get around because huge chunks of ice are moving around and grinding up everything.

Joe Mott: In the spring we probably get a slightly better success rate because bears are all we're hunting. Later is better because you see more bears. In the fall it's more of a toss-up, but you still generally see good bears.

Larry Rivers: As I said, it varies drastically from area to area. Since I'm not guiding anymore, it's best to discuss this aspect with the guide and outfitter you'll be using.

Are badly rubbed hides a problem in your area? When is the best time to hunt to avoid this problem?

Dave Leonard: In the western Arctic I've had only five or six bears that were rubbed at all, and they weren't rubbed badly.

Alaska's interior mountains have a reputation for producing good grizzlies. (Photo courtesy of Larry Rivers)

Sometimes, though, the crunchy snow can cut the hair off the bears' legs to some degree. I think that overall we have one of the areas where you see the fewest rubs on spring bears. Still, it pays to look over a bear really well before you make the final decision to shoot.

Joe Mott: We generally don't have a problem with rubbed hides like they do on the coast. We may see some animals with hair that's thinned a little, but a really rubbed bear can have a whole shoulder and all of the back essentially bare. We generally don't see that where we hunt in the interior. Early in the spring you won't see it, and that's the best time to take a really prime hide. The later in the fall you take a bear the better the coat, too, although rubs are certainly not a problem in the fall.

Larry Rivers: In the Arctic you almost never see a rubbed bear. In the Talkeetnas you'd sometimes see one rubbed, but it was rare.

How much does weather influence hunting success and how you hunt?

Dave Leonard: Quite a bit. In the spring it depends to a great degree on those overflow conditions I mentioned before, with ice breaking up on the rivers. In the fall the rivers can also flood so that everything is water bank-to-bank. In such conditions we have to hunt higher, because that's where the bears are located. In some recent years hot weather early has negatively affected our hunting, too.

Joe Mott: It influences success an awful lot. Just this past fall we got hit with thirty-mile-per-hour winds and it was raining and the fog was rolling in like crazy. We were trying to find a bush or something just to get a little shelter. In such conditions you're constantly working on your binoculars to try to keep them from fogging up, and you finally ask yourself what the heck you're doing up there. Moose and bears might be walking right by you and you couldn't see them. Anyone who's hunted Alaska will tell you that weather is a major factor in hunt success. Good or bad weather also makes a huge difference in how pleasant or difficult the hunt may be.

Larry Rivers: It depends more on the client than the weather. Some hunters will stay in the tent during bad weather, so they aren't even hunting then. Others put on their raingear and keep on glassing, so their success in moderately bad weather isn't affected adversely too much. If you've got fifty-mile-per-hour winds with blowing rain and fog and twenty-yard visibility, you just can't hunt.

Access to and from spike camp almost always is in a Super Cub or a similar plane. (Safari Press photo library)

Section IV

HUNTING GRIZZLY BEARS IN INTERIOR CANADA

Chapter 17

SELECTING AN OUTFITTER

What should a hunter look for in a grizzly outfitter/guide from interior Canada?

Darwin Cary: If I knew that for sure, I'd be the marketing king! You're always trying to figure out what attracts people to your operation. Ninety percent of our hunters are referrals from past clients. We're quite blessed in that we've been around a long time, especially when you count my parents' business, so our bookings come quite easily compared to someone who's relatively new to the industry.

Many potential clients get confused about the price of a hunt because it's not like comparing the purchase of a standard Ford truck at two different dealers. You're not buying a grizzly bear, you're buying an experience. The bear may be the end result, but how you get to that grizzly bear is where the cost lies, and we've built a lot of different infrastructure in our area. We've got twenty-one different camps with permanent cabins, plus our own airplanes and boats and such, and these things have taken many years to accumulate. These assets are what makes a hunt more comfortable and I think more successful.

If I were buying a hunt, I'd look at how much time the various employees have stayed with the outfitter. You may buy the hunt from me, but you'll actually spend very little time with me. I've got many employees—guides and cooks and wranglers and the like—who have been with me for over ten years. We've usually got a few young guys in training, but my main staff has been with me for a long time. I think that if an outfitter treats his staff well, they stick with him, and you can expect that the hunters will be treated well also.

Main base camp of Scoop Lake Outfitters. (Photo courtesy of Darwin Cary)

Ron Fleming: Your personal guide is the most important factor because so many outfitters themselves don't do any guiding. I'm one of the few who does, I think. When you meet an outfitter and he knows what he's talking about, that's great. But so many outfitters only run the business—they have very little contact with clients and the actual hunt. You might not ever see that outfitter, even though you're hunting with his outfit. The problem comes when a client is really impressed with the outfitter and looks forward to hunting with him, but ends up with some guide who may not know as much as the client does. You need an experienced, competent guide to actually be with you on the hunt.

Chris Widrig: The hunter needs to find a guide who's dedicated and will work hard to find a grizzly for him. Grizzly hunting isn't a quick-fix thing; it takes time. A good grizzly outfitter is likely to want you to stay fourteen full days so your chances are maximized. You might get lucky and get a bear in the first couple of days, but more likely the hunt will go on and on and on. A bad outfitter is likely to try to get you in and out as fast as possible, regardless of whether you got a bear. Seven days is definitely not enough time to hunt a grizzly.

What are (a) the most important single characteristic and (b) the worst possible deficiency in an interior Canadian grizzly guide?

Darwin Cary: First off, you'll want to go to an area that produces. Just because you've got a great outfit to back you up doesn't count for much if there's no game there. If you've done your homework and found an area that produces grizzlies, then you want to make sure you've got a guide with some experience who doesn't get excited under pressure.

A few years ago I had a bow hunter and we were hunting a grizzly that had been frequenting a little ridge. We had the hunter up in a tree stand, and he had put up a piece of camouflage in front of the stand. I was pretty sure the bear was somewhere nearby, so I told the hunter I'd be sitting at the base of the tree with my .375. Sure enough, the bear started coming down the ridge and he never stopped until he got within twenty-five yards of me. I was watching the bear down the barrel of my gun, waiting for the hunter to shoot—and waiting and waiting. He never did shoot, and suddenly the bear turned and ran away. It turned out the man couldn't see the bear because of the camouflage he'd put up! I should have insisted he leave that camouflage down. In so many words, you need a guide who wants you to get a bear and is willing to buck even your desires to help you achieve that.

As far as deficiencies go, it would be a major problem if the hunter lacked confidence in the guide's abilities. When things get a little hairy, there's no substitute for experience. We had a bow hunter stick a bear one year, and the hunter and guide were sneaking through the willows looking for the animal. The hunter was in front with an arrow nocked. All of a sudden there was a huge *woof!* and the bear barreled at them from twenty feet. The guide stepped around the hunter and fired twice, killing the bear. The hunter later said those shots were music to his ears—he knew his arrow had no chance of stopping the bear. In short, an indecisive guide can cost you dearly.

Ron Fleming: The most important factor is that the guide be knowledgeable of the grizzly, its habits, and the hunting area. Even if you get a good guide, if he has never hunted that

Good equipment is a necessity to outfit a hunt for an interior grizzly. (Photo courtesy of Darwin Cary)

particular area before, he's learning as he goes and the hunter is paying for him to learn! Knowing the area is a major safety factor, too: The guide has to know if there's a major swamp around that next bend or a cliff down this trail, for example.

The worst deficiency, if I had to put my finger on it, would be unfamiliarity with the area. Even if a guide doesn't know a lot about grizzlies, if he knows the area well he can usually be successful.

Chris Widrig: Persistence is a highly desirable quality. The worst characteristic would be a guy who wants to get you in and out in the shortest possible time, and to heck with your chances of success.

Is there any exceptional qualification for being an interior Canadian grizzly guide that may not apply to other types of guiding?

Darwin Cary: Grizzly bears are tremendously hard to judge. I'd never send a guy out guiding, even if he were experienced, unless he'd spent a good deal of time with other guides looking at

A good outfitter has the means to get you in and out efficiently.

bears. Evaluating these big animals is much different from judging caribou or moose. The guide must also have a huge amount of patience—for numerous reasons but especially when a big bear is spotted. He can't jump to the conclusion that it's a big boar and then find out after the shot it's got two or three cubs!

Ron Fleming: Patience is one thing that stands out, and secondarily learning everything you can about grizzlies. My daughter guided a hunter this year, and that guy never should have gotten a bear. However, she patiently watched an area she knew had to hold a big bear. She finally found the animal in the right place, got her hunter on him, and he killed that bear. That kind of success comes from knowing both the area and the bear.

Chris Widrig: A grizzly guide needs to know an awful lot about grizzly bears and their habits and life history. Grizzlies require a huge territory to survive, and in that territory they move around a lot. Grizzlies are definitely not a herd animal, so you have to know a lot about their habits and where you might find them.

Does your area boast a really good source of protein to help bears grow big (salmon streams, plentiful ungulates, large ground-squirrel population, etc.)?

Darwin Cary: Our bears are definitely meat-eaters, but we're on the Arctic watershed and there are no salmon runs here. Bears on the Pacific watershed to our west do have salmon to eat, but ours don't, and salmon-fed bears are doubtless bigger on average. Our bears weigh some fifty to sixty pounds per linear foot, whereas a coastal bear will weigh eighty to a hundred pounds per foot. A big bear in our area weighs five hundred pounds or so, but a coastal bear can weigh a thousand pounds. Our biggest positive is that salmon-fed bears are brown, while our grizzlies come with silver tips and chocolate-colored legs, and I think they're prettier.

Ron Fleming: Our area isn't known for tremendous sources of protein-rich foods, though the amount seems to be adequate and we do take some big bears. Marmots are plentiful in the summertime, moose in the spring, and there's lots and lots of high-quality vegetation. Salmon streams aren't far from us, just over the mountains some sixty miles, which is nothing for a bear. Every couple of years King Kong will come over the hill, and it's very likely he's a salmon-fed wanderer.

Chris Widrig: In the northern Yukon the bears are certainly a little protein-deficient and will eat whatever they can find. So they don't get really huge, and a seven-footer is a pretty good mountain grizzly.

What does a good interior Canadian grizzly guide do to ensure safety while hunting North America's most dangerous game?

Darwin Cary: Pack a big gun and be ready to use it. However, our grizzlies aren't overly aggressive, as some people believe. If you and I are going through the brush, probably ten bears see us for every one we see. For the most part, unless you're hunting them, just give them their space. To avoid unwanted conflict, just have a healthy respect for the animals, stay upwind, and give them plenty of room.

A fine silvertip grizzly in Ron Fleming's area. (Photo courtesy of Ron Fleming)

Ron Fleming: You've got to know grizzlies well enough to anticipate what the bear is going to do before he does it. There are things you can do to keep yourself out of a predicament. For example, if you're tracking a wounded bear, don't follow right on his trail. Do so and you've got an excellent chance of getting chewed up. If a bear is hit pretty well, he's going to run a couple of hundred yards and then double back on his trail, lie down, and wait. Be aware of that tendency and stay uphill and off the exact track if possible. Look out for little things, too, like birds, which give away a bear's presence more than any other creature might. Be especially careful if you walk in on a grizzly kill or a gut pile: If the bear is there, he's going to come after you—not because you're a human but because he's probably been conditioned to compete with other bears for his meat and you'll seem like potential competition. That can be big trouble. I've been bluffed by bears more times than I can count, but usually if you stay half calm and let the bear realize what you are, he'll back off.

Chris Widrig: We carry a backup rifle, and mine is a .45-70. You've got to stay alert when you're in grizzly country. When I got mauled by a grizzly, I wasn't even hunting grizzlies, but so often that's the way it happens.

Chapter 18

INTERIOR CANADA GRIZZLY GUIDES EVALUATE THE HUNTER

What is your favorite type of hunter [personality, physical abilities, experience level, socioeconomic status, etc.]?

Darwin Cary: I enjoy the guys who have been around the block a few times and who readily appreciate what we're providing them. Someone new to hunting often has great expectations and very little appreciation—such a person may be disappointed because we don't have caviar or the right wine on the table. The one who's hunted around a little is most appreciative of the effort we make. As for physical ability, what's in the heart is far more important. I've seen young guys come here and by their looks you'd think they'd walk you to death. But if they don't have the heart, they're done after a day or two. It takes more than physical ability to get up that hill.

Ron Fleming: If I were rating qualities, I'd position a person's patience far above his experience level. Usually that characteristic is found most often in hunters around fifty-five rather than twenty-five. I like a guy who's done a lot of hunting on his own for deer and moose and other animals. A person needn't have been on multiple African safaris; in fact, a hunter with a little less experience is much more willing to listen to you.

When you're guiding, you have to look out for basically three things: the bear, the hunter, and yourself. A guide tends to get inside himself—look at the wind, keep track of the bear he's spotted, plan a route to him, and all the other elements that go through his mind. In that process, the guide has a tendency not to keep an eye on the hunter, and that's a big mistake. You've got to make sure the client doesn't have his scope cranked up to 9X when the two of you are seventy-five yards from the bear—he'll never find the animal in the scope. We get quite a few older hunters, some so

Shooting large male bears facilitates remarkable rates of cub survival. (Photo courtesy of Ron Fleming)

old they wouldn't buy green bananas! In that case you might have to slow down and wait on them. You don't want an aging hunter huffing and puffing and trying to make a good shot.

Chris Widrig: I like a hunter who's been around the bush a little bit—especially one who's hunted and taken a lot of different animals from the North Country. Ideally, he's wealthy enough to afford it because it may take more than one hunt to be successful. When compared to a moose or caribou hunt, it's got a low chance of success even under the best of circumstances. He needs to have the qualities of experience, patience, and physical ability.

How important is it for the hunter to be in top physical shape?

Darwin Cary: It helps, but it's not very important. We use horses a lot, which allows us to get our hunters into position without so much physical exertion.

Ron Fleming: It's always helpful, but it really isn't very important.

Chris Widrig: In the spring it's very important, because we have to use snowshoes to get around—there's just no other way to do it. The snow cover is still deep, unlike areas farther south. A spring hunter should be in good shape, have a little youth to him, and not be carrying extra weight or a smoking habit. In the fall we take a good number of grizzlies while hunting on horseback. These are basically incidental kills, and you don't have to be in such great physical condition.

Should inexperienced or physically challenged hunters go after interior Canadian grizzlies? Why or why not?

Darwin Cary: I prefer someone who's done a lot of hunting, but we take plenty of inexperienced hunters. Experienced hunters may be a little more likely to understand the challenge of providing a quality hunt.

As for the physically challenged, so long as they understand their chances are reduced, we do the best we can for them. We had a paraplegic hunt moose with us last year. We made a special pack to carry him, and rigged up a special saddle so he could ride. He didn't get a moose, because he physically couldn't get up high enough to see over the willows to make the shot. Still, that guy had the time of his life, and he was such a pleasure to be around that I've offered to let him come back and try again for free. It's really a challenge to get such a hunter and the quarry in the right place at the right time, but I don't mind trying with a guy like that. There again, their most important attribute is that they have heart and really want to do it.

Ron Fleming: I can take even the most inexperienced hunter, but I have to educate them that not every bear comes with a ten-foot hide. Their expectations are often that they'll just step off the plane, then head out and shoot a ten-foot bear right away. That's highly unrealistic. It's the outfitter's job to educate them long before they arrive in camp.

Physically challenged hunters? Well, it depends on their disability, but it's necessary to have an extra person along to help deal with any special needs they might have. One person just can't do everything at the same time and still watch the bear.

Chris Widrig: Personally, I don't think so. They should hunt black bears over bait and get some experience before they take on this kind of physical hunt.

This great spring grizzly came from Ron Fleming's area in northern British Columbia. (Photo courtesy of Ron Fleming)

Is there any particular characteristic that would make you refuse to guide a given hunter on an interior Canadian grizzly hunt?

Darwin Cary: Not really. A lot of our clients are bosses and employers and thus very strong-willed. Sometimes you have to remind them that they're hiring someone's services to help them conduct a hunt, and that since they're paying good money for those services, they should make the most of them. The hunter who won't listen to the guide, and is argumentative and demanding when he really doesn't know what he's talking about, is a big negative.

I don't like judgmental people, either. We once had a judge who literally ruined his hunt because he found out his guide had gotten a DUI once, and he rode him about it the whole hunt. Well, the DUI had happened fifteen years before and was ancient history, but this judge just couldn't avoid talking about it and keeping the thing on the front burner, and in the process he ruined his relationship with his guide and consequently his whole hunt. I wouldn't accept someone like that back in my camp. That's a rare exception, though: Most hunters are among the highest-

Good firearms are a necessity to take such a great bear. (Photo courtesy of Ron Fleming)

quality people you could ever hope to meet. I'm in this business because I love meeting people!

Ron Fleming: Nothing that comes to mind right off hand. I had a guy this year pay a deposit and then not show up, leaving me holding the bag for the rest. It was too late to book anyone else, so it was just a loss. I've gone to several shows and turned down several potential clients, but in thirty-nine years of guiding, such things have been rare.

Among all the hunters who came through my camps during those years, only two were guys I wouldn't have back. One had a drinking problem, and the other one always wanted to do something illegal, such as shoot at a seagull just for fun. This last guy kept trying to go off on his own, and he tried every way in the world to get me to let him do something we both knew was illegal. When I'd refuse, he'd get mad and tell me to call a plane so he could get out of there. I'd tell him, fine, I'll call a plane, but you're still not going to shoot the seagull. I got to thinking maybe he was a sting operation from Fish and Wildlife just trying to get me to do something illegal!

Most guys are still in civilized mode when they first get here—they're used to the cell phone and the computer and the pressures of civilization, and it takes them four or five days to unwind and get into a relaxed routine. It's the outfitter's job to help them achieve this. Once the back country shows them how to loosen up and slow down, they go home a better person even if they don't get a bear. I figure we might add five years to the life of such a guy by relieving stress! Most hunters make the transition well and are a pleasure to guide.

Chris Widrig: If a hunter demonstrates from the bench that he can't shoot, he surely shouldn't be hunting a dangerous animal like the grizzly. Some hunters just can't shoot, and they should stick to less dangerous game. Most of the hunters we get are very good people, so I don't run into many personality conflicts.

What is the most dangerous thing a client can do while hunting interior Canadian grizzlies? Can you share an instance in which a client did something that put himself or the guide in danger?

Darwin Cary: I don't remember anything really dangerous that's happened. There's the occasional gut shot, and then we have to go and chase the bear, and that can be dangerous. But that's certainly not an intentional thing.

Ron Fleming: The most dangerous thing is not listening to your guide. If I tell you to stand right here while I peek around this clump of willows ahead, and I come back and you're not there, it's a huge problem. I'm worried because you're doing your own thing and maybe you've gone upwind and blown the bear out of there. Or maybe I come back a different way and you get excited and shoot me, thinking I'm the bear. It all comes down to doing what your guide tells you.

I've got a story I'll share later that was probably the most dangerous thing that's ever happened to one of our hunters, and it happened because he didn't listen to the guide.

Are you up to all the climbing and walking needed to take an interior grizzly?

Chris Widrig: What scares me more than anything is a hunter putting a shell in the chamber and never telling me about it. I can share one instance: I had a hunter up in the high country and we heard a noise down in the brush. We thought it was a bear, so I had the hunter chamber a round. Pretty soon a big bull moose stood up. It was August and the season wasn't open. I told him to unload his gun, and we kept on walking through a patch of thick brush. Pretty soon his gun went off over his shoulder! He'd purposely left it loaded, either because of the adrenaline of hearing something in the bush or whatever. Anyway, it could have cost someone his life.

Chapter 19

INTERIOR CANADA GRIZZLY GUIDES EVALUATE HUNTING ARMS

What is your favorite rifle caliber for interior Canadian grizzly bears, and do you recommend it to clients?

Darwin Cary: When potential hunters ask me that question, they've usually got an arsenal over in the corner. I always ask them which one they shoot the best. An awful lot of guys have the bigger-caliber guns but are afraid to shoot them because of recoil. If they've got a cannon but mostly shoot their .300, I tell them to bring the .300. Go with whichever one you can shoot most accurately.

Ron Fleming: I like a .300 Winchester Magnum. A bigger weapon isn't really necessary, and I personally carry a .30-06. A .30-06 with a 180-grain bullet will knock a bear down really quick. You don't really need a fast-shooting gun; you need a heavy bullet more than anything else. Still, the main thing is to bring a gun the hunter has used a lot. I'd rather a hunter come with a .270 that he's shot for the past forty years than to bring a .300 that he just takes out of the box when he gets to camp. Know your rifle well, and shoot your rifle a lot so you're proficient. And remember, it's not the size or caliber so much as the knockdown power you want.

Chris Widrig: I like the standard .300 Winchester Magnum for interior grizzlies. You need something that shoots flat but has enough power to do the job. In open alpine country you might need to make a shot up to three hundred yards, so you need to be able to get it done. Another good caliber is the .338, but if you use a heavy bullet, you're not going to reach as far as with a .300.

What is your choice as a backup weapon?

Darwin Cary: I like a .375, especially in close, but the .338 is also used commonly.

This terrific silvertip was taken on a spring hunt in northern British Columbia. (Photo courtesy of Ron Fleming)

Ron Fleming: I carry my .30-06 most of the time. If I have to go into the thick willows after a bear, I'll tote a .375. It probably isn't any more effective at short range, but it makes you feel just a little bit safer. To tell you the truth, I've carried a backup rifle only ten times or so on my successful guiding trips for grizzly, because most of the time I have enough confidence in my hunter so that I don't feel I need one. Besides, sometimes the bear's going to win, and if the hunter can't get him, then he gets away. Also, when I don't carry a gun, I've got to be more cautious, and I think that awareness has kept me out of trouble a lot of times.

Back when I was young and bulletproof, I had a hunter shoot a bear way up on a mountainside, and it ran into a really thick clump of alders. I didn't have a gun with me, but I foolishly decided to go in there anyway. I told the hunter to shoot if anything ran out the other side of those alders; if anything ran out the near side, he should shoot the second thing that came out! I eased into that tangle, and not too far in I saw the bear, lying with its head between its paws, obviously watching his backtrail. Very fortunately for me, it had already died, or I'd surely have been chewed on.

Chris Widrig: I carry something very compact that's light and easy to maneuver. I use a .45-70 with Buffalo Bore handloaded bullets. It's a really hot load for that caliber.

What is your advice on bullet weight? Bullet construction?

Darwin Cary: I'm not a ballistics guy. We use all factory loads in our backup weapons.

Ron Fleming: What you want is the biggest bullet your gun will shoot well. You need that big-bullet kind of knockdown power. In my .30-06 I use 200-grain Nosler Partition bullets, and they really do a good job. Really fast calibers that shoot smaller bullets tend to deflect too easily in thick brush, in my opinion.

Chris Widrig: The bullet has to hold together well and also hold its velocity out to three hundred yards or so. I don't have much prejudice about bullet construction. Bullet placement is so much more important than anything else.

Do you have any tips on shooting techniques in field situations?

Darwin Cary: If a guy gets nervous, and there's time, we have him dry-fire a couple of times.

Ron Fleming: I usually try to get the hunter a rifle rest. Getting him in position is a big part of shooting technique, too. You know that if a bear is up and about, he's going to be feeding, so you try to figure out ahead of time exactly where your target bear is going so you can get there and be ready for a shot. A little bit of time to get set up is worth a lot.

Chris Widrig: The first shot is generally the only one that really counts. It's critical that you have a good rest and take your time on that first shot.

Consider carefully which rifle and cartridge you'll carry in this remote country.

What advice do you give your hunters on shot placement on an interior Canadian grizzly?

Darwin Cary: We advise them to try to break down the front end. Lots of guides and hunters want to shoot bears through the heart, but a grizzly can go a long way unless the heart is literally shredded. If it's feasible, I tell the hunter to put the shot through the shoulders so that it goes on through the vitals as well.

Ron Fleming: I recommend a standard shoulder shot, though I've had hunters make a neck shot in certain situations and that's also effective, especially if the bear is facing you and turns its head to one side. When a bear is first hit, it often goes into a roll and its senses are knocked out for a brief period. That often gives me time to grab the hunter and run up just as close as we can and give the bear some more shots. If you let that bear regain its bearings and get back on its feet, it'll head into the thickest willows it can find, even if it's fatally wounded. Get in there and give the bear some more.

The glassing never stops when you're hunting interior grizzlies.

Chris Widrig: I advise a heart-lung placement, a standard boiler-room shot. I warn hunters never to shoot the animal in the head, because the skull is quite flat and bullets can bounce off pretty easily. I tell them to aim right behind the shoulder, but if they can take out a shoulder while they're doing that, that's all the better.

How many of your first-time interior Canadian grizzly hunters are intimidated by the prospect of hunting a dangerous animal? Describe some typical reactions.

Darwin Cary: They're not usually intimidated, at least not visibly. Most hunters have never been in a tight situation with a grizzly, so they don't appreciate how powerful these animals are. Most have read stories, but reading about it is far different from experiencing it. Most are blissfully oblivious, and that's probably good.

Ron Fleming: Most of them are to some degree. Before you ever get the hunter on a bear, it's the guide's job to convince him that the bear shouldn't intimidate him. Like my daughter says, a bear is just an oversize and overrated rodent! You shoot a bear in the right place and at the right time and get a good shot at the shoulder, and he'll go down as quickly as a marmot. You've got to convince the hunter that even though the bear is big, he'll go down. Big elephants go down, too, so size shouldn't intimidate.

Chris Widrig: Most of them are intimidated to some extent. For one thing, they seem to over-judge every single bear they see. In fact, with practically every bear we've ever taken, the hunter is surprised it isn't bigger when we get up to it. Hunters, especially the first time they go after grizzlies, have a preconceived notion of these animals and how big they are. The average mountain grizzly is probably less than seven feet in length.

Does it help prepare a person mentally if he has already hunted black bears successfully?

Darwin Cary: Oh, I'm sure it does. It has to, because there are many similarities. A black bear is a relatively dangerous animal, too, and having taken one or more has to have a settling effect on almost any hunter.

Ron Fleming: It would. Such hunters know something about bears—they've shot a bear and walked up to it, so they tend to be less intimidated. I took out a twelve-year-old kid who had never shot anything before, but on his first hunt he killed a pretty good grizzly. He came back at age fifteen and killed a really good eight-and-a-half-foot grizzly, a real giant. Then his dad took him to Africa, where he killed a Cape buffalo and a lion. I told his dad, kiddingly, that he'd ruined his kid. The boy's first car was a Rolls-Royce.

Guys ask if it's OK to bring a kid up here, and I tell them to bring the youngster up on a moose hunt, let him do some fishing, let him see a few bears. Kids need some maturity to appreciate killing a grizzly, in my opinion.

Chris Widrig: To a certain extent it does. For one thing, such a hunter has had some experience in judging the size of a bear. It probably also prepares them mentally, since they likely hunted over bait and so have been in close to bears already.

How do you prepare for and handle overpowering excitement in a hunter/client?

Darwin Cary: If time permits, I like to have my hunter just sit and relax a little. Every situation is different, though. As I said before, if there's time, just dry-firing helps settle them down. Sometimes there's not much time, and the excitement only sets in after the shot. Communication is the key to controlling overpowering excitement.

Ron Fleming: That is a tough one. You just have to stop sometimes and let the bear get away. If the client is shaking like a leaf and you can't get him calm enough to shoot, you've just got to call it off. Otherwise you're going to get yourself in trouble: He's going to make a bad hit, and all of a sudden you've got a major problem. It's better to let the bear walk and deal with the fallout later.

Chris Widrig: Certainly the guide has to stay calm and not get excited himself, and that's probably the most important thing in keeping the client relaxed. If the guide gets excited, you can bet the hunter, too, is going to lose it. You've got to talk to him in a very calm voice and not get worked up yourself. The majority of hunters who come to the North Country are fairly experienced already, and most of them are fairly wealthy because grizzly hunting isn't a cheap thrill. A lot of them have even been to Africa and hunted a wide variety of game already, and they're pretty level-headed. These aren't first-time deer-camp hunters we get up here, so it's usually not really a huge issue.

Do you have any wise words on bowhunting? Black-powder hunting?

Darwin Cary: I've never had a black-powder hunter, but we've had a few bow hunters over the years. The only way

Spectacular scenery and a possible big payoff makes all the hard work worthwhile.

I'll take a bow hunter is if I know he's serious and dedicated. He needs to have hunted big game before. There are a lot of "wannabe" bow hunters out there, and I go out of my way to avoid them.

Ron Fleming: We don't take bow hunters anymore, because it's just too tough in today's world. In the past we probably guided more bow hunters than any other outfit, including Fred Bear and Fred Asbell, who was head of Pope and Young for a long time. The difference is that back then we could bait, so you could almost have a bear coming in when and how you wanted. Now it's really difficult because you've got to do a conventional stalk, making it quite tough to get close enough for a bow kill.

We've had two black-powder hunters, one guided by me and another guided by my daughter. Those weapons are deadly. We did try to get the hunters a little closer than usual, but it really wasn't necessary. In both instances those big old slow bullets just flattened the bear on the spot. Still, a little more preparation is necessary to make the shot. One of the two hunters, who was very experienced, got a little rattled and couldn't get the primer in and so on. I'd advise that a guide go through some dry runs with a black-powder hunter, maybe saying something like, "Pretend that log is a bear. Let me see you get ready to shoot it." That way, I think, they're more prepared mentally and you don't get as badly rattled.

Chris Widrig: I don't take either for grizzlies.

Do you take any special precautions with bow hunters or black-powder hunters?

Darwin Cary: Sometimes you can position a bow hunter so the bear is coming past him and the guide isn't right there with him (two people are more likely to alert a bear than one). Ideally, the bear will come within twenty-five yards, and a bear usually doesn't know where the shot came from. On a spot-and-stalk hunt it's very difficult to get all the factors to come together to make a successful hunt. We've had some success by knowing that a bear has been repeatedly traveling a certain route to and from a natural food source.

Special precautions? We don't really do anything much differently from a normal rifle hunt, except for the way we position the hunter.

Ron Fleming: For certain you carry a backup weapon. Beyond that, we try to get in closer. Even with a modern firearm, however, we try to get within 150 yards or less, just to be more certain of a good hit.

Chris Widrig: As mentioned earlier, I don't take either kind of hunter for grizzlies.

Chapter 20

HUNTING GRIZZLY BEARS IN INTERIOR CANADA

Is there anything about interior Canadian grizzly hunting that sets it apart from other types of hunting?

Darwin Cary: I think it's the thrill of hunting an animal so imposing that it's critical you not mess up—if you do, you can get hurt. It's not like shooting a sheep. There's no threat of a sheep charging and running over you or something. True, bear-hunter confrontations are very rare, but whenever one occurs, it puts that little thought in the back of your mind that you'd better do it right or you could be food!

Ron Fleming: It's a very special hunt because they're a special animal. It's a privilege to be able to hunt any wild animal, but it's especially so with a bear. There aren't many of them, and they are truly the king of the woods. Every hunter ought to be equal and have the same chance every other one has, regardless of who they are. I won't let my hunters buy a bear tag just in case they see a bear. The hunt for this unique animal should be dedicated specifically to the grizzly; it should be more meaningful than an animal taken just because you happen to see one from the horse trail.

I want a client who really wants the special experience of searching for a grizzly bear. A spring hunt is a special treat because of all the rebirth of nature that's going on. The vegetation is springing to life, birds of many kinds are all around, the ducks are mating and their colors are incredible, the moose are calving, and last year we watched two nanny goats give birth to kids on a steep cliff we were glassing. It's an experience that maybe only a grizzly hunter gets to fully enjoy.

Chris Widrig: The rarity of the animal is what sets it apart more than anything. Compared to caribou or sheep or almost

Hunting grizzlies amid such spectacular scenery can be distracting—until the bear appears! (Photo courtesy of Ron Fleming)

any other animal, there just aren't that many grizzlies. When you see one, your blood boils because it's just like finding a diamond in the rough. It's an incredible treat to see any grizzly—even a family group that's off-limits to you—after hours and hours of glassing and looking. When you finally get one of these prized animals, there's no feeling quite like it.

Give us your perspective on interior Canadian grizzly hunting as a game-management tool.

Darwin Cary: In British Columbia it's a pretty diverse management situation. There are lots of grizzlies in southern British Columbia, but that's also where the bulk of the human population is located. The potential there for human-bear conflicts is great, especially with all the development. When it comes to managing grizzlies, I think the government is dropping the ball, especially up in the north where my area is located. The lawmakers are super-conservative on allocating quotas to outfitters, and as a consequence half the bears that are shot are nuisance bears. It's probable that many more are shot but not reported. We could really use more hunting to keep the population under control in a way that benefits the bears as well as both hunting and non-hunting people. Those large boars we try to take are notorious for killing cubs. If you've got a healthy, stable population where the large boars are systematically hunted and removed, the inroads on cubs are much reduced. Grizzly bear managers in British Columbia don't allow us to take enough large boars to keep the population stable and keep down the number of nuisance bears we have to take.

Ron Fleming: Bears are predators, and if you're going to manage prey species, you've got to also manage the predators. The bad part of it here is that for some reason the grizzly has become an icon and they're being managed politically instead of biologically—or, maybe more accurately, emotionally instead of scientifically. We have more grizzlies now in British Columbia than we've ever had, and they're devastating our moose population. I've got an area that consists of 2,500 square miles, and I get a quota of two bears? It's crazy.

All of our game populations are on the decline because of the manner in which predator species are being mismanaged. The thing the public doesn't realize is that it's actually bad for the bear population if we don't take out more of the older males by trophy hunting. The grizzly population in British Columbia is exploding so much that we now even have them on Vancouver Island for the first time ever. Older bears are pushing youngsters out to find a territory of their own, and bears are swimming thirty miles to the offshore islands to find a home. There are already more problem bears being shot in some places than hunters are taking.

Chris Widrig: It's quite useful if you can take male grizzlies primarily. The adult male grizzly is the number one predator of moose calves right after they're born in May. If you can take a few of these highly adapted male grizzlies out of the population, you help your moose population quite a bit. Shooting female grizzlies should definitely be avoided because they need to be up to seven years old up here before they even breed, but taking out large males helps cub survival quite a bit.

All the hard work of skinning is done on this huge spring grizzly. (Photo courtesy of Ron Fleming)

What is the most common mistake made by guided interior Canadian grizzly hunters?

Darwin Cary: I don't see an awful lot of mistakes, but if there is one, it's mistaking how acute the bear's senses are. Let's say you spot a grizzly that's totally involved in digging up the mountainside for marmots. You are a half-mile away, and yet suddenly the animal gets your wind and is gone! Grizzlies have poor eyesight, but they're smart and their noses are unparalleled.

Ron Fleming: Impatience is a common mistake. It's most dangerous when you've got a wounded bear and impatience causes you to run right in on it. It's like getting your truck stuck in a ditch—instead of horsing it around and getting it stuck deeper, you analyze the situation and decide the best way to get unstuck. You should do the same with a hit bear. Analyze the situation and come up with the safest, most likely way to retrieve the animal.

Chris Widrig: I believe it's thinking there are more grizzly bears than there actually are. Some places, especially along the coasts of British Columbia and Alaska, hold large populations, but in the interior the bears just aren't that dense.

What can a guided hunter do that would most improve the chances of taking game [patience, physical fitness, mental preparation, equipment, practice with choice of weapon, other]?

Darwin Cary: I think luck is the best thing a hunter can bring! Each hunt is different. Sometimes we have several hunters come and they don't have grizzly tags, but they see four or five grizzlies on their hunt. Then a guy who does have a tag comes and in ten days he never lays eyes on a bear. If we could figure the animals out, it wouldn't be nearly the challenge it is.

Ron Fleming: Picking the right time is by far the most important factor. That challenge is really tough for a hunter because a guide can tell him any time is good and the client has no way of knowing if that's correct or not. I could tell a guy the first of October is the best time, even if it's really not, but how's the hunter to know? Up here in the fall the best time is early September because the berries are ripe then and that's where the bears will be. The best time in the spring is May, when the snow starts melting and there's green grass on the slides.

Chris Widrig: Time of year is a highly important factor. When the bears first come out of hibernation, which in the Yukon occurs in early May, and just before they go into the den in October are the prime times to try for a good grizzly.

Besides the weapon, what kind of equipment should every hunter carry, and which item of gear is the most important?

Darwin Cary: Good raingear is very important. If you get wet you can't be warm and comfortable, and raingear keeps you both dry and out of the wind. Next is good binoculars.

Ron Fleming: Off the record, it's probably toilet paper! No, that would be good optics in both binoculars and spotting scope. The more you look at a bear the better; it's easy to make a mistake between a sow and a boar, and the better you look the more certain

The author's big interior Canadian grizzly, taken in the Yukon.

you can be. Nothing is more sickening than to shoot a big bear and find it has two little cubs. If that should happen, you might as well shoot them, too, because they're not going to make it. Something like that can turn a guy away from hunting.

Chris Widrig: In the spring in the Yukon every hunter should have a pair of hip boots because melting snow is everywhere and you're constantly in and out of the water. In the fall you need regular boots because we're usually on a horse that time of year. The most important item overall, though, is good 10X binoculars—grizzly hunting entails lots of glassing, even more so than sheep hunting, I think.

Are there any common items of equipment that you feel are unnecessary, redundant, or just plain worthless?

Darwin Cary: The second and third duffel bags! What's really ironic is that people bring far too many clothes. All you need is your hunting outfit and a clean pair of jeans to wear in camp. Generally, hunters just bring too much stuff.

Ask the Grizzly/Brown Bear Guides

Ron Fleming: The less you can carry along with you the better, so long as you cover the basics like rifle, binoculars, knife, and so on. You want to avoid anything that makes noise when you're walking. Some people bring shooting sticks, but they're not needed at all. If necessary, a hunter can shoot off the tripod of my spotting scope. Clothing should be quiet, not scratchy and noisy like most raingear. Get that raingear off during the critical time: You can dry out next winter, but right now you're hunting grizzlies. Wool is great because it's so quiet and comfortable, but some of the new synthetics are also very good. I do take a rangefinder, although we went many years without one.

Chris Widrig: I've had hunters bring predator calls, and I've never once seen them work, so I think they might be fairly useless.

Tell us your method of field-judging interior Canadian grizzlies for size.

Darwin Cary: The most reliable method is the belly—if it's dragging the ground, that's a really big bear. You also look at how wide a bear is. A young bear generally has a lot of daylight underneath the belly.

Ron Fleming: I look at the face: If a bear has a long, sloped nose and a big snout, and he's heavy in the front shoulders, then you're looking at a boar. Remember that not every bear makes nine feet; they're like people—some are big and some aren't. But if you see a boar like that with heavy front shoulders and a big head, plus he's got good fur, he's probably as big as he's going to get and could be in his twenties. One time, for example, we killed two bears, one the biggest we'd ever taken at nine feet, and the other just over seven feet. The seven-footer was twenty-seven years old and the nine-footer was eight years old. That just proves what is said above—not every man is born to be a professional basketball player, and not every bear is a buster.

Chris Widrig: Judging bear size is difficult because you don't see a large number of bears. It's a lot like judging mountain goats: It takes some years of experience before you get good at it. Any bear that appears to have big ears and is rangy is usually not a

A big bear has a big foot.

big bear. A big bear has a very big rump and a large hump, and is usually fat. The head, however, is the most important trait, so we pay a lot of attention to it. On a big bear the ears are small in proportion to the head. Still, you go by instinct a lot, and if you have to ask yourself whether it's a big bear, it's probably not.

What is the most reliable way to determine sex when no cubs are present? Give us some other methods as well.

Darwin Cary: I have the client go over and lift up the critter's tail! No, really, boars have bigger, boxier heads, and sows usually have a long nose. To make a subtle judgment on the sex of a lone bear, you have to have seen a lot of bears, and even then it's easy to make a mistake. Typically a big sow will always have cubs with her. Young bears are very difficult to judge for sex, but you're not hunting them anyway.

Ron Fleming: Usually I can see the difference in the face. A sow has a snubby nose that's not so sloped but rather is blocky. On a boar the snout is gradually sloped.

Chris Widrig: You use the size of the body and the size of the head, plus the size of the hump and the coloration. Here in the Yukon a darker bear is generally a male—sometimes they're almost black. Ninety percent of the time a straw-blonde bear is a female. On a female grizzly the face is narrow and more "foxy," and the head isn't as round as a boar's.

How do you normally follow up after the shot at an interior Canadian grizzly?

Darwin Cary: If you know the bear is hit well, you can afford to wait a while and give it time to expire. That's especially so if the bear runs off into the thick stuff, which they usually do. You really need to listen, too, because you can often follow where they go by the sound they make and the sounds of birds and other animals.

Ron Fleming: The first thing you do is run your hunter up close and try to get a couple more shots into him. Now, if he takes off, you just stop and wait for a bit. A lot of the time, circumstances will give away his escape route. One time I didn't have a clue where a bear had gone—until a couple of geese got up off a little meadow down below. Something had spooked them, and sure enough, that's the way the bear had run. You might see a moose get up and run, or something else out of the ordinary. Start out on his trail, check how much blood he's losing, and maybe you can tell something from that.

Chris Widrig: If my hunter shoots and the bear disappears into the willows, I wait at least an hour before following. There's nothing worse or more dangerous than tracking a wounded grizzly in thick willows. I try to get to high ground above where we last saw the bear, and we look for blood.

What procedure do you follow in tracking a wounded interior Canadian grizzly?

Darwin Cary: A dog is the best method, but we don't have one, unfortunately. The main thing is to make certain your hunter understands he really has only one shot—in our thick country it

Traditionally, the width of the front paw in inches plus one [inch] is thought to equal the square of the hide in feet.

usually isn't possible to get a good second shot unless the bear actually goes down. After the bear disappears, all you can do is follow the blood trail and hope he's well hit. If he isn't, you're going to find a live bear at uncomfortably close range. We've been very fortunate over the years, and I actually can't remember us losing a wounded grizzly.

Ron Fleming: I leave the hunter sitting and try to pick up the trail, maybe a blood spot or whatever. I move the hunter up and then have him wait at any blood I find. I then get off to one side—preferably a high side to stay above the bear—and go around a bit, maybe a hundred feet or so, before dropping down to try to pick up his trail. Once I find it, I whistle for the hunter to move up to the new location. When the bear enters a thick willow clump, I don't go in right away. I circle around it and see if I can pick up the trail on the other side. If not, there's a good chance he's in there. You do have to go in there, but at least you know what you're getting into.

Chris Widrig: You take the wind into consideration, and you stay off to one side of the animal's trail as much as possible. If you're following blood, you have to stay fairly close to the track, of course. I've tracked wounded grizzlies for miles and miles, and if an animal isn't badly wounded, there's an excellent chance his wound will heal. If it's just a flesh wound, he'll go forever. We've taken bears that had old wounds, and we've dug old bullets out of others. If he's hit badly, there's going to be a lot of blood and he's going to lie down pretty quickly. Still, tracking any wounded bear is a potentially dangerous situation.

Chapter 21

SPECIFIC GUIDING AREAS FOR HUNTING GRIZZLY BEARS IN INTERIOR CANADA

Describe your home guiding area and any distinctions that set it apart.

Darwin Cary: Our guiding concession is two and a half million acres in size and is accessible only by airplane. We have three planes of our own to help us move hunters around within the area. We've built cabin facilities in most areas because I got tired of buying tents, which the bears were always tearing apart. Now we repair cabins, which they also tear apart. We hunt part of the Rocky Mountain Trench and the Cassiar Mountains. We seek grizzlies from the valley floors right up into the high alpine country, because grizzlies are wherever you find them.

Ron Fleming: It's a really neat area. It's so remote that the nearest road is 165 miles from our border. We fly in by float plane, and we don't use horses. All our camps are on lakes, so we use boats extensively. In the spring we have to wait until the ice gets off the lakes before taking any hunters in. The mountains have really steep slides, so it's real mountain-goat country. Avalanches come down in winter and wipe these slides clean—they've done that for the past thousand years, probably. The soil there is really fertile because the avalanches serve just like a cultivator. The grass and wild rhubarb will be two feet high at the bottoms of the slides, while at our camp across the lake there's still two feet of snow. If a bear is going to feed, he's going to those slides across from camp. You can go up in a plane and see that the whole country is white except for the slides. We've taken twenty-seven bears from that same spot over the years. We're never hampered by resident hunters, because it's too hard to get in there.

A fine grizzly frequents the avalanche slides in guide Ron Fleming's area. (Photo courtesy of Ron Fleming)

Chris Widrig: It's very close to the Arctic Circle, and the whole area is mountainous with deep, narrow valleys. It holds a good population of grizzlies. One reason is that we're along the Northwest Territories border, and grizzly hunting there has been closed for thirty years, so we've got a good reservoir of bears coming over all the time. Still, these are interior grizzlies, and the densities are fairly low compared to coastal grizzlies. One thing about our area is different: The color variation of grizzlies here is really striking—we've got everything from blonde to black.

How much of a role do food sources play in hunting bears in your area?

Darwin Cary: In September we follow the berry crop and try to stay near a valley where there's been some carrion, such as a moose kill. You take advantage of any food source that might attract bears, keeping in mind that it's prohibited to hunt a bear that's actually on a carcass.

Specific Guiding Areas for Hunting Grizzly Bears in Interior Canada

Ron Fleming: Ninety percent of our hunting is done around food sources. In the spring it's the avalanche slides and the vegetation there, and in the fall it's the berries. The kind of slide you look for is one with lots of big boulders, which tend to retain the sun's heat and make the vegetation grow.

Chris Widrig: Food sources play a big role. The berries start to ripen in early fall, and the bears really start to hit the patches then to put on lots of fat. In the spring the grizzlies frequent the south-facing slopes where the new green grass is emerging. So even though our bears are protein-deficient to some extent, lacking salmon streams, we still focus on areas where we know they'll be feeding. There are some areas where the cranberries will overwinter underneath the snow, and the bears know these places. We always take a look at such spots to see if a bear is working them.

How many of your bears are taken incidentally (as opposed to being the primary species sought)?

Darwin Cary: We have a lot of guys come on a moose and goat hunt, during which success is almost guaranteed in our country. Our bears are almost all taken on a harvest-fee basis, because if a person wants only a bear, he'll likely go over to the coast, where both the size and numbers of bears are better. I don't want hunters to come and pay me a big price for a grizzly hunt and then not find the size or age bear they want. I'd rather they do the moose-goat combination hunt, get their money's worth from that, and take a grizzly if they see a really good one. With that in mind, you might say that most of our grizzlies are taken on a trophy-fee basis, and that's "incidental" in a way.

Ron Fleming: Maybe 10 percent, probably less. That's because in the fall we have one combination hunt during which the hunter is also after moose. I prefer to have a hunter who really wants to hunt grizzly bears and not just bump into one. In a rare instance where we don't fill our two tags in the spring, I might have an incoming hunter in mind that I advise to buy a grizzly tag, but usually I just roll the tag over to the next year and book a hunt dedicated to just grizzlies.

A happy hunter and guide with another great trophy from British Columbia. (Photo courtesy of Ron Fleming)

Chris Widrig: We take on average about three each year while hunting other species in the fall. The spring hunt, of course, is for only one hunter and it's only for grizzly. That would mean that three-fourths of our bears are taken incidentally and one-quarter are the primary species sought.

What kind of terrain is ideal for hunting interior Canadian grizzly bears?

Darwin Cary: It's a matter of getting up where you can actually glass. If the country is thick and you're down low, there's a good chance you'll never see them. Typically, when we're moose and goat hunting, the bears are up on the mountainsides rooting around. We sometimes spot them above timberline and make a stalk on them.

Ron Fleming: The best places are open slopes that are green in early spring because of avalanches. That's also where the best berries are located.

Chris Widrig: Each fall the bears are concentrated in the river valleys where all the berries are getting ripe, so you need to hunt that kind of terrain. In the spring they're up on the south-facing slopes where the grass and lichens are turning green, so that's where we find them. Later in the spring, when the moose start calving, the bears move down along the rivers so they can prey on newborn moose.

You can't bait grizzlies in the Yukon, so you've got to have open country so you can see the bears; without it, you really don't have much of a chance. You're not going to see them down in the trees. You try to pick an area with a lot of south-facing slopes where the grass is greening up and the bears are out feeding. In the fall it's legal to hunt a gut pile after a hunter has killed a moose, though you can't move the remains to improve your chances. You've got to take out all the meat, of course, or it's considered baiting.

Describe your typical camp setup and routine.

Darwin Cary: Everybody except sheep hunters stays in a cabin, and in most places we use horses. Hunters with bear tags have to be ready to pack up quickly and move if one of our guides spots a good grizzly working a different camp. All our camps are a little different in the way they've been set up. I have a crew in each camp, including a cook, a guide, a wrangler, and so on. I try to keep crews together if they work well together, and that's almost an art in itself.

Ron Fleming: We have all cabins—we don't use tents. I have five camps that we rotate with only one group of four hunters in my area at one time in the fall. The next group of four hunters goes to a different camp, so we hunt from any given camp only once a year, and every new group of hunters gets to hunt where no one else has hunted that year. In the spring I take only one hunter to a camp at a time for a grizzly hunt, and then a second one comes for the next hunt; that way they're not there at the

Nobody can complain about the scenery while hunting a grizzly with Chris Widrig. (Photo courtesy of Chris Widrig)

same time competing for the same bear. Our cabins include a cookhouse with a bedroom on the back, where my wife Brenda and I stay. We have two hunter cabins and a guide cabin, as well as a shower house, meat house, and storage shed. There are two boats and motors at each camp as well. We run the operation as a family, with my daughter and son-in-law as the two guides and Brenda doing the cooking.

Chris Widrig: In the spring we fly in and set up a camp on a high riverbank where we have a good view. We want a place where we can glass right from camp, and we spend hours at it. I'm an early riser and it's always daylight in the spring, so I'm up at 4:00 A.M. looking for bears. We often move up or down the river and sit on a hill to glass, and we may stay right there in that location all day long, just glassing different sections.

What is your success rate on trophy animals?

Darwin Cary: We've got three grizzly tags per year, and we typically fill two of them.

Ron Fleming: I'd say about 90 percent. We improve our chances by picking both the time and the place to hunt, and by trying to ensure we have a serious hunter.

Chris Widrig: On grizzly hunts it must be about 50 percent over the years. It's hard to put a percentage on the fall hunts, because lots of our hunters have grizzly tags then and we do take quite a few bears. We do see a lot of bears, though—at least a few on every hunt and sometimes ten or more.

Describe your usual hunting method and any common variations.

Darwin Cary: It's always a spot-and-stalk hunt. When you're chasing goats, you're always looking for the grizzly bear. It's the same when you're hunting moose. You may go days on end without seeing a bear, but all of a sudden there he is. When we've got seven or eight camps full of hunters and one is after a grizzly, the grizzly guy actually has all those eyes looking for his bear.

Ron Fleming: It's really a tough deal. First thing we do when we get up in the morning is go and glass those avalanche slides. We built one particular camp right across the lake from them so we could watch them. You get out the lawn chair and give the slides a good glassing for an hour or so, and then you go in and have breakfast. After breakfast, it's back to the lawn chair for more glassing, until you're just burned out from it. From noon to 3:00 P.M. I have the guys go out fishing or go for a walk or something, and then in the evening we hit it again with the glassing. When we see a good bear, we do some figuring on how to intercept him, and we usually can.

Chris Widrig: Glassing is the primary method of finding a grizzly, but in the fall we often simply spot one while we're hunting other species. In that case we judge whether it's a bear we should go after, and if so, we leave the horses and set up a stalk to try to get a shot.

Tell us your method of getting close enough to a bear for a shot.

Darwin Cary: First you try to figure out what the bear is doing, and then you figure in the wind and how to stay out of sight.

Ron Fleming: It's pretty open country, so you check the wind and climb up so you can see him. I know where a bear will cross nine out of ten times, and we're there waiting when he does. There are times when an adverse wind prevents you from going after a bear, but we usually can make a stalk. We do pretty much the same thing in the fall.

Chris Widrig: It's always a stalking situation, and the closer you can get the better. I like to get within two hundred yards or so, but not closer than thirty yards, and always take the wind into consideration while getting into position.

Do you have both a spring and a fall season in your area?

Darwin Cary: We don't hunt the spring season even though it's still open. When our permits got limited so severely, the logistics just killed that hunt. Unless you can take five or six hunters, a spring season just doesn't make much sense.

Ron Fleming: Obviously we do.

Chris Widrig: Yes.

If so, which season [spring or fall] offers the best hunting in your area? Early or late in either season?

Darwin Cary: We only hunt the fall, as I said, for logistical and practical reasons.

Ron Fleming: Spring is the best time, one reason being that you spend all the time looking for a bear. In the fall you lose a day here and there because you spot a moose and go after it, and that takes up a couple of days. Then you head out again and see

Grizzly country has some awesome scenery.

a good goat, and you're off after it. So by the end of ten days in the fall, you might have hunted bears only a few of those days.

Chris Widrig: I'd say 1–14 May is the best time to hunt in the spring because only the large males are out of the dens that early and you don't have to worry so much about sows. In the fall the best time is the second and third weeks of September because the berries are ripe and the bears are moving around a lot feeding and putting on fat for the winter.

Are badly rubbed hides a problem in your area? What period is best for avoiding this problem?

Darwin Cary: Since we hunt only the fall, rubbed hides are never a problem.

Ron Fleming: I've never seen a rubbed hide in our area in the spring. You can have some left-over guard hairs in the fall that make the hide look like it's rubbed, but they're usually pretty good even then.

Chris Widrig: I've never even seen a rubbed hide in our area. I think if we hunted up into June we'd see some rubbing, but we're finished before then.

How much does weather influence hunting success and how you hunt in your area?

Darwin Cary: Very little. We've got mountains eleven thousand feet high both east and west of us, but the Cassiar Mountains are only six or seven thousand feet high. Weather can certainly move in on us, but it generally blows through fairly rapidly.

Ron Fleming: Hot weather is the only major adverse factor. If it's really hot, bears tend to stay down in the timber to feed and they don't come out on the slides so we can see them.

Chris Widrig: The influence of weather is negligible in the spring—we have twenty-four hours of daylight then and the weather is usually great. You can have some spring showers, but they're usually not a factor.

Section V

HUNTING BARREN-GROUND GRIZZLY BEARS

Chapter 22

SELECTING AN OUTFITTER

What should a hunter look for in an outfitter/guide for barren-ground grizzly bears?

James Pokiak: I think the most important things in an outfitter are honesty, the price of the hunt, and the success rate of the operation. These factors vary widely when you're talking about barren-ground grizzly hunting.

What are [a] the most important single characteristic and [b] the worst possible deficiency in a barren-ground grizzly guide?

James Pokiak: Knowledge of the area would be the most important positive factor. These areas are big places and you

Packed and ready to go out for barren-ground grizzly.

Good equipment is a necessity to cover the long distances involved in hunting barren-ground grizzly.

have to know yours well if you're to be consistently successful. The worst deficiency would be dishonesty, and unfortunately, some outfitters for barren-ground grizzly are certainly that way. They don't tell the truth about how they conduct their hunts.

Is there any exceptional qualification for being a barren-ground grizzly guide that may not apply to other types of guiding?

James Pokiak: I don't think so. Again, though, it depends on the individual's knowledge of the area and the quality of his equipment.

Does your area boast a really good source of protein to help bears grow big [salmon streams, plentiful ungulates, large ground-squirrel population, etc.]?

James Pokiak: The ungulates are plentiful here, and the ground-squirrel population, too, is very good. The bears don't lack for protein sources. There are lots of roots and berries, too, so I think our grizzlies overall are very well fed.

What does a good barren-ground grizzly guide do to ensure safety while hunting North America's most dangerous game?

James Pokiak: For one thing the hunter needs a big enough rifle shooting a heavy enough bullet to stop the bear quickly. Also, we try to get close enough for a good shot—but not dangerously close. It's important to make a good first shot, too.

Chapter 23

BARREN-GROUND GRIZZLY GUIDES EVALUATE THE HUNTER

What is your favorite type of hunter (personality, physical abilities, experience level, socioeconomic status, etc.)

James Pokiak: From my standpoint the most important qualities are the first two you've listed. I like a hunter with some personality who really enjoys the hunt. He also needs to have a good degree of physical ability because it's not a really easy hunt—we spend many hours riding a snowmobile or sometimes in a sled. The hunter also needs to be able to walk a good amount; the final stalk can be pretty long and there's always snow on the ground, making progress harder.

Riding long distances on a snowmobile is required to hunt barren-ground grizzlies.

The outcome can be a spectacular Arctic grizzly if one is persistent.

How important is it for the hunter to be in top physical shape?

James Pokiak: It's pretty important, for the reasons I mentioned in the previous question.

Should inexperienced or physically challenged hunters try for barren-ground grizzlies? Why or why not?

James Pokiak: I believe everybody should have a chance to do so, even if they're inexperienced or physically challenged. Again, the ability of the guide to accommodate this type of hunter is a major consideration, and that factor is highly variable among different outfitters. I had one hunter who had to be helped in and out of the sled as well as on and off the snowmobile. We had to expend quite a bit of extra effort in assisting him physically, but we were able to get him a bear.

Is there any particular characteristic in a hunter that would make you refuse to guide him on a barren-ground grizzly hunt?

James Pokiak: We hunt in extremely remote locations, and I don't like to take a person whose health could be problematic. If a prospective client had a really bad heart and needed medication just to walk around, for example, I'd be reluctant to expose him to the rigors of a grizzly hunt. In most cases I would probably still do it, but I'd have to know in detail about the health problem ahead of time. I don't want to be surprised by a hunter's condition when he shows up in Tuktoyaktuk for a barren-ground grizzly hunt. Dealing with a heart attack when you're a few hundred miles away from town would really be a nightmare.

What is the most dangerous thing a client can do while hunting barren-ground grizzlies? Can you share an instance where a client placed himself or the guide in danger?

James Pokiak: It's just plain dangerous when the client doesn't listen to me. There's always a reason we do things, or don't do some things, and it's necessary to just trust your guide. We don't live in very forgiving country and we're not hunting a forgiving animal, so if a hunter insists on doing things his way, he can quickly get into trouble.

Chapter 24

BARREN-GROUND GRIZZLY GUIDES EVALUATE HUNTING ARMS

What is your favorite rifle caliber for barren-ground grizzlies, and do you recommend this caliber to clients?

James Pokiak: I like best the bigger calibers such as the .375 and the .338 because a decent shot with one of them generally puts the bear down solidly. Lots of hunters come with smaller calibers, though, and if they can shoot them well, these are fine.

What is your choice as a backup weapon for barren-ground grizzlies?

James Pokiak: I've actually used a pretty small backup weapon, a .257 shooting 100-grain bullets. I recently purchased a .30-06 to use for backup because it's a little bigger. Usually backup isn't necessary in the terrain we hunt, but I always carry my rifle just in case.

You need an adequate weapon to take the bear that made this fresh track.

Persistence and a steady shot produced this fine barren-ground grizzly.

What is your advice on bullet weight? Bullet construction?

James Pokiak: The minimum size I recommend is 180-grain. I don't have a bullet design or brand that I particularly recommend.

Do you have any tips on shooting techniques in field situations?

James Pokiak: It's happened more than once that my hunter misses the first shot and then the animal takes off. We try to get a good standing first shot, but if the animal sees us and takes off, or if the first shot misses, the bear will be running away fast. In this case it's important that the hunter be able to hit a moving target, so clients should practice for this possibility.

What advice do you give your hunters on shot placement?

James Pokiak: I always tell my hunters to hold right behind the shoulder and put a good shot through the heart-lung area.

How many of your first-time barren-ground grizzly hunters are intimidated by the prospect of hunting a dangerous animal? Describe some typical such reactions.

James Pokiak: Most of my hunters are already fairly experienced, so it hasn't been a problem. I really haven't had to deal with such a reaction so far.

Does it help a person prepare mentally if he has already hunted black bears successfully?

James Pokiak: I think so. At least that person has already hunted one kind of bear, so he's somewhat prepared for a more dangerous kind of animal. A bear is a bear, and it's got to help some.

How do you prepare for and handle overpowering excitement in a hunter/client?

James Pokiak: Again, this hasn't been much of a problem. I think that's probably because of the generally high experience level of hunters who come to the Arctic to hunt barren-ground grizzlies.

Do you have any wise words on bowhunting? Black-powder hunting?

James Pokiak: I've had a couple of people come up who used both methods. The biggest difference is how close you have to get to take the bear. Of course, those are single-shot weapons, so it's essential to make that first shot count.

Do you take any special precautions with bowhunters or black-powder hunters?

James Pokiak: Not really. I haven't guided many such hunters, so I'm not an expert in this kind of hunting. I just make sure that I'm close enough behind the client so I'm in position to use my weapon as a backup if I must.

Chapter 25

HUNTING BARREN-GROUND GRIZZLY BEARS

Is there anything about barren-ground grizzly hunting that is particularly significant to you [i.e., sets it apart from other kinds of hunting]?

James Pokiak: There is really no "spiritual" significance attached to hunting grizzlies, as there may be with polar bear hunting. It's very much like other kinds of hunting, except that, for example, the grizzly is more aggressive than the polar bear. Hunters and guides must keep that in mind.

Give us your perspective on barren-ground grizzly hunting as a game-management tool.

James Pokiak: It's a very positive factor in every way. We have very good management tools in place. My only problem with the system is that sometimes the game department doesn't act on complaints and concerns voiced by outfitters in the field. But the management aspect is very good. We work with the managing authorities to make certain the bear population remains at a level that allows a sustainable harvest every year.

What is the most common mistake made by guided barren-ground grizzly hunters?

James Pokiak: The biggest mistakes almost always are rooted in the hunter not listening to the guide, or pressuring the guide to conduct the hunt differently from the way we know works best. The occasional hunter seems to think he knows more about hunting barren-ground grizzlies than I do. If that happens, it can be a problem.

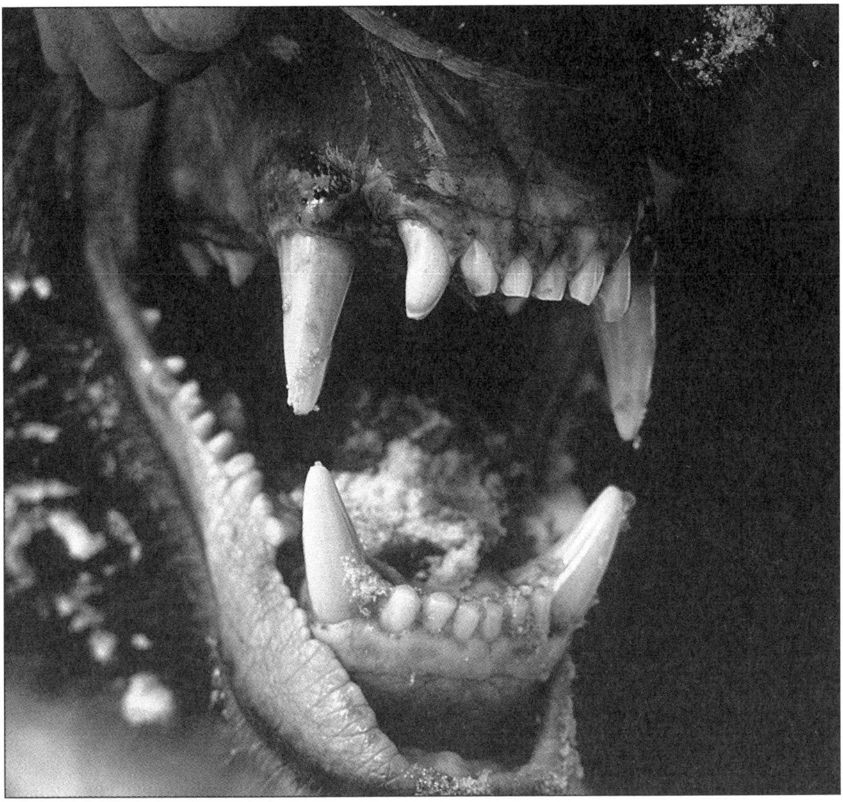

The teeth of a barren-ground grizzly can crush anything.

What can a guided hunter do that would most improve the chances of taking game (patience, physical fitness, mental preparation, equipment, practice with choice of weapon, other)?

James Pokiak: Once more, the first two items you list seem to be the best answers. Bear hunters have to be patient, and they've got to get in good enough shape to handle the rigors of a long, difficult Arctic hunt. Hunting this animal is very demanding, especially if you go east from Tuktoyaktuk. Hunting to the west of there isn't so bad because you can basically start hunting as soon as you leave town. If we go east, though, it takes twelve hours of snowmobiling just to get to the actual hunting area. That's a long time on a snowmobile and it can take a lot out of you, so the patience and physical stamina needed to do that are quite important to success.

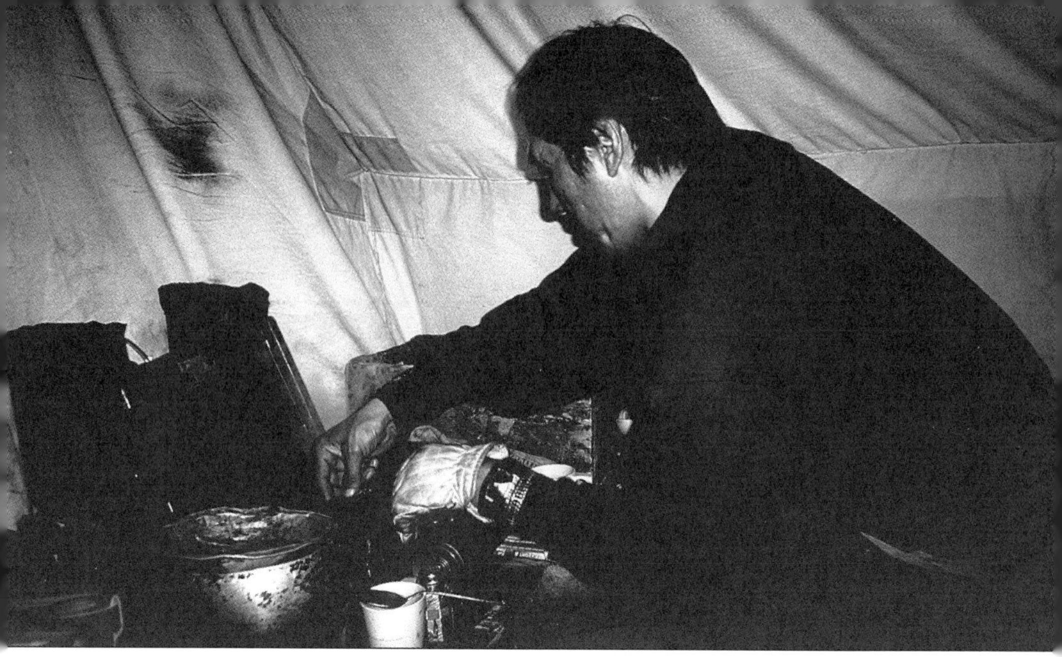

Cooking is done inside the tent because of the extreme cold.

Besides the weapon, what kind of equipment should every hunter carry and what is the most important single item?

James Pokiak: I'd have to say every hunter should carry along a really good, sharp knife. In a bad situation, some matches or a lighter to start a fire can be life-saving, so I'd rank them very high on the equipment list.

Are there any common items of equipment that you feel are unnecessary, redundant, or just plain worthless?

James Pokiak: I don't know how the other outfitters do it, but when I get my clients into town I usually go over their equipment carefully with them because sometimes they show up with two or three bags. We go through it all and trim it down to what they really need, leaving here in town what I feel they don't need out there.

Tell us your method of field-judging the size of barren-ground grizzlies.

James Pokiak: Mainly we go by the track size; most of the time we cut a track and follow it, so we need to know pretty much what size bear we're following. If we spot a bear in the distance, we can tell if it's a big boar by the size of the head relative to the body, and also by the size of the hump—the sows up here don't have much of a hump.

What is the most reliable way to determine sex when no cubs are present? Give us some other methods as well.

James Pokiak: Generally the hump on a male is a lot bigger than on females. I've seen enough of them to know that the bigger the hump, the bigger the bear most of the time. As I said, female barren-ground grizzlies usually don't have much of a hump on their back.

How do you normally follow up after the shot at a barren-ground grizzly?

James Pokiak: It depends on the terrain. Up here there's always snow cover during the grizzly season, which really helps us. There are no sizable trees up here except pretty far south, but there are some areas with high willows. A few times we've had to work a bear out of one of those patches. You try to get up high so you can see down into the brush and find the bear. It's important to use the terrain to your advantage.

What procedure do you follow in tracking a wounded barren-ground grizzly?

James Pokiak: Unless you're right at the tree line, where the country starts to get thicker, it's usually no problem to track a wounded bear. Our terrain is pretty wide open, and visibility is usually exceptional. During the spring bear season we always have snow on the ground, as I said.

Chapter 26

SPECIFIC GUIDING AREAS FOR HUNTING BARREN-GROUND GRIZZLY BEARS

Describe your home guiding area and any distinctions that set it apart.

James Pokiak: Our area extends from the Yukon border on the west all the way to the Horton River on the east. It's mainly open, rolling terrain with no significant mountains. Along the coast there is hardly any vegetation taller than a foot or so, but to the south you can get into some low trees and fairly thick stands of willow. A major distinction is the enormous size of the area.

You also guide for polar bears. Which is a bigger challenge—the polar bear or the barren-ground grizzly?

James Pokiak: I hate to tell you this for inclusion in a brown bear book, but I consider the polar bear a much bigger challenge than a grizzly, for a number of reasons. Where we chase polar bears, the ice is always shifting and the terrain can be terribly irregular, with areas of rough ice that we call rubble. Also, you can have problems sometimes with open water. Of course, on guided polar bear hunts we have to use dog sleds, and that presents a different set of challenges. Where we hunt grizzlies, the terrain is rolling but regular and we can use snowmobiles all the time to find a bear. These factors make the polar bear a much bigger challenge.

How much of a role do food sources play in hunting bears in your area?

James Pokiak: Most of our hunting is simply looking for tracks or trying to spot a bear, so food sources are not a big part of it. We know which areas the bears use, though, and of

Typical camp setup from which to hunt a barren-ground grizzly.

course you find them where the food is. Sometimes the bears will key in on a herd of muskoxen or caribou, and we also know where these animals are located. Still, our primary method is to go to a likely area and cover it well, looking for tracks, so we don't specifically think about hunting a food source, the way grizzlies are hunted in other locations.

How many of your bears are taken incidentally (as opposed to being the primary species sought)?

James Pokiak: None of them are taken incidentally. It's like a polar bear hunt. Every barren-ground grizzly hunt is dedicated to that animal. We do sometimes combine it with a hunt for other species, though, such as muskoxen, but the bear is always the priority animal.

What kind of terrain is ideal for hunting the barren-ground grizzly?

James Pokiak: I like rolling terrain that has some good, high hills facing the south. Rivers are also excellent places to find a good bear.

Describe your typical camp setup and routine.

James Pokiak: We sometimes have no choice but to stop and set up camp wherever we happen to be, because of weather or visibility or other factors. We like to set up camp in one spot, hunt in different directions from there, and then move the camp when we've covered that part of the area well. In that case, camp is just a place to eat and sleep. If the weather's nice, you try to get an early start and make the most of it. If it's snowing or foggy, you have to stay in camp and wait it out.

What is your success rate on trophy animals?

James Pokiak: I run about 90 percent on trophy barren-ground grizzlies.

Describe your usual hunting method and any common variations.

James Pokiak: The first thing you must decide is which direction you're going to travel that day. I take various things into consideration in making that decision. You have to be aware of where the muskoxen will be, because these are animals the bears will likely be going after as a food source, and you could cut a good track there. You might have reasons to travel to the north and check along the coast, or you might want to go in some other direction—it depends on many factors, both tangible and intangible. You need to stay on high terrain as much as possible so you can see a long way.

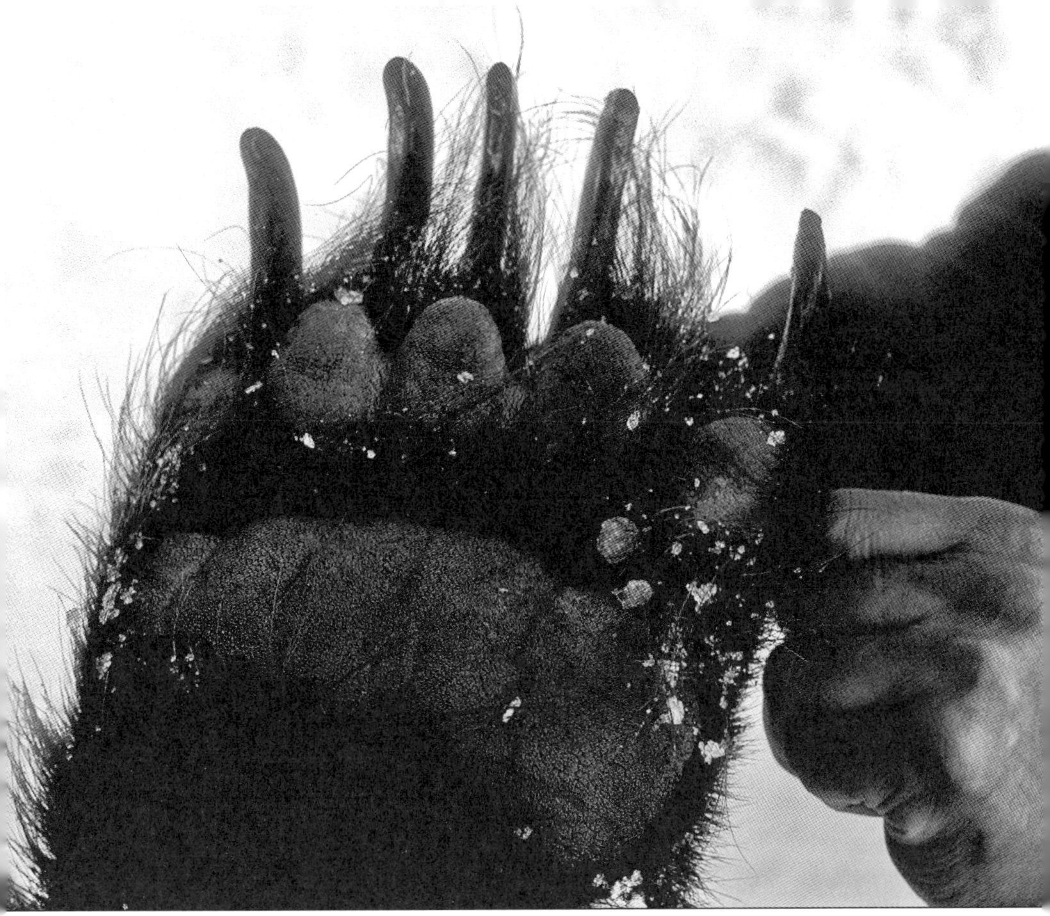

The claws on this magnificent bear were over five inches long.

Tell us your method of getting close enough to a bear for a shot.

James Pokiak: By law we must stalk the animal on foot the last mile or so after we locate it. We're required to leave the snowmobile once the animal we want is spotted, and try to work our way in closer for the shot.

Do you have both a spring and a fall season in your area?

James Pokiak: Yes, we have both. In the fall we're restricted to hunting near water, using a boat and an outboard motor. If the hunter is unsuccessful on a fall hunt, the tag can be carried forward and used the next spring for a second hunt, and that's a big advantage.

If so, which season (spring or fall) offers the best hunting in your area? Early or late in either season?

James Pokiak: The best time is actually in the spring, and we get started the third week of April. In terms of seeing more bears, the first week of May is the best time. However, I'll point out that the earlier in the spring the hunter comes, the longer the claws of his bear will be—at that time the bears haven't been out of the winter den long enough to wear the claws down by digging for food. When they first emerge, the claws are often five inches long, but the hungry animals begin to wear them down pretty quickly.

Are badly rubbed hides a problem in your area? When is it best to hunt to avoid this problem?

James Pokiak: None of our hunters has ever taken a bear that was significantly rubbed, so it's just not a problem.

How much does weather influence hunting success and how you hunt?

James Pokiak: Weather can surely be a significant factor, especially snow and fog, which can reduce visibility to the point you're stuck in camp. You can sometimes waste several days just waiting out the weather. Most of the time, though, the weather cooperates enough for us to get the job done. I don't think we've ever had anyone fail to get a bear purely because of the weather.

Section VI

PARTING SHOTS BY THE GRIZZLY/BROWN BEAR GUIDES

Chapter 27

FAREWELL FROM THE GRIZZLY/BROWN BEAR GUIDES

Do you have any unusual bear hunting stories to share?

Dennis Harms: My most unusual client ever was a ten-year-old girl I had on a hunt two years ago. I was really reluctant to take her but ended up being quite surprised at how well she did. She certainly had no trouble keeping up—if anything, she was always stepping on my heels—and her dad had taught her to shoot a .308 quite well.

On about the third or fourth day of the hunt this big bear came along below the crest of a mountain we were on. She and her dad and one of our guides took off after it, but I didn't think there was any chance they'd catch up to it because it was moving pretty fast.

The bear came to a creek, leaped off the bank into the water and caught a deer, then came back into sight dragging its catch. It dragged the deer about a hundred yards into another little creek and out of sight. I got the attention of the three hunters, caught up to them, and we were able to sneak to within thirty-eight yards of this giant bear. We got this little girl rested down on a pack, and she made a terrific shot and got her bear. It squared an honest ten and a half feet!

Gary "Butch" King: This story's key element involves not having enough firepower to stop a bear. It all occurred back in the '70s. I had a .458 as my backup weapon, and we had a hunter with a .30-06 who had wounded a bear. It was a really big bear that we found out later squared ten feet eight inches.

Basically, I got elected to go in and try to mop up the mess. The bear had gone into the worst possible location—really thick vegetation. I got into a situation where the wind was quartering downhill from my right and the bear was somewhere above me on my left. I had a choice: I could try to move into the wind and sneak up on him through the brush, or else I could get above him and let him wind me. If I chose that latter option, I realized that one of two things would happen: Either he'd blow out of that spot and, hopefully, go to another spot that was better, or he'd charge and come through an opening that should give me fifty yards or so to stop him. With my .458 I felt fairly confident I could do that.

I chose the latter option, and started through a narrow hourglass spot where the bushes converged. All of a sudden the brush started shaking—that bear was obviously coming. It broke out of the thick stuff at a distance of about twenty feet, and I only had time to turn and shoot from the hip. I hit him and stopped him in his tracks, but it knocked me backward, and I, too, went down. I heard the pop of the hunter's gun, and by the time I got turned back toward the bear he had regained his footing and was right on top of me. I had the butt of the gun on the ground, and I'm not even sure who chambered the round, me or the Almighty, but the gun went off and broke the bear's back, and the huge animal fell right on my hip boots and pinned me to the ground. I heard the hunter's gun go off again, and then I was more afraid that he was going to shoot me!

I crawled out from under that big old bear and had a little talk with my hunter.

Mike Munsey: One of my most memorable hunts took place several years ago. It was early spring and the bears were just coming out of their dens. We spotted a very large male hanging around his den up quite high on the mountain in what looked like pretty deep snow. It was early in the day, so we decided to make the climb. Once we got close to the bear, we realized the snow was frozen enough that we could walk on top without falling through, if we were careful and walked gingerly. We approached to within about a hundred fifty yards below and to the left of the bear; with no cover between us and him, I decided we weren't going to get any closer. I told my hunter he had better shoot from there. He shot and hit the bear, and it immediately started running downhill toward us! I don't think the bear was attacking—he was simply hit pretty hard and downhill was the

Hunting a spring grizzly in British Columbia is sometimes a horseback affair.

only direction he could run. Also, he didn't know where we were but just happened to be angling right toward us.

I started shooting but didn't hear my hunter shooting, so I looked back and he was running away! Problem was, as he ran in six feet of snow, he kept breaking that crust and falling through all the way to his crotch. Needless to say, the bear was covering ground a bit faster than he was. I yelled at the man to start shooting at the bear, which by this time was about twenty yards from him. Now the bear realized where we were and began running straight downhill, paralleling us and no longer a threat to our lives. My hunter detected this, snapped out of it, and joined me in firing until we finally killed the animal. The man was pretty quiet as we skinned the bear, and he never mentioned the episode again.

Scott Newman: Anyone who's been mauled by a brown bear will probably share that story, if he lives to tell about it. It was April 2004 and the last day of a ten-day hunt. A couple of hours of daylight remained when we spotted a "shootable" bear, so I parked the skiff well downwind and left my nephew, Levi, there to keep it from being stranded as the tide receded. We made the final stalk on foot and closed the distance to 132 yards by rangefinder. We couldn't get any closer because the bear was behind a logjam and the open beach separating him from us had no cover.

I got my hunter to set up on a solid log and we waited a long time, hoping for a good presentation. The wind swirled and seemed to be changing directions, so I decided to try a little different approach. We could see the bear intermittently between openings in the logs, and I knew it was a large boar. I got worried we could lose the opportunity due to a fickle shift in the wind, so I moved with my hunter down the beach for a better view. Just as I moved, the bear looked over the pile of logs. All of a sudden he hoisted himself up right on top of the logs, where he stood without moving for about five seconds. I glanced at the hunter, who didn't have his rifle ready, and then I slowly moved my head to look back at the bear. It took about two steps toward us and then, unexpectedly, the hunter fired! It was such an easy shot, and he had a good rest, so I wasn't worried. It appeared the bear was hit hard, but I told the hunter to keep shooting. After he emptied his gun, I shot a couple of times with my .416, just to be certain, and I believed I had hit the bear behind the front shoulder. I reloaded and headed to where the bear had disappeared into dark timber up ahead.

I was more concerned at that point about making sure we got the bear and could wind up this hunt, because I had another hunt in two days. I was confident the bear was either dead or almost so, so I left the hunter on the beach and proceeded into the timber. There was a good blood trail, but some of it was dark red, which concerned me. I walked easily through the timber following the trail, avoiding brush so as to stay silent. All of a sudden I could actually smell the bear. I stopped cold, thinking I could see him up ahead, but it turned out to be a stump. I took another quiet step—thinking the bear ought to be dead by now but fully aware that if he wasn't, I could be walking into a very dangerous situation. I had just processed this thought when I heard a twig snap, so I slid off the safety of my rifle. There was an instantaneous *whooshing* sound as the bear inhaled deeply and then charged.

I first saw the brush move about ten yards away. My thoughts then were that I had to make this shot count. This was the real deal. The bear was moving so fast I couldn't focus on him—he was just a big brown blur. At six to eight feet from me he already had his front leg in position to hit me, his head was down, and his chest looked huge. I leaned forward and fired at his chest, the concussion of the 400-grain Swift A-Frame flattening the hair there. Still he didn't go down, and now he was right on me!

I backed up a couple of steps to reload, but for some reason the bolt wouldn't work. All of a sudden I found myself on my back, kicking at the bear and trying to get my gun reloaded. At first I thought I'd be able to reload, shove the barrel in his throat, and finish him. He grabbed my foot and then bit down, crushing it badly and causing me to scream out. He pulled back and my boot came off, so he came at me again. I shoved my useless gun into his mouth and he chomped down hard on the stock, then began gnashing back and forth, biting my arms and hands. When he released me, I fell back, my thoughts on my three little daughters and how I'd let this situation go from bad to worse. The bear then grabbed me by my inner thigh, picked me up, and gave me a hard head shake. I felt blood running like a hot river down my thigh.

Then the huge animal dropped me, took two slow steps to my left, and started to turn the other way. He turned partly back my way and I was sure he was coming back to finish me. For a split-second we were eye to eye with less than three feet separating us. I could see pure hate in those eyes, more anger than I've ever seen in an animal. Still, he wavered, barely able to hold his head up. I saw my opportunity and grabbed my gun again, but despite my efforts I couldn't get it to function. The firing pin was jammed in the fired position, and I realized I had no chance of finishing this bear.

The bear was only a few feet away and I didn't want him to grab me again, so I did the only thing I could: I took off running, and was able to do so despite my crushed ankle. Thank God

I had my VHF radio in my pocket; I called the Coast Guard. Within a couple of hours they had me in the Sitka hospital, where I had extensive surgery and spent several days in intensive care. My nephew returned to the attack site the next day with another guide and the hunter, and they found the bear lying dead on my boot.

I've pretty much recovered from my wounds now and I'm back at it, maybe with a little different perspective than before. I try not to let that incident interfere with what I do, but it's always in the back of my mind.

Alisha "Mutts" Rosenbruch-Decker: There are several that come to mind, but one experience in particular stands out—how I killed my own brown bear (which happens to be the largest we've taken in over forty years).

Over many years of watching hunters come on a quest to find a trophy brown bear, I developed a desire to take one of these tremendous trophies myself. Somehow this quest developed into a search for that one "perfect" bear for me. I wanted to take only one of these giants in my life. For a brown bear guide to harvest his or her own bear, all the stars must line up just so.

My quest for the perfect bear spanned nine years in all. In some of those years I could manage just a day or two of hunting—when hunters would finish early and leave the field. Not all of those years were that way, though. One fall I hunted thirty-six days in a row and looked at ninety-seven different brown bears. Among all those bears, there was one old boar I absolutely would've taken, had there been a chance, but I think it was simply not yet meant to be.

In May of 2004, when exceptional weather and other conditions combined to produce fantastic hunting success, a group of French clients all killed beautiful bears and flew out of camp early. I suddenly had two days to hunt. The first day, however, a very aggressive storm prevented our even leaving our yacht, *Alaskan Grandeur*. This reduced my 2004 brown bear hunt to only one day.

It's amazing how differently you hunt when you are on your own. With an exact plan in mind, my Dad and I left the boat together about 7 in the evening, after the drainage winds had switched to produce an offshore flow. We walked softly along a long stretch of shoreline with a specific destination in mind. It was a magical evening along that stretch of beach, and we saw, stalked, and consequently turned down two huge boars that would have squared over nine and a half feet. In a moment of self-reflection I dared ask myself, *Do you really even want to kill one of these bears? Why are you turning down such huge animals?*

I had an answer shortly. A meadow at the head of one bay was transected in many places with trees. Dad and I eased up along a shallow slough and then split apart to cross a narrow band of trees so we could watch both sides as darkness fell. I had just eased through the line of trees when I heard a soft whistle with an urgent tone. I responded in kind, and as I eased back through the trees, another whistle came, then another. Dad hadn't heard my response and needed my attention! By now it was now a little after 10:00 P.M. and getting very dark. As I joined him, a shadow that had emerged through the scattered trees and onto the grass flat was just disappearing. It was a nervous animal that sensed something was not quite right, but it was not really spooked.

I remember seeing a young button buck disappearing close behind that bear. A bit deflated, we remained quiet and retraced our steps back down the slough. We stopped just short of the skiff's anchor line, not wanting this perfect evening to end. I stared into the darkness up the small creek dividing the grass and watched a shadow again emerge from the tree line but this time staying close to a cutbank. Just the top of his back was exposed, but when I saw its length my breath caught up short. I grabbed Dad, and as the bear crossed the creek we nearly ran to get closer. Darkness was quite thick now but served perfectly as cover allowing us to get close on a completely open tidal flat. When we were sixty yards away, we both sat down and got ready. Even with superb optics, I simply could not see well enough to shoot, so we had to run closer.

The bear was walking downstream now on the far side of the creek, and we were going to lose him if something didn't happen soon. We gained another thirty yards, but at a range of thirty-two yards I was still having an awful time finding my cross hairs on that black mass. By some miracle the bear found some sedge to feed on and stopped momentarily while we made one more move. At the river's edge, now twenty-three yards from this amazing animal, I set up again, but it was still too dark.

Now, I can't explain what happened next, except that miracles do still happen. On this dark night there was actually a full moon behind the overcast . . . and when the moment was right, a break in the clouds revealed its almost blinding brightness. Truly, it was like midday! As the full effect of the light washed over the bear, I squeezed the trigger. At the shot he spun in place, roaring. I shot twice more and Dad once before the great creature dropped and lay where he had been feeding. Shortly after the shooting ended, clouds once more obscured the moon and inky blackness returned. I'll never forget the full effect of walking up to that massive, magnificent creature lying there that night.

It was interesting that neither of us had ever discussed the bear's size. Big is simply big, and it remained completely unspoken that this was the bear I had been searching for over the past nine years. Admittedly, I shed some tears that night; actually, both of us were moist around the eyes. To take such an animal was truly a spiritual experience for me. My emotions of awe and respect were mingled with joy at the harvest and sadness at the loss of the life of such an animal.

We were not able to so much as roll this old boy over, and I wanted to just stay all night and relish the moment, but a spring tide following the full moon quickly drove us to higher ground and back to the skiff. The next morning was another discovery, to actually see this animal in detail! As we walked up to him, a young Sitka blacktail button buck was bedded down on an open gravel bar a mere eighteen yards or so from the fallen bear. That buck stayed put until I walked right up to the bear. Even then it retreated only a short way and stayed close the entire time we were there.

That old boar squared out at just over 10 feet, 4 inches (and measured over 11 feet claw tip to claw tip), with a $27\frac{10}{16}$-inch skull. The Alaska Department of Fish and Game aged him at 27 years. Perfection, I thus discovered, is attainable.

Tracy Vrem: I have one story that is a testament to how tough these bears can be. It happened twenty years ago. One of my guides was in a spike camp with a hunter, and over several days they had seen two big bears in the area kind of chasing each other around. A day or so later the men found one of the bears stationary on some kind of kill. They made a stalk and shot the bear, a very nice one that squared 9 feet, 8 inches. This one had killed another boar that measured over 9 feet, which happens fairly often, but what was unique was that the smaller bear had only three legs. At some point in its life it had lost its hind leg just below the knee joint, but a pad had grown over the stub and the animal had survived for some years in that condition. Not many wild animals, especially predators, can survive for years on only three legs.

Guy Anttila: One evening we spotted three grizzlies on a mountainside, one about a six-footer, one about seven and a half feet, and the last a solid nine-footer. The big one, we noticed, was rubbed, which was unusual in the early part of the season. He seemed to walk stiff-legged as if he had rheumatism. Our comments went like this: "Look at that old guy—he must have lost his hair in the den already and he can hardly walk. I'm surprised he made it through the winter." Although he appeared to be easily a Boone and Crockett-size bear, his skull likely measuring more than twenty-five inches, he had no guard hairs, and on the first day of the hunt we weren't about to chase him.

The next morning we were back glassing on the same mountain, and on the snow atop an avalanche slide we spotted a flurry of activity. It was the medium-size bear, backed up toward a rock face with the old guy in full attack mode. The battlers repeatedly raised up on their hind legs, trying to get a good grip on one another with their mouths. The one defending himself was hitting the larger bear in the head and face to avoid getting gripped solidly. It was obvious that if the old guy had any aging problems, he had been cured overnight. The smaller bear wanted to get away, but the old guy always cut off his escape, keeping his prey up against the rock face.

We set up our spotting scopes to watch the fight, and after about fifteen minutes it became obvious that the smaller bear was slowly losing his strength. Finally a solid blow by his opponent sent him down in the snow. The old guy seized the opportunity and pounced with straight, stiff forearms, putting all his weight onto the ribs of the smaller bear. He repeated this maneuver several times, and when he stepped back the smaller bear hardly moved. It would have been easy for the big guy to finish the fight quickly right there by crushing the smaller bear's skull with a bite, but it now became the type of game that you see when a house cat has a mouse. He would grab the downed bear by an ear and flip him completely over. He did this four or five times, leaving the other lying on his back.

Then the old bear grabbed hold of his victim's testicles, which stretched a long way before snapping. Then I heard a sort of loud whisper from my hunter: "Guy, there's no way I'm going up on that mountain!"

I was flying past the spot a couple of days later and found that the dead bear had been rolled and dragged down the mountain about a hundred yards from the kill site. It lay on its side, and I could see that the top side of one hind leg had been eaten and I could also see the ribs. The older, bigger bear was lying beside his kill, sound asleep.

Peter Klaui: All of them are unusual! I've had all kinds of situations happen, though. We had one scenario where a guide and hunter were stalking a bear that another guide and hunter hadn't been able to get to. The pair crossed a river carrying their boots and were in position to take the shot when all of a sudden a sow and a cub came walking out of nowhere, crossed the river, and headed right toward them. When the animals were about fifty yards away, the guide started waving his arms wildly, trying to haze them off. The cub saw him and spooked, but the sow was looking back at the boar the hunters wanted, which was fishing in a pool upstream about a hundred fifty yards away. Fortunately, the sow also spooked and she and the cub disappeared across the river. A minute later, the hunter shot and down went the big boar!

That wandering sow and cub could have meant the end of the hunt, but Lady Luck smiled and the hunter wound up with a big, big win. In a period of about five minutes he went from sitting calmly in place, waiting for a grizzly to come out, to being in the thick of some pretty exciting action.

Dave Leonard: I had an Austrian hunter who shot a really nice moose up in the Arctic just as it was getting dark. When he pulled out this huge pig-sticker knife and said, "I must help," I suddenly felt more than a little gun-shy. Here's why: The week before, a German hunter had been helping me skin a sheep, and his knife slipped and he stabbed me right in the calf of one leg. I ended up bleeding pretty badly, but I got through that hunt and was healing up well enough to take this Austrian hunter out for moose.

Well, I told the Austrian he could help best by watching for a bear with his gun ready—mostly so I could keep his knife from doing a repeat of the week before. I pointed down the game trail and told him to watch that way, more to give him something to do than anything else. I got all the guts and blood out, by which time I was covered in gore and the moose was really steaming as it cooled. You could actually see the steam drifting down the hill, on past the hunter, and out of sight down the trail. The hunter turned to me, tapped me on the shoulder, and said, "Oh, look, here comes the grizzly"—almost as if he fully expected to see one!

The bear was about twenty feet away, hunkered down and actually stalking us! I shot between his front legs and he turned and ran twenty feet down the trail, but he didn't want to leave. This moose was like manna from heaven to that bear, and he wanted it badly. We shot several more times, but it was dark and we had to get going. I explained to the hunter that the bear was going to steal his moose that night, but we'd try to steal it back if possible. He didn't quite understand what I was telling him, but he accepted it. The guy did have a bear tag but not for that area.

The next morning we hiked back in there, and sure enough the bear had raked up all the moss in the area on top of the moose, bitten off a bunch of willow branches to add to the pile, and was lying on top of "his" moose. We shot up a box and a half of bullets trying to keep this bear at bay while we did our job on the moose. We quartered it up and carried it out while one of us stood guard, firing as necessary.

This really nice brown bear is from the Alaska Peninsula.

Another time one of my hunters drew blood on a grizzly bear but didn't actually harvest it. We were on snowshoes, going in to a bear's moose kill. The air was crystal clear and the temperature about twenty-five below zero. We got within about seventy yards of the kill and were trying to pinpoint where both the bear and the carcass were. I spied the bear, pointed him out to the hunter, and we were checking the wind and planning what to do.

About that time I heard a wolf howl, and then another and another. The pack was coming in to the same kill, and right away there were eleven wolves all around us. They dropped down off a little bluff, and the bear stood up on his hind legs, trying to look bigger than he was to intimidate the wolves. Several wolves got on one side of him and the others went to the other side. Some kept the end with teeth busy while others ran in and tried to bite the bear on the butt. He'd wheel around to try to get to them, and then the other group would seize him by the butt. They were really trying to run him off the kill, and they finally succeeded.

In the meantime, a wolverine climbed down from one of the trees and grabbed a bite of moose, and so did a group of ravens. While the wolves were keeping the bear busy, everybody else was eating moose!

My hunter was so entertained he said, "Man, this is just like something out of *National Geographic!*"

We moved back toward the river because I figured the bear might circle around and come at us from behind. Well, here came the bear just thirty yards away. The hunter fired but hit a twig and the bullet barely grazed the bear. Both of us broke through the crusted snow about that time, and we had a hard time getting off another shot. There was hardly any blood, and what little there was rapidly dried up and stopped as we followed the bear. We searched all day, and I even got in my airplane and followed the track for several miles, but we didn't get that bear.

Joe Mott: I've forgotten so much I can hardly remember anything! I do recall a couple of little stories:

One spring we had seen a bear feeding on a moose kill, and we spent the whole day sitting underneath a spruce tree in a hole in the snow caused by the tree's shelter, watching for that bear to come out. We waited eight or ten hours and saw martens and birds coming and going but no bear. I finally figured the animal had eaten the best of the moose and was probably gone, and I shared that thought with the hunter. The moose kill was on the other side of a creek from us, so we got on our snowshoes and headed over to check things out. We made a big circle around the place to get a good look at the kill, staying in the open the whole time so we could see the kill. The area was semi-open but had quite a few big spruce trees with holes underneath them where the snow didn't collect, some of those holes four or five feet deep.

I was wound tighter than a two-dollar watch, watching for the bear but seeing nothing. We were seventy-five feet from the kill when the hunter said, "There's the bear." I looked to my left, and twenty yards away, coming out of one of those holes underneath a spruce, was the bear. The sleepy, confused look on his face said clearly, "Who the heck woke me up?"

"Well, shoot him!" I told the hunter. He did, and the bear fell back into the hole! We had a terrible time dealing with this bear in that hole—you don't just drag a bear weighing about eight hundred pounds out of a hole! We had to skin the critter down in the hole, in fact.

We had another situation where a bear had killed both a cow and a calf moose down close to a river. I knew exactly where the bear was, but the snow was terribly crunchy, like walking on cornflakes, and we were trying to be quiet. We even put cloth covers on the snowshoes to try to keep down the noise. Nothing really helped, though, no matter how hard we tried.

After a while the hunter said, "Hey, Joe, here comes the bear!" That bear just wasn't thinking we were any threat to him; he seemed to be thinking about a third moose and more meat to add to the pile. It was a perfect setup because we were trying to ease up on him and here he was coming to us! And of course we got him.

Larry Rivers: One time we had four guys in a tent (they wanted to hunt together). In those days we used the old Eureka tents held up by plastic cords. Well, a sow and a cub came into camp. The cub fell on one of the cords and the tent pulled outward and then sprang back. The bears thought that was hilarious, so they started doing it just for fun. The guys inside stayed as quiet as they could, and for two hours those bears played with the tent cords. The game went on so long the men finally decided they'd have to kill that sow, so they unzipped the tent slowly—and the sow stuck her head in the opening! The guide had been complaining about how little room there was in the tent with five people sleeping in it, but he later told me he couldn't believe how much room you could get between four hunters and the door of the tent when something like that happens!

They tried shooting the rifle without killing the bears, but that never works because the noise of the shots doesn't bother the animals. We even moved the camp the next day, but the bears followed and repeated the whole thing the next evening during a storm. One shot went through the roof of the tent and rain dripped in all night. In the morning, when the hunters could finally see to shoot the bear, it and the cub were gone—naturally. The clients left the field the next morning. They said they wouldn't take a million dollars for the experience, but wouldn't give you five cents to repeat it.

Another time I was sleeping in a tent alone and a bear started pushing on the nylon outside. I keep a round in the chamber while I sleep, but I keep the bolt open. I also keep a knife handy, not to use on an intruder but so I can cut a hole in that nylon baggie and get out of there if I need to. In this case I crawled over by the door and could hear the bear breathing. I zipped open the bottom of the door and could see the bear's claws right there. I took a big firecracker called a "seal bomb," which fishermen use to drive seals out of the fishing nets, and tossed it between that bear's front legs. When it went off, he switched ends and took off running.

As the bear ran off, I used a shotgun to shoot a "popper" at him. A popper is like an M-80 firecracker that's fired from a shotgun in place of lead. These are also used to chase seals away from fishing nets. I aimed it at the bear's butt, but it went over his head and exploded right in front of that critter. Again he swapped ends and came right back at me, letting out an indignant *woof!* as he went by!

Darwin Cary: I was only twenty-one and guiding for my parents when I was taken by boat up a river about ten miles. I was then to hike up over a mountain pass to a spike camp where there was a guide, a wrangler, and a family group that was hunting. I had been with them the first few days of their hunt but had to return to base camp to do some flying. Now I was on my way back. On my hike, which would take about four hours, I had my backpack but no rifle.

I had crossed the mountain pass and was still a couple of miles from the spike camp when I went through a cluster of willows maybe a couple of hundred yards long, following a horse trail. A really pretty grizzly appeared about thirty feet off the trail—hunting grubs, I guessed—and I just looked at him and he at me. I kept on walking, not really giving the bear a second thought because he was behaving himself.

A couple of hundred yards down the mountainside, in a place where the trees were fairly sparse, I heard this noise behind me, turned and looked, and the bear was a hundred fifty yards away and charging me full-bore. I had two choices, either turn and confront him or try to climb a tree. I was in great shape, and there was a tree thirty yards away, so I decided to climb it. The bear had to run a hundred fifty yards and I had to run only thirty, but we reached the tree at the same time!

As I tried to pull myself up in the branches, the grizzly bit my right foot and tore away my boot, along with half the sole of my foot. That bear then climbed that tree, dispelling the myth that grizzlies can't or won't climb trees. Next thing I knew he was right underneath me, and I started kicking at him with my left foot. Every time I'd kick, he'd bite me, and he wound up tearing away my entire left calf, including all the tendons. He got hold of my knee and I got him in a headlock, but I couldn't handle him. I decided to jump, which I did, and landed on my backpack, which broke my fall without even hurting my back.

All I had was my folding skinning knife, so I got ready to fight to the death. For the moment, though, I just lay there and played dead as the bear came down the tree. He walked over to me and started sniffing me, starting at my feet and then moving right up to my face. I had my knife down at my side, ready to fight as soon as he started to do anything. He just sniffed me real good and then walked away, and to this day I have no idea where he went.

I took my pack apart and got out some twine. Then I took my shirt and wrapped it around one leg and my T-shirt around the other, and put on tourniquets to stop the bleeding. Tendons a foot long were hanging out of my left calf, which was spewing copious blood. I crawled around and found a stick to try to make a crutch, but even with two of them I couldn't walk. I decided to just crawl. I checked my watch and loosened my tourniquets every fifteen minutes or so, but kept on going, and it took me four hours to crawl to the spike camp.

When I was five hundred yards from it, I called loudly and they heard me. I said to them that the mosquitoes were eating me alive, and they thought that was so inappropriate in view of the major injuries the bear had inflicted. One of the wranglers started back for base camp right away while the others cared for me, and the next morning a helicopter came in and got me. I spent the better half of the next year recovering and undergoing rehabilitation. I lost more than fifty pounds almost immediately from that injury.

Ron Fleming: One spring we were watching a sow with two little cubs feeding on a rockslide just across from us. Some two miles farther away we spotted another sow on a different slide, and she had two older cubs with her. I'd actually seen her several years in a row. Those cubs were about three years old and pretty good-size animals, one blonde one and one dark one. Up above them was a cliff some two hundred feet high, and on the cliff face was a bench perhaps twenty feet wide; above that was another solid rock face. In springtime bears like to get up high where the vegetation is greening and the first shoots are nice and tender.

The far group was feeding along together with the dark cub in front, the lighter one maybe ten feet behind, and the sow bringing up the rear. My hunter had his scope on them, watching. All of a sudden he let out an expletive and said, "I can't believe this!" As he described it, the lighter cub had turned to look back at the sow, because maybe she had growled at it or something, and when it turned it caught its foot in the rocks. It struggled to get free, and when the foot broke loose, the cub tripped and fell off the cliff! It came down tumbling and banging against the rocks, broke its neck, and was lying there dead!

The odds of that happening at all have got to be incredibly low, but to have a guy watching it all through a spotting scope is almost unbelievable. Even without the scope I could see the bear plummeting through the air just like a rag doll until it hit. The old sow just went over to the edge and looked, a reaction that seemed to say, "Oh, well, I guess that happens." And she simply went back to feeding again. The bottom line is that bears—just like people—trip and fall sometimes!

Chris Widrig: I have spent all of my adult life in the wilderness, hunting, guiding, or trapping. I have seen grizzly bears on many occasions, and have had many successful hunting trips with my clients. But until this episode, I had never faced a really dangerous situation, a close call where my life was threatened. In hindsight, this first head-on meeting could have been my last.

It was 1 August 1999, and in our packstring heading out of base camp were two hunters with their wives, myself and another guide, and eleven horses. We intended to ride north to hunt sheep in the headwaters of Dolores Creek. After hunting there, we would travel east over a high pass and descend into the Snake River valley. Everybody had a horse except me. There was just too much gear, so my horse was used for packing and I walked the entire way, about seventy miles. I am in fairly good shape and didn't mind doing that.

On the way, we ran into a sow grizzly and a very small cub right on the trail about a hundred yards ahead of us. She stood up and looked at us, and eventually we made a wide detour around her. Those were the first bears we'd seen. I did not have a gun on this trip, either, but both hunters did. They were riding right behind me, and since the guide had a gun as well, I figured we had enough firepower. I didn't really want to carry a gun on such a long walk.

Both hunters had enjoyable, successful hunts and bagged nice rams.

On 9 August we broke camp, packed up, and started to ride toward the Snake River. For several days the weather had been very warm, but that day a low fog hung over the landscape, visibility was restricted, and a light rain was falling. We had almost reached the summit of the pass, where we would begin the descent to the river. I was walking about a hundred yards ahead of the horses along a well-defined trail. There were no trees up there, just scrub willows up to about my waist. The willows were well spaced, not really thick.

Suddenly I heard a *woof!* and spied a sow and cub standing up in the willows really close, maybe thirty paces away! I immediately realized that without a rifle, I was in trouble. The horses and hunters were a hundred yards behind me, rifles in the scabbards. I yelled "Bear, bear!" as loud as I could and immediately ran. I could not run back to the horses since I had actually walked past the bear and she was between me and the horses. For about

Boats are used for hunting spring grizzlies in both British Columbia and the Yukon.

fifteen seconds I ran uphill on soft, spongy tundra, then looked back. The sow was with the cub and I thought they would move away, so I kept on running. When I glanced back again, I saw the horses rearing up and panicking, with the hunters trying to get hold of the reins and get the animals under control while also trying to get their rifles out of the scabbards. I must have established a personal best sprint time because afterward one hunter made the remark that I was speeding away like Carl Lewis!

I glanced over my shoulder again and this time saw that the bear was quickly coming after me. Then I could hear her right behind me, making a noise sort of like a cross between a growl and a snapping of teeth—probably she was doing both these things. I stopped, turned around, and tried to make myself look as big as I could. I saw the hunters and horses from the corner of one eye, but now my focus was on her. I didn't know where the big two-year-old cub was.

The sow came within about four steps and reared up as I stood facing her. Then she lunged for me, going right for my face. I looked straight into her yellow eyes, and with her ears flattened back, she was hissing and snapping her teeth. The last image my mind recorded was her gaping mouth and large fangs, and I could smell her foul breath. I put my hands up to protect myself, and she bit into my left hand before coming right for my face and eyes. She bit three times into my face around my eyes and nose, each bite extremely painful. I did not pass out and can remember every second of that attack. I could feel bones being crushed and breaking. I fell backward, and I think she had me in some sort of bear hug.

My eyes were closed for days after that, and I wondered if I would ever be able to see again. My recollections of the attack from that point on are based on what I felt, heard, and smelled. When I was down she started biting into my back in several places, but could not really get through my clothing, including a Gore-tex raincoat, to do any damage. But then she bit into my left leg, just below the knee, and broke it. At that point I fought no more—I simply gave up. Lying on my back, I thought it was all over. She swiped me with one of her paws, hitting my upper right leg very close to my groin. I thought she had bitten me there, but later the surgeons told me that these wounds were claw marks.

Shortly after that I heard a shot and the bear left me alone. One of the hunters had finally got his rifle out and fired and the bear disappeared.

I was convinced I was history: I could feel blood pouring from my face and had lost my vision. I thought I had serious head injuries, perhaps even damage to my brain cavity, since the bear had got into my head pretty good. Getting me out of there was an ordeal, but the hunters and one of the wives took good care of me. My clothes were soaking wet from walking in the rain all morning and then falling on the swampy ground. One of the hunters took all his dry clothes off, as well as my wet ones, and dressed me in his dry clothes. This may have been a life-saving idea.

James Pokiak: We've had very few unusual things happen on our grizzly hunts. We did have a father-son hunt one year, and the father brought his wife along. There was a lot of complaining from the older guy about the fumes from the back of the snowmobile and such. It turned out that the wife was basically tougher than he was!

What is the most dangerous situation you or your bear hunters have encountered? What was the outcome? Why did it occur, and could it have been avoided?

Dennis Harms: Very fortunately, we've never had anyone injured. We did have one situation when guide Kevin Atkins and his hunter had sneaked up on a really good bear. The hunter shot and hit the bear pretty well, and then was able to hit it again as it disappeared. It was pretty late, but the men could see an awful lot of blood. It was getting dark, so they decided to leave the track and return the next morning.

I joined the group then, and when we started tracking again, the vegetation was so thick we had to go pretty much single file along a narrow trail. Kevin was in the lead. We could see where the bear had lain down two or three times to ambush us, but had then gotten up and moved on. Ultimately the bear charged Kevin from about fifty feet away, and he shot it twice, stopping the charge. It still wasn't finished, though, so I stepped up and ended it. That situation was really dangerous because had that bear picked a better ambush spot, like the ones it had chosen earlier, it could have been on us before we could shoot. You prevent that kind of thing by making a killing shot in the first place.

Gary "Butch" King: The story I told in answering the previous question is the most dangerous situation I've encountered. It's actually the only time anyone in my operation has ever been touched by a bear. The whole incident happened as the result of a lousy first shot, plus the assistant guide letting the bear leave the arena without firing a backup shot.

Mike Munsey: The most dangerous situation that I or my guides or hunters have ever encountered didn't involve an actual bear hunt but weather. The weather can change so quickly here on Kodiak Island that you can find yourself in a dangerous situation regardless of how careful you are. The temptation to stay out a little later and hunt a little longer is so great that you overlook hazardous conditions. Then, when you do decide to return to camp, you keep going regardless of the weather because the thought of having to spend the night on the beach is so unappealing.

I have never had a situation where a guide or client had to spend the night out without shelter because of the weather, but it's always a risk because here on Kodiak we use boats to get around. It's vital that you always watch the weather and make sure you leave before it gets too bad. It's also important to carry emergency gear—radio or satellite phone, survival suits, emergency rations, etc.—at all times.

Scott Newman: My mauling was by far the most dangerous situation I've ever been a part of. It was the result of multiple "malfunctions," from poor shot placement initially to a busted rifle. You should do all in your power to avoid these and other such errors, and never forget how powerful brown bears are.

Alisha "Mutts" Rosenbruch-Decker: Several years ago my father, my brother, and I spent thirty-seven solid days hunting brown bears for ourselves. One day in mid-October we left the boat early with the intention of going clear to the headwaters of a river system. On the way in, near the mouth of the stream, a large sow bear was fishing with a pair of two-year-old cubs. We attempted to go around in an effort to avoid disturbing them, but she heard us and *woofed* the cubs to the woods.

That day was amazing! We saw an incredible number of bears, and my brother took a huge old boar that squared just over nine feet, but what was truly special about the animal was its color—it was blue, the color of a glacier bear! But that is a story for another time.

We were late coming out and darkness had already fallen. A storm was coming in and it was pouring rain with gusting wind. We each had a small mini-mag flashlight. Just as we broke into the open area of the estuary's grass flat, we all heard it again—a gruff *woofing,* as when a sow sends off her cubs.

I clenched the little light in my teeth and we split up, standing our ground and staying ready for whatever might come. This sow, apparently the same one we had spooked earlier in the day, came at us from about a hundred and twenty yards out. One of us probably should have fired, but none of us wanted to harm this sow. She stopped only twelve paces away, slapped the ground in an impressive display of power, and went her way with another gruff *woof!*

Looking back, one of us probably should have fired either into the ground at her feet or in the air to try to spook her. If one of us had turned to run, no doubt she would have pounced on that person like a dog on a rabbit. The real saving grace, though, was that none of us broke. Some situations like that may be unavoidable. Different animals simply have different tolerance levels, and it is not always possible to know how close you're getting to an animal. The key is how you react.

Tracy Vrem: The most dangerous thing we encounter is the hunter who refuses to take the cartridge out of the chamber of his rifle, so the guide ends up walking along with a loaded gun pointed at his back. That's my biggest fear in bear hunting. I haven't had many close calls from bears.

There was one time, though, when I was charged, sort of. A German hunter and I had stalked a bear that was fishing in a creek. The hunter made a great shot, but the bullet passed all the way through the animal and splashed the water on the other side of it. I don't think the bear was really charging us—more likely it simply wanted to get away from the danger it perceived where the bullet hit the water. But it sure was coming our way fast. It died about twenty-five feet from us. We both emptied our rifles into the bear, and thank goodness there was a little incline it had to come up. The disturbing thing was that my rifle malfunctioned in the middle of all this, so I was essentially out of commission. Fortunately the animal was well-hit by the initial shot.

Guy Anttila: Our last fall-season hunters had left, so my wife Elsie and I decided to play for a couple of days—taking videos of bears. We went to a location where I had watched bears on a previous day, and spotted a medium-size sow with a large cub.

The youngster was probably three years old and normally would not be hanging around the mother any more. Both bears were fishing and they seemed to be loosely attached, staying within fifty or sixty yards of each other. Elsie and I were hiding in a pile of logs on a gravel bar about fifty yards from them.

After about thirty minutes the sow had apparently had her fill and she headed out, probably to bed down for the day. She ended up on our side of the creek, passing about forty yards from us without spotting where we were hiding, and continued on into the brush. The cub, realizing its mother had left, took off in a run to catch up and also disappeared into the brush. I knew that if the bears continued in the same direction, they would cut our scent probably a hundred to a hundred and fifty yards back in the bush where the wind was taking our human odor. It really didn't matter, I figured, because we had enough videos of them. With the bears gone, we were standing alongside the log pile discussing the camera.

Elsie, the gunbearer, had leaned her .375 against the log pile between the two of us. Some minutes had gone by when, in my peripheral vision to the left, I caught a movement in the brush some sixty-five yards away. It was the sow in a full run, charging up the scent trail without even having seen us. I dropped the camera and reached for the gun. While doing this I instinctively shouted at the sow, which was automatic to me because bears sometimes take a run at you when they see movement. They may think they're looking at prey, and a shout often stops them in their tracks as they realize their mistake.

However, this situation was different. The bear knew what we were and had no hesitation about what she was going to do about it. It was a silent charge, and my shout only pinpointed her target. She was running so hard a plume of sand was kicking up behind every leap. Slow motion kicked in as my rifle centered on her head, which she was carrying in a low position. I pulled slightly to the right side of the head and touched off the shot when she was some twenty-five yards away. She piled over backward, the slug actually knocking her rearward a few feet. She tried to get up, but her left front leg was not cooperating.

This seemed to frustrate her, and she roared for the first time. I lined up on her for a second shot, which killed her.

Right then, for the first time, I noticed that her big cub was being very vocal, prancing around near the brush line. The cub was the size of an average black bear, and I assume it had been participating with its mother in killing food other than fish. The cub obviously didn't understand that its mother was dead, and seemed to think it needed to finish whatever had been started, so with a lot of noise it, too, started a charge at us. I obviously didn't want to kill the cub unless it became absolutely necessary. I yelled at the top of my voice, keeping the rifle aimed at it. The cub finally came to a skidding halt about thirty yards right in front of us. It stood there roaring, snapping its teeth, and looking around for its mother. I didn't think it had the confidence to follow through with the charge, so I held back on the shot. The cub then turned around, walked back a short way, still looking for its mother, and then wheeled around and took another run at us with a lot of sound effects. Again I held off on the shot because the bear didn't seem to have adequate confidence, and it stopped, a few yards farther back than on the first charge. It repeated this run one more time but with less noise, and again stopped, even farther back. By now I was sure I would not have to kill the cub.

British Columbia regulations state that bears killed in self-defense will be confiscated, but it was late in the year and the hair on the sow's pelt was probably four inches long and gorgeous. I decided to skin her, even knowing I would have to give up the hide to the game department. The cub was now standing quietly some ten to fifteen yards away, on the opposite side of its dead mother. As we approached the sow, the cub did the same thing from the other side, charging and roaring at us. I wanted to drive the cub away, so I picked up a fist-size stone and bounced it hard off the cub's back. Its only response was to move closer to the sow. I hit it with another stone, and the cub moved right up to the sow and lay alongside her.

Both Elsie and I were quite touched by the situation, and we decided to walk away, keeping an eye on the cub. The youngster got some blood on the side of its face in the process of snuggling up to its dead mother, and suddenly started licking vigorously at blood coming from the bullet wound. Both Elsie and I stepped back and realized that this was nature taking its course. The mother bear might be one of the last meals the cub would have before denning. No sooner had that thought crossed our mind than we saw a large boar coming down the creek. We realized that in fact the cub would be run off by the bigger bear. Oh, well, that creek was still full of spawning fish, which the cub could catch and load up on before denning.

Peter Klaui: I guess that sow and cub coming toward my guide and hunter, described earlier, would be near the top of the list. We go far out of our way to minimize the potential for danger, and for the most part we've been successful.

Dave Leonard: I've had a few close calls, but we've never had a hunter or guide mauled by a bear. We've even had bears charge us and others have doubled back on us, but they've never touched us. I'd say the most dangerous things generally happened when the hunter didn't listen to instructions and either the bear almost got us as a result or else we had a rifle accidentally discharge. A couple of times I've almost had my head blown off in such situations. My greatest danger is always from my own hunters. We do everything humanly possible to minimize it, but still the risk is there.

Joe Mott: I really haven't had anything dangerous happen. People are amazed that I've taken a hundred bears and never had one attack me or even charge me. Bears in Alaska don't like people—they don't like the way we smell or the way we look. They take off at the first sign of trouble, and when they reach a safe distance they look back to see if whatever disturbed them is a real concern. If it is, they keep on trucking. If not, they go back to whatever they were doing before. But I can't say I've ever had any bad experiences.

Larry Rivers: There's not much you can do to avoid such situations; if there were, you probably wouldn't be in such a situation. One time we shot a bear and it dropped over a bluff and landed in the ocean, where it swam around a point. We ran down and followed it around the point to where we thought it had come out. We couldn't find the bear, which had climbed a steep rock cliff a hundred and fifty feet high. When we started back, I saw some rocks rolling, looked up, and there was the bear just fifty feet away. The bear charged, and both I and the client shot—my shot coming from the hip, actually. Luckily we killed it, so close to us that it rolled up and knocked our legs out from under us.

Darwin Cary: My mauling is the only close call I or my guides have ever had.

Ron Fleming: We had one close call that happened because the hunter failed to follow instructions. It occurred back when we were able to hunt over a gut pile, which we can't do now. An earlier hunter had killed a moose and a bear was feeding on it. We put a newly arrived bow hunter in a one-man tree stand over the kill site. The situation prevented having a guide right there with him, so I and one of my guides backed the boat out into the nearby lake far enough to avoid scaring the bear but close enough so we could see the hunter. We'd told the hunter to blink his flashlight when he was ready to come out and we'd come get him, but not to come out of the tree until we arrived with the gun.

Well, it got pretty late—darkness was gathering, the perfect time for the bear to come out—and the guy started blinking his flashlight at us! Apparently he thought surely the bear wasn't coming in that night. He looked around, couldn't see a bear but could hear the boat coming, so he used a string to lower his bow to the ground. Then he turned around and climbed down himself. When he picked up his bow and turned around, ten feet in front of him was a nine-foot bear!

We were just getting to shore in the boat when we heard all this commotion, yelling and roaring, and we figured the hunter had fallen out of the tree and the bear had him. We went tearing in there, and there's the hunter, up the tree way past the tree stand! He told us later he looked at his bow and thought to himself, *Here's this bear and all I've got is this piece of stick!* He gave a loud yell and shot up that tree like a squirrel! I guess it startled the bear, too, or it surely would have chewed on him instead of letting out a roar and taking off. The guy was totally spooked after that and didn't want to hunt anymore.

Wherever you hunt brown bears or grizzlies, it's always lots of glassing amidst dazzling panoramas.

We killed that same bear the next spring, and it turned out to be the biggest bear we've ever killed, a genuine nine-foot mountain grizzly. I think it's still in the top twenty-five in Boone and Crockett. But we easily could have lost a hunter on that deal. That whole scene could have been avoided if the hunter had just followed instructions.

Chris Widrig: The time I was mauled is by far the most serious incident I've been involved in. Other than that, I've never really been seriously charged by a grizzly.

James Pokiak: We haven't really had any truly dangerous situations develop. We try to do everything right so bad things don't happen, and so far they haven't.

What do you see as the most critical environmental/management/public relations issues affecting the future of hunting these magnificent bears?

Dennis Harms: That would be the politics of it. We all fervently hope nothing gets started like the ballyhoo with wolves. The state of Alaska just flat lost the ability to manage wolves twenty years ago, and that resulted in some incredibly bad consequences for ungulates. The Board of Fish and Game and the Department of Fish and Game have tried time and again to regain control, but the antis stop them every time with injunctions and other court actions. I can envision something like this happening with bears, too. It hasn't yet, but it could, and it would be a disaster for the bear population because it's been proven beyond doubt that hunting bears is good for the population as a whole. You can have hunting, bear viewing, and a high population of bears if you follow a good, effective management regimen. So I see politics as the biggest obstacle that might adversely affect bears and bear hunting.

Gary "Butch" King: Ballot-box biology is the biggest fear that we have as guides. The management we have in place right now is far superior to any other possible scheme, and it's based on forty years of intensive management in the area. The entire management regimen for the Alaska Peninsula, which is devised right in my area, consists of an annual survey and count done by the Alaska Department of Fish and Game. It's based on several criteria. For decades they've done this count in mid-August every year, counting single bears, family groups, and so on. Biologists get a good idea of how many bears there are. They watch every year to discover any trends. Also, every bear killed has a tooth pulled for aging, the sex is identified, and the skull is measured. This gives a wealth of information that is valuable in determining the direction of the population. All these things go into the equation to determine the number of days the season will be open. The trend is an increasing number of bears, and seven opportunity days have been added to our fall season just recently based on the data.

Mike Munsey: My biggest concern is antihunting groups and the possibility they will eventually get hunting closed or greatly restricted on federal refuge lands. Regardless of how good the bear population is here on Kodiak and on the Alaska Peninsula, or how good hunting is for the state and the economy, I can see a time when the wrong people get into office and wind up lending a sympathetic ear to antihunting groups. That would be the end. Let's hope I'm being a fatalist.

Scott Newman: Access to bears is critical. Several places in Alaska are dedicated to viewing bears, and there's a basic conflict between people who want to see bears and people who want to hunt them. I do feel good about the management of brown bears by the Alaska Department of Fish and Game—they're doing a good job. The land is managed by the federal government while the wildlife is managed by the state.

Alisha "Mutts" Rosenbruch-Decker: Brown bear hunting, now and for future generations, requires a delicate balance that must constantly be monitored and massaged. Probably the single most important element to ensure a healthy bear population for generations to come is protection of their habitat. Clear-cut logging and similar habitat destruction and encroachment are the most harmful issues facing these bears. Loss of old-growth habitat clearly has been shown to displace bears, and the resulting damage to salmon streams and riparian areas directly impacts wild salmon stocks.

We do not have to look far to discover what has been done in other areas. Washington, Oregon, and British Columbia have severely reduced or eliminated their old-growth stocks, and the result has been catastrophic to both salmon and the land-based animals that rely on them. If we as a nation are not willing to set aside some unspoiled temperate old-growth rain-forest tracts, then our children and grandchildren will be denied the very thing that so many of us hold so dear—the chance to experience a place more magical and unspoiled than many people believe possible.

Additionally, brown bear management needs to include areas for public viewing and enjoyment. Reserves, sanctuaries, and parks are important to brown bear hunting because they allow the general public opportunities to see and enjoy these animals. It is very important that guides, outfitters, and hunters all support and protect these areas because the future of hunting hangs in the balance. Management of brown bears has undergone a lengthy evolution to reach where it is today. Guides and outfitters, along with hunters, must have the fortitude and dedication to adhere to this management plan.

Tracy Vrem: I think the most critical thing is maintaining habitat for the bears. The parks created by Jimmy Carter we could do without, but the refuges are good news for hunters and wildlife. The only problem is the word "refuge," a term the antihunters have seized upon to try to stop hunting. These lands should be given some other name, like "sportsmen's preserves" or "wildlife reservoirs."

Food sources are important, to: If anything ever happened to the salmon runs, for example, you'd see a crash in bear numbers and decreased growth and reproduction. Right now the state is doing a tremendous job of managing salmon, so I don't foresee a problem anytime soon. It's also critical for brown bears to have enough room to roam without having human encounters that result in defensive kills.

Guy Anttila: We need to get back to scientific management instead of political management. We can't have biologists guessing how many tags should be given to outfitters based on the lowest possible number they can justify.

Peter Klaui: That's a broad question. If the government would manage bears scientifically and keep politics out of it, there would be grizzly bear hunting forever. I think every government should have as part of its mandate a provision that management of any species will be done scientifically, not based on public opinion or emotion. The question is how many bears does the public want? An independent study by a group of experts from outside British Columbia determined that the data being used in the province was excellent, and that in fact biologists were using low figures on the inventory of bears and conservative quotas were being issued.

There are a minimum of seventeen thousand grizzlies in British Columbia, and we take less than 1 percent of them on sport hunts. That level of take is totally sustainable, and any resource managed in that manner is perpetuated indefinitely. Places where grizzlies are scientifically managed—like Alaska, British Columbia, and Russia—are the only places good numbers of these bears still exist. They don't exist in California, but they weren't killed off by sport hunters. No, it was the general public and the government that killed them off, and scientific management played no role.

Dave Leonard: I'd have to say the progress of man. I'm not down on mining, but there's no question human exploitation of the land affects grizzlies. We're in a national preserve, so we don't have to worry about it right in my area, but it can sure affect bears all around that area. Another thing that's a danger to the bears is treating them like a predator to protect ungulate populations. We need to watch that concept so it doesn't get out of control.

Joe Mott: Now you're getting political. The animal-rights bunch and hard-core environmentalists just don't understand how positive an influence grizzly hunting is for the bear population. Grizzly hunting is a true trophy hunt—it's not a meat hunt at all, and a lot of people have a bad problem with that. Well, grizzly bear meat generally is barely edible—though sometimes it isn't bad and sometimes it's terrible. Still, we need to hunt them, and we need to educate the public and maintain good public relations or we could lose the privilege to hunt grizzlies.

Larry Rivers: It's all political. It's just a shame that people can lose their jobs if they vote for quality scientific game management, but that's the world we live in. The environmentalists want to paint hunters as far worse than they really are, and hunters want to portray themselves as far better than they are. The truth is, unfortunately, that there are a lot of slob hunters out there that give us all a bad reputation. Nobody on either side deals in the truth, and it's the bears that suffer. There are times we need to shut down hunting for the good of the bears, and there are times we need more hunting, again for the good of the bears. But nobody wants to deal in pure honesty on either side.

Darwin Cary: If they ever, for political reasons, banned hunting outright, we'd lose all our true conservationists. God bless the antihunters, because deep down they think they're doing what's best. But when you give $1,000 to Greenpeace or most other environmentalist organizations, not a penny of that money gets back to actual conservation. If we ever see a ban on hunting, we will have lost the people most interested in the welfare of our wild resources. It would be a terrible tragedy that most city folks just wouldn't understand.

Ron Fleming: It's all strictly politics. A lot of our last election was about grizzly bears. One party promised to close all grizzly hunting, and the other promised to open grizzly hunting. The latter party got seventy-seven out of seventy-nine seats in the government, so we've got grizzly hunting. The antihunters have a strong voice and they're more vocal, but their numbers are weak, and we can usually counter them effectively if we get motivated.

Chris Widrig: I think we're heading for far more restrictions. The grizzly generates strong emotions, especially in people who don't understand the benefits of hunting them—you know, the teddy bear and similar ideas. It's a fairly rare and low-density animal, no matter where they live. In the Yukon you'll probably always have some level of grizzly hunting, but the take will be lower and some areas will lose their grizzly hunting altogether due to public pressure.

James Pokiak: The biggest concern I have is the ability of another country to put a stop to what we do in our own area.

A successful grizzly/brown bear hunt can truly produce the trophy of a lifetime.

This is happening right now with polar bears, and it could also happen to our grizzly hunts at some point. We live here and we have to make a living with what we have here, and that's primarily our wildlife. That hasn't changed throughout all our history. It isn't right for another country to try to dictate how we use our own resources, but that's what's happening.

Do you have any parting words of wisdom for future bear hunters?

Dennis Harms: Shoot to kill!

Gary "Butch" King: Do your homework. If you're looking to hunt big trophy bears and you find any consistency in the names of the outfitters that keep coming up, there's probably a really good reason for that. Those people are most likely to have mastered the logistics well enough to consistently conduct quality hunts. Beware of pup-tent gypsies! People who have a fiduciary commitment to the area and the quarry are the ones you should seek out as an outfitter.

Ask the Grizzly/Brown Bear Guides

Mike Munsey: Book early. The best hunts usually go first. If a guide has only one spot left for a season, there might be a reason that hunt is still open. Ask how much experience your guide has in the area you'll be hunting. And check references!

Scott Newman: Travel light, hunt hard, and shoot straight!

Alisha "Mutts" Rosenbruch-Decker: Perhaps the only thought I can impart to future bear hunters would be this: Expect to be touched by these magnificent animals in a way you have never been affected by any other hunting experience. If you come on a hunt and take in every aspect of it and embrace the challenge, then you will go away changed, whether you take an animal or not.

Tracy Vrem: You get out of your hunt what you put into it. Get in the best shape you can before you come so you can walk thirty minutes without having to stop and rest. Sometimes a bear comes easy, but sometimes it's a tough hunt. Hunters need to come with the attitude that they're going to help their guide find the bear by being a diligent glassing partner.

Guy Anttila: Hunting grizzlies is a huge privilege no hunter should take lightly. And it's a unique experience no hunter should miss.

Peter Klaui: We need more future bear hunters! Some people say there's nothing to shooting a bear, but I disagree. Hunting grizzlies in Canada and Alaska is true hunting, and it's a privilege to participate. There are things out of our control and you may not kill a bear, but in our situation hunters normally have a good opportunity.

Dave Leonard: Always respect the bears; shoot straight, quickly, and often; and for heaven's sake, don't get scratched!

Joe Mott: Know your rifle and be in shape.

Larry Rivers: No, I don't have a whole bunch of wisdom to share.

Darwin Cary: Learn to live the moment and enjoy the outdoors. I see far too many people who are just concerned about killing something and not truly enjoying the experience. Go hunting and just enjoy it.

Ron Fleming: All hunters have to remember that it's a privilege to be out hunting grizzly bears, and you don't have to get one that's eight or nine feet to have a good hunt.

Chris Widrig: You have to have patience. Don't expect more than the terrain and the bears are willing to give you. Seeking these animals is simply not like hunting other animals, and you've just got to enjoy the hunt whether you get a bear or not. Be aware that on interior grizzlies, it may take more than one trip to be successful.

James Pokiak: Just make sure, when you come up here, that you're physically able to withstand the elements, and that you have the patience and endurance to stick with it long enough to find your trophy.

SAFARI PRESS